CORRECT
WRITING

Form 2

CORRECT WRITING

Second Edition

Form 2

Eugenia Butler
University of Georgia

Mary Ann Hickman
Gainesville Junior College

Lalla Overby
Brenau College

D.C. Heath and Company
Lexington, Massachusetts
Toronto

This work is a revision of *Correct Writing,* Forms A, B, C & D, by Edwin
M. Everett, Marie Dumas, and Charles Wall, all late of the University of
Georgia.

International Standard Book Number: 0-669-01627-6

Preface

TO THE TEACHER

Correct Writing, Second Edition, Form 2 is a revision and enlargement of earlier editions. Notable changes in this edition of *Correct Writing* have been made in order to meet universal needs in colleges which now find it mandatory to return to the teaching of basic grammar, punctuation, and mechanics before moving on to instruction in composition and rhetoric. With this need in mind the authors have amplified the book to a considerable degree through the addition of definitions of terms and more thorough explanations of the principles involved in sentence structure. These definitions and explanations come at the earliest mention of a term, so that students will not have to continue their study of a grammatical principle without a clear understanding of what they have already been told. Discussions which may be enlarged upon in other chapters carry convenient cross-references that point the reader to further information available on a given topic.

The format for this edition of *Correct Writing* combines the best features of a handbook of grammar and composition with a workbook of exercises. Wherever it has been possible, the exercises have been simplified to make them more than usually illustrative of the grammatical principles involved. The exposition of the various aspects of grammar and sentence structure is presented to the student in as simple terms as possible and is more extensive than that in most other workbooks. Although the discussion of many aspects of grammar is not intended to be exhaustive, information in this present book is complete enough for a student to grasp and to learn without having constantly to rely on the instructor's further discussion. The Glossary of Faulty Diction is an especially useful feature, and it is accompanied by exercises so that it may be used both for a reference and for study.

The treatment of punctuation is a distinctive adjunct of this book, since it serves as a follow-up to the chapters in which the basic principles of sentence structure are discussed. When students reach this lesson on punctuation, they will already have learned most of the rules in the lesson, which can then serve as a review of the subject instead of a listing of arbitrary rules to be memorized. There are, however, numerous occasions when it seems appropriate simply to cite a rule without attempting theoretical explanations which would defeat the purpose of the text as an elementary handbook for composition. A rule governing punctuation, grammar, or sentence structure may be susceptible to modification or exception, but it is nonetheless useful for being arbitrarily stated. If students do not know that their sentences contain comma splices, they are hardly prepared at that stage of development to explore the subtleties of such a construction.

A central point which should emerge through a student's careful use of this text is that the study of grammar and of sentence elements is of value primarily as a means of improving communication and understanding.

TO THE STUDENT

This book is a combination textbook, workbook, and reference handbook. It contains a great deal of information in the various chapters that precede the exercises. It is a workbook in which you will be able to write your answers concerning grammatical principles which you have just studied. When you have worked all the exercises as well as the Review and Achievement Tests, you will still have a convenient reference handbook in which you can check points of grammar, usage, punctuation, and mechanics whenever you need to.

Working conscientiously through the chapters and exercises of this book will put you well on your way to a mastery of grammar and usage, which in turn will help you to write and speak accurately and effectively.

Contents

DIAGNOSTIC TEST

In the following sentences identify the part of speech of each *italicized* word by writing one of the following numbers in the space at the right:

1 if it is a noun,	*5* if it is an adverb,
2 if it is a pronoun,	*6* if it is a preposition,
3 if it is a verb,	*7* if it is a conjunction,
4 if it is an adjective,	*8* if it is an interjection.

1. I have lost my *book.* ....
2. You have been working *too* hard. ....
3. *Both* Betty and Jean went to the convention. ....
4. Do *you* have a date for this weekend? ....
5. *After* the game we are going to a party. ....
6. Irene *broke* her arm. ....
7. I knew *that* you wanted to go. ....
8. *Well*, I do not know about that. ....
9. Our Florida trip was *expensive.* ....
10. The sheriff and his men searched the woods *for* the little girl. ....
11. *When* did you decide to attend the Georgia State University? ....
12. *I* was not sure how Bill would react to the problem. ....
13. Professor Wright excused me from the final *examination.* ....
14. John *recently* moved into a new home. ....
15. Graduation day is a joyous occasion for *everyone.* ....
16. Linda's arrangement *of* wildflowers won first prize. ....
17. The Beta Club *will sponsor* a tennis tournament. ....
18. *Hey*, I want to watch the end of the game. ....
19. How many books did you read last *semester*? ....
20. Either Ann *or* Sue will wash the car. ....
21. *Oh*, I understand your position. ....
22. The miners *barely* escaped the avalanche. ....
23. *Each* member of the team played well. ....
24. The violence in the movie *shocked* the audience. ....
25. *Each* of the students prepared a written speech. ....

Each of the following sentences either contains an error in grammar or is correct. Indicate the error or the correctness by writing one of the following numbers in the space at the right:

> *1* if the case of the pronoun is incorrect,
> *2* if the subject and verb do not agree,
> *3* if a pronoun and its antecedent do not agree,
> *4* if an adjective or an adverb is used incorrectly,
> *5* if the sentence is correct.

26. A group of scientists are visiting the White House.   ....
27. Every student has their favorite subject.   ....
28. I studied real hard for the test.   ....
29. My aunt baked a chocolate cake for my brother and I.   ....
30. Can you direct me to the music hall?   ....
31. Ralph did good on his theme.   ....
32. Cold weather, snow, and sleet have taken its toll this winter.   ....
33. Did you read about Zelda's award?   ....
34. Each of the members of the panel expressed their views clearly.   ....
35. Bruce is real anxious to attend the Highland games this summer.   ....
36. The boy along with his dog had already clambered into the truck.   ....
37. Neither of his daughters have an interest in politics.   ....
38. Between you and I, a successful vegetable garden is hard work.   ....
39. Newton cannot run the mile as fast as him.   ....
40. I prefer cheese that tastes sharply.   ....
41. Last weekend the bass surely were biting at Lake Hartwell.   ....
42. Sitting on the chest was a lamp and several magazines.   ....
43. The League of Women Voters announced their support of the revised constitution.   ....
44. I certainly hope that I did good on the sociology test.   ....
45. I have not heard who is invited to the reception for the ballet company.   ....
46. The media has been concerned with the lack of an energy policy.   ....
47. We feel badly about forgetting to stop for you this morning.   ....
48. Everybody is planning to bring their lunch to the committee meeting.   ....
49. Who have you asked to introduce the guest speaker?   ....
50. We do appreciate you meeting the bus.   ....

Each of the following sentences either contains an error in sentence structure or is correct. Indicate the error or the correctness by writing one of the following numbers in the space at the right:

1 if the sentence contains a dangling modifier,
2 if the sentence contains a misplaced modifier,
3 if the sentence contains a faulty reference of a pronoun,
4 if the sentence contains faulty parallelism,
5 if the sentence is correct.

51. I hope to get up early, study, and to leave for the mountains by noon.   ....
52. After reading the morning paper, another cup of coffee seemed in order.   ....
53. The mornings have grown chilly which is a sure sign of fall.   ....
54. To completely stop the noise of the crowd was impossible.   ....
55. The music at River Inn was soft, soothing, and I thoroughly enjoyed it.   ....
56. Margaret has only read the opening chapter of the book.   ....
57. Because his father is a lawyer, he also hopes to practice it.   ....
58. After gathering up my beach towel and magazines, the sun came out again.   ....
59. The committee which meets frequently hopes to make a full report.   ....
60. He is a boy with ambition and who has an attractive personality.   ....
61. She thinks that her job in the antique shop is more interesting than Hannah.   ....
62. Stretched out on the couch, Wilson nodded over his book.   ....
63. One cannot be sure when you will need a second language.   ....
64. To make good coffee, careful measurement is necessary.   ....
65. Her books were stacked all over the room which made cleaning difficult.   ....
66. We either plan to spend the afternoon skiing or scuba diving.   ....
67. A poem was read to the group which was very hard to understand.   ....
68. We went for a walk around the block every morning, but this soon became a bore.   ....
69. The exhausted runner almost ran the full distance before collapsing.   ....
70. By taking the pills the doctor had given him, his leg soon stopped aching.   ....
71. The man who was weeding the garden carefully stepped over the brick wall.   ....
72. After she saw my new skateboard, Maggie began to compliment me and saying that she wanted one just like mine.   ....
73. When the dog knocked over the garbage can, it was strewn all over the yard.   ....
74. Kleer-Kleen Shampoo will leave your hair more unmanageable than any other, which is saying a great deal.   ....
75. To be successful in business, ambition is definitely needed.   ....

Each of the following sentences contains an error in punctuation or mechanics, or is correct. Indicate the error or correctness by writing one of the following numbers in the space at the right:

1 if a comma has been omitted,
2 if a semicolon has been omitted,
3 if an apostrophe has been omitted,
4 if quotation marks have been omitted,
5 if the sentence is correct.

76. Rachel Suzanne and Marian have a pet gerbil in their apartment. ....
77. Shirley Jackson's short story The Lottery has a shocking ending. ....
78. Marty knowing her way around Williamsburg led the visitors straight to the Governor's Palace. ....
79. The heavy awkward knot in the rope was hard to untie. ....
80. I am planning to fly to Geneva in July however, I do not know the exact date. ....
81. Alex wants to save enough money to go to Canada for Christmas for he has always wanted to make that trip. ....
82. Johns flying lessons are progressing well; he plans to solo in about two weeks. ....
83. Did Maria mean it when she answered, I don't think so? ....
84. Remember Mildred that you are supposed to go to the dentist today ....
85. I am told that the Rotary Club meets on Wednesdays for lunch. ....
86. If I had known where to look for my keys I could have saved a great deal of trouble. ....
87. Foster asked, "How many *t*s are there in the word *etiquette*?" ....
88. The frightened puppy had its tail tucked between its legs. ....
89. I want you to understand, Helen said, why I cannot support your point of view. ....
90. Although I avoided him the whole evening he insisted on having a private talk with me. ....
91. To tell the truth I have never liked okra. ....
92. Tim taught us some wonderful sea chanteys, including Eddystone Light. ....
93. Mrs. Morris my history teacher has two children. ....
94. He heard a noise and turned to see a rhinoceros rushing toward him. ....
95. Why dont we try to swim across the lake this afternoon? ....
96. Uncle Bill while watching the television debates went to sleep. ....
97. Her latest hairdo is a hideous mess it looks like a beehive. ....
98. The used car dealer sold me a lemon and she steadfastly refuses to discuss the problem with me. ....
99. Hamilton is a member of the so-called Peanut Brigade. ....
100. The news reporter called his informant a courageous man the informant's enemies called him a traitor. ....

CORRECT
WRITING

Form 2

The Parts of Speech 1

Our own language is one of the most fascinating subjects that we can investigate, and those of us who speak and write English can find pleasure in seeking to understand its various aspects. The concern of this book is Standard English and its use in contemporary writing. The study and description of Standard English, based on the thoughtful use of language by educated people, provide standards for correct writing. Although the English language is flexible and continually changing, it is possible to follow certain principles and to observe certain characteristics of usage which can make grammar a relatively exact study and one which can widen the scope of the individual in a satisfying way.

An understanding of the accurate and effective use of English is important not only for communication but also as a vital element of creative thought. Because words are used in the formulation of conscious thought, precise grammatical usage promotes clear thinking and insures logical and systematic transmission of ideas.

Knowledge of Standard English and its acceptable forms is basic to the education of all college students. Learning grammatical terms is an essential first step toward understanding what is correct and what is incorrect in speech and writing. The best place to begin this learning of terms is with the various elements that make up a sentence, elements called **parts of speech**. Any word's identification as a part of speech depends upon its usage within a sentence. The names of the eight parts of speech are as follows:

noun	adverb
pronoun	preposition
adjective	conjunction
verb	interjection

1a Noun

A **noun** (from Latin *nomen*, name) is the name of a person, place, thing, or idea. All nouns are either proper nouns or common nouns. **A proper noun** is the name of a particular person, place, or thing and is spelled with a capital letter:

John F. Kennedy	London, England
California	The Washington Monument
The Vatican	O'Keefe Junior High School

A **common noun** is the name of a class of persons, places, things, or ideas, and is not capitalized:

girl	home	dog	disgust
teacher	park	automobile	friendship
student	street	honesty	poverty

Nouns may also be classified as **individual** or **collective**. **Collective** nouns name groups of persons, places, or things that function as units:

flock	dozen
jury	the rich
team	club

Finally, nouns may be classified as **concrete** or **abstract**. The **concrete** noun names a person, place, or thing which can be perceived by one of the five senses. It can be seen, felt, smelled, heard, or tasted. Here are some examples of concrete nouns:

door	woman	scream
dress	city	snow
tree	odor	museum

An **abstract** noun is the name of a quality, condition, action, or idea. The following are examples of abstract nouns:

beauty	truth	kindness
fear	loneliness	campaign
dismissal	hatred	courtesy

A noun is said to belong to the **nominative**, the **objective**, or the **possessive case**, depending upon its function within a sentence. Subjects are in the nominative case (The *truck* stopped), objects are in the objective case (He saw the *parade*), and nouns showing possession are in the possessive case (That car is *John's*). As you can see, there is no difference in form between nouns in the nominative and the objective cases. The possessive case, however, changes a noun's form. (See Chapter 11 for a thorough discussion of case.)

A noun may be **singular** or **plural**, forming its plural generally by the addition of *-s* or *-es* to the end of the singular form (*girl, girls; potato, potatoes*).

Nouns, together with pronouns and other words or expressions that function as nouns, are sometimes called **substantives**.

1b Pronoun

A **pronoun** (from Latin *pro,* for, and *nomen,* name) is a word used in place of a noun. A pronoun usually refers to a noun or other substantive already mentioned, which is called its **antecedent** (from Latin *ante,* before, and *cedere,* to go). Most pronouns have antecedents, but some do not.

Pronouns are divided into seven categories:

PERSONAL PRONOUNS: I, you, he, it, they, etc.

DEMONSTRATIVE PRONOUNS: this, that, these, those

INDEFINITE PRONOUNS: each, anyone, everyone, either, etc.

INTERROGATIVE PRONOUNS: who, which, what

RELATIVE PRONOUNS: who, which, that

REFLEXIVE PRONOUNS: myself, yourself, herself, themselves, etc.

INTENSIVE PRONOUNS: I *myself,* you *yourself,* she *herself,* they *themselves,* etc.

The personal pronouns have differing forms depending upon whether they are subjects (*I* will help Mr. Curtis) or objects (Gene told *him* to leave) or show possession (The red coat is *hers*). These differences in form, which are seen only in the possessive case of nouns, occur in all three cases (*nominative, objective,* and *possessive*) of pronouns.

Personal pronouns, like nouns, are singular and plural, but their plurals are irregularly formed: I, *we*; she, *they*; it, *they*; etc. The following table shows the various forms of the personal pronouns:

SINGULAR

	Nominative	*Objective*	*Possessive*
1st person	I	me	my, mine
2nd person	you	you	your, yours
3rd person	he, she, it	him, her, it	his, her, hers, its

PLURAL

	Nominative	*Objective*	*Possessive*
1st person	we	us	our, ours
2nd person	you	you	your, yours
3rd person	they	them	their, theirs

1c Adjective

An **adjective** (from Latin *adjectivum,* something that is added) modifies, describes, limits, or adds to the meaning of a noun or pronoun (*strange, lovely, three, French, those*). In other words, adjectives modify substantives. The articles *the, a,* and *an* are adjectives. Nouns in the possessive case (*Martha's* book, the *cat's* whiskers) and some possessive forms of the personal pronouns are used as adjectives:

my	our
your	your
his, her, its	their

Many demonstrative, indefinite, and interrogative forms may be used as either pronouns or adjectives:

DEMONSTRATIVE: this, that, these, those

INDEFINITE: each, any, either, neither, some, all, both, every, many, most

INTERROGATIVE: which, what, whose

When one of these words appears before a noun or other substantive, describing it or adding to its meaning (*this* cake, *those* gloves, *any* person, *some* food, *which* dress), it is an adjective. When the word stands in the place of a noun (*Those* are pretty roses), it is, of course, a pronoun.

Adjectives formed from proper nouns are called **proper adjectives** and are spelled with a capital letter **(German, Christian, Biblical, Shakespearean).**

1d Verb

A **verb** (from Latin *verbum,* word) is a word used to state or ask something and usually expresses an action (*spoke, tells, ran, argued, fights*) or a state of being (*is, seemed, existed, appears*). As its Latin origin indicates, the verb is *the* word in the sentence, for every sentence must have a verb, either expressed or understood.

TRANSITIVE AND INTRANSITIVE VERBS

A verb is called **transitive** if its action is directed toward some receiver, which may be the object of the verb or even its subject. (*David flew the plane,* or *The plane was flown by David.* Whether *plane* is the subject or object of the verb, the fact remains that David flew the plane, making *plane* in both sentences the receiver of the verb's action.)

NOTE: The term *action* should not be misinterpreted as always involving physical activity. The so-called "action" of a verb may not refer to a physical action at all: Mr. Lee *considered* the plan, Amanda *believed* Frank's story, Louise *wants* a new car. The verbs *considered, believed,* and *wants* are transitive verbs; and their objects *plan, story,* and *car* are receivers of their "action," even though there is no physical action involved.

A verb is called **intransitive** if its action is not directed toward some receiver. (*Lightning strikes. Mother is ill.*) Most verbs may be either transitive or intransitive, simply depending on whether or not a receiver of the verb's action is present in the sentence: *Lightning strikes tall trees* (*strikes* is transitive because *trees* is its object). *Lightning strikes suddenly* (*strikes* is intransitive because no receiver of its action is present).

LINKING VERBS

There is a special group of intransitive verbs which make a statement not by expressing action but by indicating a state of being or a condition. These verbs are called **linking verbs** because their function is to link the subject of a sentence with a noun, pronoun, or other substantive that identifies it or with an adjective that describes it. A subject and a linking verb cannot function together as a complete sentence without the help of the substantive or adjective needed to complete the thought; for example, in the sentence *Dorothy is my sister* the word *sister* is necessary to complete the sentence, and it identifies *Dorothy,* the subject. In the sentence *Dorothy is vigorous* the word *vigorous* is necessary, and it describes the subject.

The most common linking verb is the verb *to be* in all its forms, but any verb that expresses a state of being and is followed by a noun or an adjective that identifies or describes the subject is a linking verb. Following is a list of some of the most commonly used linking verbs:

appear	grow	seem	taste*
become	look	smell	
feel	remain	sound	

You will notice that those verbs referring to states of being perceived through the five "senses" are included in the list: *look, feel, smell, sound,* and *taste.* (Sally *looks* happy, I *feel* chilly, The coffee *smells* good, The ticking of the clock *sounded* loud, The plum pudding *tastes* spicy.)

ACTIVE AND PASSIVE VOICE

Transitive verbs are said to be in the **active voice** or the **passive voice**. **Voice** is the form of a verb that indicates whether the subject of the sentence performs the action or is the receiver of the action of the verb. If the subject performs the action, the verb is in the *active voice* (*Andy ate soup for lunch today*). If the subject receives the action, the verb is in the *passive voice* (*Soup was eaten by Andy for lunch today*).

TENSE

Tense is the form a verb takes in order to express the time of an action or a state of being, as in these examples: *Helen walks* (**present tense**); *Helen walked* (**past tense**). These two tenses, present and past, change the verb's simple form to show the time of the verb's action. The other four of the six principal tenses found in English verbs are formed through the use of **auxiliary** (helping) verb forms like the following:

am	is	were	have	had
are	was	will	has	been

The use of these auxiliary verbs creates **verb phrases** (groups of related words that function as single parts of speech). These verb phrases enable the writer to express time and time relationships far beyond those found in the simple present and past forms: She *has gone* to the office; Maggie *will ride* with me; You *must finish* your dinner; He *had expected* to win the prize; I *am planning* a trip.

CONJUGATION OF VERBS

Showing all forms of a verb in all its tenses is called **conjugation**. Any verb may be conjugated if its **principal parts** are known. These are (1) the first person singular, present tense, (2) the first person singular, past tense, (3) the past participle. (The **participle** is a verbal form which must always be accompanied by an auxiliary verb when it is used to create one of the verb tenses.)

---

*These verbs are not exclusively linking verbs; they may also be used in an active sense, possibly having objects, as in the following:

The dog cautiously *smelled* the food in its bowl.
We *looked* everywhere for the lost key.
Sharon *felt* the warmth of the log fire across the room.
Nick *tasted* the chowder and then added salt.

The principal parts of the verb *to call* are (1) *call*, (2) *called*, (3) *called*. The first two of these provide the basic forms of the simple tenses; the third is used with the auxiliary verbs to form verb phrases for the other tenses. The conjugation in the **indicative mood** (that form used for declarative or interrogative sentences) of the verb *to call* is given below:

ACTIVE VOICE

Present Tense

Singular	*Plural*
1. I call	We call
2. You call	You call
3. He, she, it calls	They call

Past Tense

1. I called	We called
2. You called	You called
3. He, she, it called	They called

Future Tense

1. I shall (will) call	We shall (will) call
2. You will call	You will call
3. He, she, it will call	They will call

Present Perfect Tense

1. I have called	We have called
2. You have called	You have called
3. He, she, it has called	They have called

Past Perfect Tense

1. I had called	We had called
2. You had called	You had called
3. He, she, it had called	They had called

Future Perfect Tense

1. I shall (will) have called	We shall (will) have called
2. You will have called	You will have called
3. He, she, it will have called	They will have called

PASSIVE VOICE

Present Tense

1. I am called	We are called
2. You are called	You are called
3. He, she, it is called	They are called

Past Tense

1. I was called	We were called
2. You were called	You were called
3. He, she, it was called	They were called

Future Tense

1. I shall (will) be called	We shall (will) be called
2. You will be called	You will be called
3. He, she, it will be called	They will be called

Present Perfect Tense

1. I have been called	We have been called
2. You have been called	You have been called
3. He, she, it has been called	They have been called

Past Perfect Tense

1. I had been called	We had been called
2. You had been called	You had been called
3. He, she, it had been called	They had been called

Future Perfect Tense

1. I shall (will) have been called	We shall (will) have been called
2. You will have been called	You will have been called
3. He, she, it will have been called	They will have been called

NOTE: You have probably noticed that in the future and future perfect tenses the auxiliary verb *shall* is used in the first persons singular and plural. Traditionally, written English has required this usage, but contemporary grammarians now suggest that the distinction need be made only in formal written English and that *will* may usually be used throughout a conjugation. For emphasis, however, *shall* may occasionally be needed, especially to express strong determination or invitation:

We *shall* overcome!

Shall we dance?

PROGRESSIVE TENSES

To express an action or state in progress either at the time of speaking or at the time spoken of, forms of the auxiliary verb *to be* are combined with the present participle (See Chapter 4, Section C) as follows:

Progressive Present Tense

1. I am calling	We are calling
2. You are calling	You are calling
3. He, she, it is calling	They are calling

Progressive Past Tense

1. I was calling	We were calling
2. You were calling	You were calling
3. He, she, it was calling	They were calling

This process may be continued through the various tenses of the active voice, as indicated below:

> PROGRESSIVE FUTURE TENSE: I shall (will) be calling, etc.
>
> PROGRESSIVE PRESENT PERFECT TENSE: I have been calling, etc.
>
> PROGRESSIVE PAST PERFECT TENSE: I had been calling, etc.
>
> PROGRESSIVE FUTURE PERFECT TENSE: I shall (will) have been calling, etc.

In the passive voice, the progressive is generally used only in the simple present and past tenses:

> PROGRESSIVE PRESENT TENSE: I am being called, etc.
>
> PROGRESSIVE PAST TENSE: I was being called, etc.

In the remaining tenses of the passive voice, the progressive forms—though feasible—become awkward (I shall be being called, I have been being called, etc.).

AUXILIARY VERBS *TO BE* AND *TO HAVE*

As you have seen, the verbs *to be* and *to have* are used to form certain tenses of all verbs. Following are the conjugations of these two auxiliary verbs in the indicative mood, active voice:

The principal parts of *to be* are (1) *am*, (2) *was*, and (3) *been*.

Present Tense

Singular	*Plural*
1. I am	We are
2. You are	You are
3. He, she, it is	They are

Past Tense

1. I was	We were
2. You were	You were
3. He, she, it was	They were

Future Tense

1. I shall (will) be	We shall (will) be
2. You will be	You will be
3. He, she, it will be	They will be

Present Perfect Tense

1. I have been	We have been
2. You have been	You have been
3. He, she, it has been	They have been

Past Perfect Tense

1. I had been	We had been
2. You had been	You had been
3. He, she, it had been	They had been

Future Perfect Tense

1. I shall (will) have been	We shall (will) have been
2. You will have been	You will have been
3. He, she, it will have been	They will have been

The principal parts of the verb *to have* are (1) *have,* (2) *had,* and (3) *had.*

Present Tense

Singular	*Plural*
1. I have	We have
2. You have	You have
3. He, she, it has	They have

Past Tense

1. I had	We had
2. You had	You had
3. He, she, it had	They had

Future Tense

1. I shall (will) have	We shall (will) have
2. You will have	You will have
3. He, she, it will have	They will have

Present Perfect Tense

1. I have had	We have had
2. You have had	You have had
3. He, she, it has had	They have had

Past Perfect Tense

1. I had had	We had had
2. You had had	You had had
3. He, she, it had had	They had had

Future Perfect Tense

1. I shall (will) have had	We shall (will) have had
2. You will have had	You will have had
3. He, she, it will have had	They will have had

MOOD

Mood is the form a verb may take to indicate whether it is intended to make a statement, to give a command, or to express a condition contrary to fact. Besides the **indicative** mood shown in the conjugations above, there are the **imperative** and the **subjunctive** moods.

The **imperative** mood is used in giving commands or making requests, as in *TAKE me out to the ball game.* Here *TAKE* is in the imperative mood. The subject of an imperative sentence is *you,* usually understood, but sometimes expressed for the sake of emphasis, as in *You get out of here!*

The **subjunctive** mood is most often used today to express a wish or a condition contrary to fact. In the sentences *I wish I WERE going* and *If I WERE you, I would not go,* the verbs in capitals are in the subjunctive mood.

1e Adverb

An **adverb** (from Latin *ad,* to or toward, and *verbum,* word) usually modifies or adds to the meaning of verbs, adjectives, and other adverbs. Sometimes, however, it may be used to modify or qualify a whole phrase or clause, adding to the meaning of an idea that the sentence expresses. The following sentences illustrate the variety of uses of the adverb:

He ran *fast.* [*Fast* modifies the verb *ran.*]

The judges considered the contestants *unusually* brilliant. [*Unusually* modifies the adjective *brilliant.*]

She sang *very* loudly. [*Very* modifies the adverb *loudly.*]

The doves were flying *just* outside gun range. [*Just* modifies either the preposition *outside* or the whole prepositional phrase *outside gun range.*]

He had driven carefully *ever* since he was injured. [*Ever* modifies either the conjunction *since* or the whole clause *since he was injured.*]

Unfortunately, she has encountered rejection everywhere. [*Unfortunately* modifies the whole idea expressed in the sentence and cannot logically be attached to a single word.]

1e Preposition

A **preposition** (from Latin *prae,* before, and *positum,* placed) is a word placed usually before a substantive, called the *object of the preposition,* to show relationship between that object and some other word in the sentence. The combination of a preposition, its object, and any modifiers of the object is called a **prepositional phrase** (*in the mood, on the porch, of human events, toward the beautiful green lake*). You will see how necessary prepositions are to our language when you realize how often you use most of the ones in the group below, which includes some of the most commonly used prepositions:

about	between	over
above	beyond	past
across	but (meaning *except*)	since
after	by	through
against	concerning	throughout
along	down	to
amid	during	toward
among	except	under
around	for	underneath
at	from	until
before	in	up
behind	into	upon
below	like	with
beneath	of	within
beside	off	without
besides	on	

Ordinarily a preposition precedes its object, as its name indicates. Although a sentence ending with a preposition is frequently unemphatic or clumsy, it is in no way contrary to English usage. *She asked what they were cooked in* is better English than *She asked in what they were cooked.*

1g Conjunction

A **conjunction** (from Latin *conjungere,* to join) is a word used to join words or groups of words. There are two kinds of conjunctions: **coordinating conjunctions** and **subordinating conjunctions.**

COORDINATING CONJUNCTIONS

Coordinating conjunctions join sentence elements of equal rank. In the sentence *She was poor but honest* the conjunction *but* joins the two adjectives *poor* and *honest.* In *She was poor, but she was honest* the conjunction *but* joins the two independent statements *She was poor* and *she was honest.* The common coordinating conjunctions are the following:

    and   but   or   nor   for

Yet in the sense of *but,* and *so* in the sense of *therefore* are also coordinating conjunctions. **Correlative conjunctions,** which are used in pairs (*either . . . or . . . , neither . . . nor . . .*) are coordinating conjunctions also.

SUBORDINATING CONJUNCTIONS

Subordinating conjunctions introduce certain subordinate or dependent elements and join them to the main or independent part of the sentence. In *Jack has gone home because he was tired* the subordinating conjunction *because* subordinates the clause that it is part of and joins it to the main part of the sentence, *Jack has gone home. If, whether, while, unless, although, as, before, after,* and *until* are common examples of subordinating conjunctions.

NOTE: Words like *however, therefore, nevertheless, moreover, in fact, consequently, hence,* and *accordingly* are essentially adverbs, not conjunctions; they are sometimes called **conjunctive adverbs.**

1h Interjection

An **interjection** (from Latin *inter,* among or between, and *jectum,* thrown) is an exclamatory word like *oh, ouch, please, why, hey* thrown into a sentence or sometimes used alone. An interjection is always grammatically independent of the rest of the sentence. Adjectives, adverbs, and occasionally other parts of speech become interjections when used as independent exclamations (*good! horrible! fine! what! wait!*).

Exercise 1   NOUNS AND PRONOUNS

Write in the first blank at the right any *italicized* word that is a noun and in the second any that is a pronoun.

	NOUN	PRONOUN
EXAMPLE: *Someone* forgot to close *the gate*.	gate	someone
1. *We* took *three* rolls of *film* during our vacation.	film	we
2. Come early if *you* want *supper*.	supper	you
3. *I* listened carefully to *every word* the professor said.	word	I
4. The reporter *asked her* for an *interview*.	interview	her
5. *Everyone* values *success* in his own way.	success	Everyone
6. *He* is a *friendly individual*.	friendly	he
7. The professor gave *me* my *examination* early.		he
8. *Some students* like to study by *themselves*.	students	themselves
9. Did *you understand* his *question*?	question	you
10. *I missed* the five o'clock *train* yesterday.	train	I
11. Saving *money* is *difficult* for *him*.	difficult	him
12. *These* are the *suggestions for* the party.	suggestion	these
13. *What* is the telephone number of the *hospital*?	hospital	what
14. Norrine took *me* for a *ride* on her *new* motorcycle.	ride	me
15. *Everybody* loves the *zoo*.	zoo	Everybody
16. *Who* broke the *glass bowl*?	glass	who

13

17. The *jury* said *he* was *not* guilty.

jury   *he*

18. Jamie *went* with *me* to the *Kentucky Derby.*

Kentucky   *me*

19. Bob has a *friend who traveled* through Mexico on a bicycle.

friend   *who*

20. *Bill* made *me* a model airplane *for* Christmas.

Bill   *me*

Exercise 2   PRONOUNS

In the sentences below identify the *italicized* pronouns by writing one of the following abbreviations in the space at the right:

P for personal,   *Inter* for interrogative,
D for demonstrative,   *Inten* for intensive,
I for indefinite,   *Ref* for reflexive.
Rel for relative,

EXAMPLE: Where have *you* been?   ....*P*....

1. *Who* has read *Zen and the Art of Motorcyle Maintenance*?   ...*Inter*...

2. *We* regretted that you could not come.   ....*P*....

3. *Everyone* is ready.   ....*I*....

4. I *myself* selected the gift.   ....

5. I could not make *myself* work the problem.   ....

6. They had prepared a plan by *themselves.*   ....

7. *These* are my favorite flowers.   ....

8. Irene asked *us* to wait.   ....

9. Students *who* fail have usually not studied.   ....

10. Tipper said that he could not tell *anyone* his secret.   ....

11. He earned a reputation *which* ruined his career.   ....

12. *That* is a serious accusation to make.   ....

13. *What* is your family bringing to the picnic?   ....

14. If you apply *yourself*, you will succeed.   ....

15. Neither my brother nor *I* can attend the reunion.   ....

16. Where did you buy *those*?   ....

17. Jimmy can manage *it* quite well.   ....

15

18. Jane received all the help that *she* needed. ....

19. *What* should I do? ....

20. This was *something* that he could not understand. ....

Exercise 3   ADJECTIVES AND ADVERBS

In the following sentences underline once all the adjectives and words used as adjectives except the articles *a, an,* and *the*. Underline all adverbs twice.

EXAMPLE: She is very stubborn.

1. Jake wore a light blue suit.

2. We seriously considered every suggestion.

3. The main dish was a very large salad.

4. Jan recently bought a new truck.

5. A small-town student often feels lost in a university.

6. The old man quietly entered the room.

7. In a big city driving is very often dangerous.

8. Autumn leaves are always beautiful.

9. The father spoke softly to the little children.

10. I live in a high-rise apartment only two blocks from the college.

11. He has extremely bad manners.

12. Hilda makes fresh bread daily.

13. The biology professor carefully explained the test.

14. Many citizens complained loudly.

15. She works actively with the tennis team.

16. He suddenly lost his balance.

17. He seldom goes to a soccer game.

18. The afternoon traffic moves slowly.

19. He wandered blindly down the busy street.

20. The practical student carefully plans ahead.

Exercise 4   VERBS

In the first column at the right, write the verbs in the following sentences. In the second column write *A* if the verb is in the active voice, *P* if it is in the passive voice. In the last column write *T* if the verb is transitive, *I* if it is intransitive.

	VERB	A/P	T/I
EXAMPLE: Mary was elected president.	*was elected*	*P*	*T*
1. Sam baked a cake.			
2. Henry is angry.			
3. The argument became violent.			
4. Celestine lives quietly in her old mountain cabin.			
5. The artist has not achieved success.			
6. The train will remain empty until tomorrow.			
7. I can see no way around the difficulty.			
8. Paula was admitted to the Mercer University Law School.			
9. He refused the fraternity's invitation to membership.			
10. The Appaloosa horse is one of the world's oldest breeds.			
11. They are at their best in a social situation.			
12. The coach had been given a trophy by the team.			
13. The lazy professor was brought before the board.			
14. The wildcat has finally been caught.			
15. Marge wanted a car for graduation.			

16. We must become aware of our
    responsibilities.   ....

17. Reading enlarges one's horizon. ....

18. We drove carefully through the snow. ....

19. Our definition of leadership definitely
    excludes the gang leader.   ....

20. I stood up and slowly moved toward the
    door.   ....

Exercise 5   PREPOSITIONS

Write the prepositions in the following sentences in the spaces of the first column to the right. Write the objects of the prepositions in the second column. If a sentence contains no preposition, leave the spaces blank.

	PREP.	OBJECT
EXAMPLE: Mario is among my many friends.	*among*	*friends*
1. Do not throw the ball in the house.		
2. The professor read a poem to us.		
3. The conservative is usually against any changes.		
4. The final choice was between Frank and Clyde.		
5. Betsy stumbled down the stairs.		
6. Everyone went home except me.		
7. We planted twenty acres of soybeans.		
8. Once in the apartment, I felt safe.		
9. Our cat chased Ed's dog around the house.		
10. Mrs. Jefferson had a long talk with her son's teacher.		
11. Before the race the drivers were tense.		
12. My supervisor said that she was pleased with my work.		
13. The traffic helicopter flies over the city every day.		
14. Everyone asked questions but me.		
15. The little girl hid behind the tree.		
16. The speaker's criticism was aimed at the school board.		

17. Walking through the woods is a delightful experience.   ....

18. He made his confession under stress.   ....

19. Do you know anything about physics?   ....

20. I recently moved to Split Silk, Georgia.   ....

Exercise 6 CONJUNCTIONS

In the following sentences there are both coordinating and subordinating conjunctions. Write the conjunction in the space at the right, and after it write *C* if it joins sentence elements of equal rank or *S* if it joins unequal elements.

EXAMPLE: Both the faculty and the students were frustrated by the regulations.

Both...and, C

1. Last summer I read *The Lives of a Cell* and *The Ascent of Man*. ....

2. When the snow melts, there will be flooding. ....

3. Shakespeare is a writer with wit and imagination. ....

4. As the sailor walked toward the village, he saw his ship in port. ....

5. If you have never been to San Francisco, you will be quite enchanted. ....

6. When Peter stayed here, he wanted his own room. ....

7. He did not like the movie, nor did I. ....

8. The people were delighted because they had an heir to the throne. ....

9. Before I could answer the door, the stranger rushed in. ....

10. Although the night air was chilly, we slept outside. ....

11. I came because I was worried about you. ....

12. Please wait for me at the hotel until I call. ....

13. If I call you tomorrow, perhaps we can have lunch together. ....

14. Irene thought that you had left. ....

15. I can go, or I can stay here. ....

16. Although he lost the race, he will always remember the challenge. ....

17. I do not have the time to go, but Wayne is going. ....

18. Before you walk to the store, make a grocery list. ....

23

19. When the ground dries, I will plow my garden.   ....

20. Both you and I will attend the meeting.   ....

Exercise 7   REVIEW OF PARTS OF SPEECH

In the following sentences identify the part of speech of each *italicized* word by writing one of the following abbreviations in the space at the right:

N for noun,	*Adv* for adverb,
V for verb,	*Prep* for preposition,
P for pronoun,	*C* for conjunction,
Adj for adjective,	*I* for interjection.

EXAMPLE: Those books are *mine*.   *P*

1. New York taxicab drivers are a unique *group* of people.   ....

2. *After* a moment, the crowd stepped aside.   ....

3. *Oh*, that will be very good.   ....

4. As she waited patiently, *she* remembered only the good times.   ....

5. According to the gossip, the owner was indeed *eccentric*.   ....

6. The pyramids are an example of *Egyptian* architecture.   ....

7. Leon seemed thinner *and* paler than usual.   ....

8. She turned *abruptly* and walked off.   ....

9. The *outside* of the house needs painting.   ....

10. The man *with* the beard moved cautiously toward the door.   ....

11. The children are waiting *outside*.   ....

12. I *have finished* reading her latest novel.   ....

13. *We* visited Magnolia Gardens this spring.   ....

14. My grandparents used an *old-fashioned* icebox.   ....

15. The soccer clinic will be *jointly* sponsored by J and J Sporting Goods and the
    recreation department.   ....

16. The Morgan horse *is known* for its endurance.   ....

17. I enjoy the beauty of the *countryside*.   ....

18. *What*, have you lost your keys?   ....

19. *When* Beverly Sills appeared on stage, the audience gave her a standing ovation.   ....

20. *Neither* his home *nor* his barn is painted.   ....

Exercise 8   REVIEW OF PARTS OF SPEECH

In the following sentences identify the part of speech of each *italicized* word by writing one of the following abbreviations in the space at the right:

N for noun,	*Adv* for adverb,
V for verb,	*Prep* for preposition,
P for pronoun,	*C* for conjunction,
Adj for adjective,	*I* for interjection.

EXAMPLE: I found *myself* unable to cope with the situation.   *P*

1. You must stay *outside* the house.   ....

2. The trapped animal freed *itself*.   ....

3. I enjoyed reading the book, *but* I did not see the movie.   ....

4. I have several pieces of Steve Blair's *pottery*.   ....

5. Sam made *himself* a wheelbarrow.   ....

6. If we have a garden next summer, we will build a *compost* box.   ....

7. *Did* you *see* the game between Marquette and the University of North Carolina?   ....

8. *Oh*, I can hardly wait for spring vacation.   ....

9. An Italian artist painted "The Adoration *of* the Magi."   ....

10. I think that I brought the *wrong* key.   ....

11. *Everyone* is working hard on the project.   ....

12. The rain *stopped* before we got up.   ....

13. For a moment he could *not* remember where he was.   ....

14. He scarcely noticed *me*.   ....

15. They stared at each other for several *minutes*.   ....

16. Wayne apologized *for* his remark.   ....

17. *Neither* his friends *nor* his enemies believed his story.   ....

18. *Ah*! Now I understand why you were late. ....

19. Despite the warning, the man *moved* toward the door. ....

20. Existentialism is probably the *most* popular philosophy of our time. ....

Recognizing Subjects, Verbs, and Complements 2

2a The Sentence

A **sentence** is made up of single parts of speech combined into a pattern which expresses a complete thought. In other words, a sentence is a group of words that expresses a complete thought. In its simplest form this complete statement is an independent clause or a **simple sentence**.

2b Subject and Predicate

Every simple sentence must have two basic elements: (1) the thing we are talking about, and (2) what we say about it. The thing we are talking about is called the **subject**, and what we say about it is called the **predicate**. The subject is a noun, a pronoun, or some other word or group of words used as a noun. The essential part of the predicate is a verb—a word which tells something about the subject. It tells that the subject *does* something or that something *is true* of the subject. Therefore, a subject and a verb are the fundamental parts of every sentence. In fact, it is possible to express meaning with just these two elements:

> Pilots fly.
> Flowers bloom.

In each example the verb says that the subject does something. The sentences are about pilots and flowers. What does each do? The pilots fly; the flowers bloom.

2c Finding the Verb

Finding verbs and subjects of verbs in a sentence is the first step in determining whether or not a group of words expresses a complete thought. Therefore, look first for the verb, the most important word in the sentence, and then for its subject.

The verb may sometimes be difficult to find. It may come anywhere in the sentence; for instance, it may precede the subject, as in some interrogative sentences (*Where is my pencil?*). It may consist of a single word or a group of two or more words; it may have other words inserted within the verb phrase; it may be combined with the negative *not* or with a contraction of *not*. To find the verb, however, look for the word or group of words that expresses an action or a state of being. In the following sentences the verbs are in italics:

My friend *stood* by me. [The verb *stood* follows the subject *friend.*]

By me *stood* my friend. [The verb *stood* precedes the subject *friend.*]

My friend *was standing* by me. [The verb *was standing* consists of two words.]

My friend *cannot stand* by me. [The verb *can* is combined with the negative adverb *not,* which is not part of the verb.]

Did my friend *stand* by me? [The verb *did stand* is divided by the subject.]

2d Finding the Subject

Sometimes finding the subject may also be difficult, for, as we have just seen, the subject does not always come immediately before the verb. Often it comes after the verb; often it is separated from the verb by a modifying element. Always look for the noun or pronoun about which the verb asserts something and disregard intervening elements:

Many of the children *come* to the clinic. [A prepositional phrase comes between the subject and the verb.]

There *are flowers* on the table. [The subject comes after the verb. The word *there* is never a subject; in this sentence it is an *expletive,* an idiomatic introductory word.]

In the room *were* a *cot* and a *chair.* [The subject comes after the verb.]

In an imperative sentence, a sentence expressing a command or a request, the subject *you* is usually implied rather than expressed. Occasionally, however, the subject *you* is expressed:

Come in out of the rain.

Shut the door!

You play goalie.

Either the verb or the subject or both may be **compound**; that is, there may be more than one subject and more than one verb:

The *boy* and the *girl* played. [Two subjects.]

The boy *worked* and *played.* [Two verbs.]

The *boy* and the *girl worked* and *played.* [Two subjects and two verbs.]

In the first sentence the compound subject is *boy* and *girl.* In the second sentence there is a compound verb, *worked* and *played.* In the third sentence both the subject and the verb are compound.

2e Complements

Thus far we have discussed two functions of words: that of nouns and pronouns as subjects and that of verbs as predicates.

A third function of words which we must consider is that of completing the verb. Nouns, pronouns, and adjectives are used to complete verbs and are called **complements**. A complement may be a **direct object**, an **indirect object**, a **predicate noun** or **pronoun**, a **predicate adjective**, an **objective complement**, or a **retained object**.

A **direct object** is a noun or noun equivalent which completes the verb and receives the action expressed in the verb:

> The pilot flew the plane. [*Plane* is the direct object of *flew*. Just as the subject answers the question "*who?*" or "*what?*" before the verb (Who flew?), so the direct object answers the question "*whom?*" or "*what?*" after the verb (Flew what?).]

An **indirect object** is a word (or words) denoting the person or thing indirectly affected by the action of a transitive verb. It is the person or thing to which something is given or for which something is done. Such words as *give, offer, grant, lend, teach,* etc., represent the idea of something done for the indirect object:

> We gave *her* the book. [*Her* is the indirect object of *gave*. The indirect object answers the question "*to (for) whom or what?*" after the verb *gave* (Gave to whom?).]

Certain verbs that represent the idea of taking away or withholding something can also have indirect objects:

> The judge *denied him* the opportunity to speak in his own defense.
>
> Father *refused Frances* the use of the car.

A **predicate noun** (also called **predicate nominative**) is a noun or its equivalent which renames or identifies the subject and completes such verbs as *be, seem, become,* and *appear* (called linking verbs):

> The woman is a *doctor*. [The predicate noun *doctor* completes the intransitive verb *is* and renames the subject *woman*.]
>
> My best friends are *she* and her *sister*. [The predicate pronoun *she* and the predicate noun *sister* complete the intransitive verb *are* and rename the subject *friends*.]
>
> Mary has become a *pilot*. [The predicate noun *pilot* completes the intransitive verb *has become* and renames the subject *Mary*.]

A **predicate adjective** is an adjective which completes a linking verb and describes the subject:

> The man seems *angry*. [The predicate adjective *angry* completes the intransitive verb *seems* and describes the subject *man*.]

An **objective complement** is a noun or an adjective which completes the action expressed in the verb and refers to the direct object. If it is a noun, the objective complement is in a sense identical with the direct object; if it is an adjective, it describes or limits the direct object. It occurs commonly after such verbs as *think, call, find, make, consider, choose,* and *believe:*

> Jealousy made Othello a *murderer*. [The objective complement *murderer* completes the transitive verb *made* and renames the direct object *Othello*.]
>
> She thought the day very *disagreeable*. [The objective complement *disagreeable* is an adjective which describes the direct object *day*.]

A **retained object** is a noun or noun equivalent which remains as the object when a verb which has both a direct and an indirect object is put into the passive voice. The other object becomes the subject of such a verb. Although either object may become the subject, the indirect object more commonly takes that position, and the direct object is retained:

> The board granted him a year's leave of absence.
> He was granted a year's leave of absence.
>
> [In the second sentence the verb has been put into the passive voice, the indirect object of the first sentence has become the subject of the second, and the direct object has been retained.]
>
> The teacher asked the student a difficult question.
> A difficult question was asked the student.
>
> [In the second sentence the verb has been put into the passive voice, the direct object of the first sentence has become the subject of the second, and the indirect object has been retained.]

Exercise 9   SUBJECTS AND VERBS

In each of the following sentences underline the subject once and its verb twice. Then copy
the subject on the first line and the verb on the second line at the right of the sentence.

	SUBJECT	VERB
EXAMPLE: Students are encouraged through discussions with their academic advisors.	Students	are encouraged
1. After colliding with an iceberg, the *Titanic* sank.		
2. Have you ever ridden on a snowplow?		
3. The blue sky turned a soft gray.		
4. Self-discipline is an admirable character trait.		
5. Lynn was chosen hockey captain.		
6. A group of students from Gainesville Junior College will tour Greece this summer.		
7. According to Keats, "a thing of beauty is a joy forever."		
8. These suggestions are timely and stimulating.		
9. Despite the warning, the strikers left the plant.		
10. Why do you want pickles in your salad?		
11. In earlier days a man's word was his bond.		
12. Any successful business needs satisfied customers.		
13. I appreciate your help and advice.		
14. Jake returned to his hotel room quite late.		
15. In the cabin were two beds, a chair, and a table.		
16. The specimens were examined by the biology students.		
17. My mother and I have season tickets to the opera.		

18. Neither the student nor the professor was happy about the test grades.

19. Arlie, in the meantime, will help you.

20. Shari's mother lit the Sabbath candles.

21. New courses will be added and others changed during the school year.

22. Tommy, as well as his three sons, attended the NCAA tournament in St. Louis.

23. Ed patiently waited for Jan.

24. I hurried to class but forgot my books.

25. Part of the blame is yours.

26. There are several pieces of fruit on the table.

27. Where did you find my book?

28. The mayor and the union met every day last week.

29. Earl, in the beginning, agreed with the politicians.

30. Have you visited the Peabody Museum?

31. Duke University is planning an alumni party.

32. A number of student leaders were present.

33. The committee took action last Monday.

34. War movies draw large crowds.

35. He was temporarily suspended from class.

Exercise 10   SUBJECTS AND VERBS

In each of the following sentences underline the subject(s) once and their verb(s) twice. Then copy the subject(s) in the first column and the verb(s) in the second column at the right of the sentence. Use only as many lines as are needed.

	SUBJECT(S)	VERB(S)
EXAMPLE: Kyle visited Israel and learned about his ancestors.	Kyle	visited
		learned

1. The Seacrest Inn overlooks the rugged Maine Coast.

2. His attitude and work have been criticized.

3. Rue and her family go to Atlantic City every spring.

4. My nephew broke his arm and could not play baseball.

5. Are you and Frances going to Canada this year?

6. John and I are having a grand time.

7. I stood in the rain and waited for the bus.

8. We will leave early in the morning and return late Sunday.

9. Hockey and soccer are my favorite sports. ....

....

10. Both the bus driver and the driver of the car were at fault. ....

....

11. Ralph patted the little dog. ....

....

12. A college education is priceless but expensive. ....

....

13. Neither the President nor the Dean is on campus. ....

....

14. We are having problems with our hand tiller. ....

....

15. Did you plant corn this year? ....

....

16. Tobacco is a major crop in North Carolina. ....

....

17. Andy and his friends spent a week at the beach. ....

....

18. The carpenter cut each plank carefully. ....

....

19. Baylor University has an excellent academic program. ....

....

20. I am late for my dental appointment.   ....

    ....

21. My sister hates country and western music.   ....

    ....

22. Our class is planning an overnight trip to the mountains.   ....

    ....

23. What have you done with my sunglasses?   ....

    ....

24. Our term papers are due next week.   ....

    ....

25. The police and the parents understand our problems.   ....

    ....

26. Lois hurried to the meeting.   ....

    ....

Exercise 11   DIRECT OBJECTS AND PREDICATE NOUNS

In each of the following sentences underline the complement. In the blank space write *DO* if the complement is a direct object and *PN* if it is a predicate noun.

EXAMPLE: Dr. Hammock is a psychology <u>professor</u>.   *PN*
....

1. I paid my lab fee yesterday.   ....

2. Will you give me her address?   ....

3. Tommy has become a vegetarian.   ....

4. We are planning a summer tour of Australia.   ....

5. The new chef prepared a delicious dinner.   ....

6. The weather was the cause of the airplane crash.   ....

7. What action do you suggest?   ....

8. The boy by the door is my brother.   ....

9. The film was a chilling tale of murder.   ....

10. Eudora Welty read a selection from her works.   ....

11. Have you hiked the Appalachian Trail?   ....

12. I am a stockholder in a large aircraft corporation.   ....

13. Sarah played tennis Saturday.   ....

14. Warren is an accountant with Arthur Andersen and Company.   ....

15. He solved the problem.   ....

16. Sugar does not have any food value.   ....

17. Max Ernst is a prominent American landscape artist.   ....

18. Everyone knows her.   ....

19. Will Merle become president?   ....

20. Angie will cultivate the garden tomorrow.   ....

21. She is her father's favorite child. ....

22. My only exercise is tennis. ....

23. Henry has been our secretary for some time. ....

24. I watched the game on television. ....

25. The coach's daughter is a natural athlete. ....

Exercise 12   INDIRECT OBJECTS AND OBJECTIVE COMPLEMENTS

In each of the following sentences identify the *italicized* complement by writing in the space at the right one of the following abbreviations:

IO if it is an indirect object
OC if it is an objective complement

EXAMPLE: The Rabbi read the *children* stories from the Bible.   *IO*
....

1. The class elected Joseph *president.*   ....

2. He sent *me* his recipe for chocolate mousse.   ....

3. I bought *you* a new CB radio.   ....

4. Did Roger paint his house *purple*?   ....

5. Lynn wrote *me* a letter explaining her new job.   ....

6. Becky cannot find her *classmates* an apartment.   ....

7. The professor considered her logic *faulty*.   ....

8. Did you bring *him* his coat?   ....

9. Our book club selected Joyce Carol Oates *author* of the year.   ....

10. Did you give the *kittens* any milk?   ....

11. Smith College mailed *Kyle* a catalogue.   ....

12. The audience gave *Marilyn Horne* a standing ovation.   ....

13. She wanted her wedding dress *simple*.   ....

14. The governor appointed Mr. Oxford a *Regent.*   ....

15. Karl won the *family* a trip to Hawaii.   ....

16. The faculty presented *Dr. Butler* a first edition of Faulkner's masterpiece.   ....

17. The blind student is teaching *us* Braille.   ....

18. Mary Jane ordered her *husband* a Porsche for an anniversary present.   ....

19. The Dean thought the faculty member *insubordinate*.   ....

20. Jane considered her sister very *selfish*.   ....

Exercise 13   COMPLEMENTS

A. In each of the following sentences identify the *italicized* word by writing one of the
following abbreviations in the space at the right:

PN if it is a predicate noun,   IO if it is an indirect object,
PA if it is a predicate adjective,   OC if it is an objective complement.
DO if it is a direct object,

EXAMPLE: The desire to travel made Ulysses *restless.*   *OC*

1. I recently reread C. S. Lewis's *The Screwtape Letters.*   ....

2. He buried his *head* in his hands.   ....

3. The young man was too *faint* and *dizzy* to protest.   ....

4. Newman is my little brother's *name*.   ....

5. Her mouth was *dry* with fear and tension.   ....

6. Did the hockey team elect *Grace* co-captain?   ....

7. He weighed his *words* carefully.   ....

8. I thought the president's speech *insulting*.   ....

9. They sent *Aubrey* to Washington.   ....

10. We gave *Jimmy* the room upstairs.   ....

11. Paula has always been a *leader*.   ....

12. The outfielder quickly threw the first *baseman* the ball.   ....

13. Threepio is a delightful *robot*.   ....

14. I found his conversation quite *boring*.   ....

15. I will read *you* a story about the magic land of Narnia.   ....

B.   Write sixteen sentences, four of which contain direct objects; four, indirect objects; four, predicate nouns; four, predicate adjectives. In the space at the right, write *DO* (direct object), *IO* (indirect object), *PN* (predicate noun), or *PA* (predicate adjective) as the case may be.

1. ....

2. ....

3. ....

4. ....

5. ....

6. ....

7. ....

8. ....

9. ....

10. ....

11. ....

12. ....

13. ....

14. ....

15. ....

16. ....

The Sentence 3
Fragment

3a Grammatical Fragments

If you are not careful to have both a subject and a predicate in your sentences, you will write sentence fragments instead of complete sentences. Observe, for example, the following:

> A tall, distinguished-looking gentleman standing on the corner in a pouring rain.

> Standing on the corner in a pouring rain and shielding himself from the deluge with a a large umbrella.

The first of these groups of words is no more than the subject of a sentence or the object of a verb or preposition. It may be part of such a sentence, for example, as *We noticed a tall, distinguished-looking gentleman standing on the corner in a pouring rain.* The second group is probably a modifier of some kind, the modifier of a subject, for instance: *Standing on the corner in a pouring rain and shielding himself from the deluge with a large umbrella, a tall, distinguished-looking gentleman was waiting for a cab.*

Another type of fragment is seen in the following illustrations:

> Because I had heard all that I wanted to hear and did not intend to be bored any longer.

> Who was the outstanding athlete of her class and also the best scholar.

> Although he had been well recommended by his former employers.

Each of these groups of words actually has a subject and a predicate, but each is still a fragment because the first word of each is a subordinating element and clearly indicates that the thought is incomplete, that the thought expressed depends upon some other thought. Such fragments are subordinate parts of longer sentences like the following:

> I left the hall because I had heard all that I wanted to hear and did not intend to be bored any longer.

The valedictorian was Alice Snodgrass, who was the outstanding athlete of her class and also the best scholar.

He did not get the job although he was well recommended by his former employers.

3b Permissible Fragments

A sentence fragment is usually the result of ignorance or carelessness. It is the sign of an immature writer. But, on the other hand, much correct spoken and written English contains perfectly proper fragments of sentences. The words *yes* and *no* may stand alone, as may other words and phrases in dialogue; there is nothing wrong, for example, in such fragments as the following:

The sooner, the better.

Anything but that.

Same as before.

Interjections and exclamatory phrases may also stand alone as independent elements. The following fragments are correct:

Ouch!

Tickets, please!

Not so!

3c Stylistic Fragments

There is another kind of fragment of rather common occurrence in the writing of some of the best authors. It is the phrase used for realistic or impressionistic effect, the piling up of words or phrases without any effort to organize them into sentences: "The blue haze of evening was upon the field. Lines of forest with long purple shadows. One cloud along the western sky partly smothering the red." This kind of writing, if it is to be good, is very difficult. Like free verse, it may best be left to the experienced writer. Students should learn to recognize a sentence fragment when they see one. They should use this form sparingly in their own writing. And they should remember two things: first, that the legitimacy of the sentence fragment depends upon whether it is used intentionally or not, and second, that in an elementary course in composition most instructors assume that a sentence fragment is unintended.

Study carefully the following sentence fragments and the accompanying comments:

A large woman of rather determined attitude who says that she wishes to see you to discuss a matter of great importance. [This is a typical fragment unintended by the writer, who seems to have felt that it is a complete sentence because there are a subject and a predicate in each subordinate clause.]

He finally decided to leave school. Because he was utterly bored with his work and was failing all his courses. [Here the second group of words is an unjustifiable fragment. It is a subordinate clause and should be attached to the main clause without a break of any kind.]

There were books everywhere. Books in the living room, books in the bedroom, books even in the kitchen. [The second group of words is a fragment, but it may be defended on grounds of emphasis. Many writers, however, would have used a comma or colon after *everywhere* and made a single sentence.]

Exercise 14   THE SENTENCE FRAGMENT

Indicate in the space at the right by writing *C* or *F* whether the following groups of words are complete sentences or fragments of sentences. Rewrite any fragment making it a complete sentence.

EXAMPLE: The Grand Canyon National Park located in Arizona.   .....*F*....

   The Grand Canyon National Park is located in Arizona.

1. California, a state which attracts many of my friends.   ....

2. The tournament features more than thirty international tennis stars.   ....

3. If you have never painted before.   ....

4. After the play, which was over at ten o'clock.   ....

5. During his illness he never lost his sense of humor.   ....

6. While still a girl living in Apple Valley.   ....

7. Albert studied music with the best teachers of the day.   ....

8. His three marriages, two of which were short-lived.   ....

9. T. S. Eliot, having won an honored position among modern poets.   ....

10. One of the collection's most fascinating books.   ....

11. Be sure that you eat at Ma Hull's in Atlanta.   ....

12. While they were in Michigan, they visited Mackinac Island.   ....

13. Though the characters are well developed.   ....

14. The object of the meeting, which will be short.   ....

15. Attempts have been made to telephone the camp.   ....

16. Charlemagne, the first ruler of the Holy Roman Empire, who died in 814.   ....

17. The small but growing collection of rare stones.   ....

18. An issue that must be faced by the next generation.   ....

19. Alfalfa, one of the oldest crops in the world.   ....

20. During the afternoon we went to a movie.   ....

21. Although the debate over human rights is an ancient one.   ....

22. If you cannot find the book which I told you about.   ....

23. The raven, which is a frequent subject of poetry.   ....

24. These reports, together with Jake's record.   ....

25. Even though the first opera of the season was not well known.   ....

Exercise 15   THE SENTENCE FRAGMENT

Some of the following groups are fragments. Some are fragments and sentences. Some are complete sentences. Rewrite in such a way as to leave no fragments. If the group of words is already a complete sentence, leave it as it is.

EXAMPLE: I enjoyed reading Dickens's novel. Because it carried me from one adventure to another.

I enjoyed reading Dickens's novel because it carried me from one adventure to another.

1. When I got home. I looked everywhere for my riding boots.

2. Mike missed his ride. Because he was not ready.

3. When the play was over and we left the theater.

4. The man-made lake almost complete. Which will be stocked with fish.

5. Walking to the pitcher's mound. The team's manager said something to the veteran pitcher.

6. I plan to leave the city. After I visit the Smithsonian tomorrow.

7. Ted bought fifty acres in the country. In order to breed Thoroughbred horses.

8. The Mount Rushmore Memorial with its carved heads of Washington, Jefferson, Lincoln, and Theodore Roosevelt. It attracts many visitors.

9. I recently finished reading a biography of Flannery O'Connor. A great American author.

10. Mt. Everest, which is the world's highest mountain. It is located in Tibet.

11. Because of the beautiful scenery, we will travel U.S. Highway 81 on our way to Vermont.

12. The city workers' strike finally ending. The workers returned to their jobs.

13. An exchange student using a ham radio. He helped save the Panamanian vessel *Rhinoceros.*

14. Winning the Pulitzer Prize in Letters in 1940, John Steinbeck. The book was *The Grapes of Wrath.*

15. I was late for the Standard Federal Board meeting. My clock having stopped.

Exercise 16   THE SENTENCE FRAGMENT

Complete or revise the following sentence fragments in such a way as to make complete sentences.

EXAMPLE: Cranberries, a treat at any time and always served with our Thanksgiving turkey.

> *Cranberries, a treat at any time, are always served with our Thanksgiving turkey.*

1. As we strolled down the winding path.

2. Travelers on I-75 who have the time and the inclination.

3. When my brother visited the Bowdoin campus.

4. In remote places people who enjoy eating venison.

5. By choosing this horrible back road.

6. Giles and Judy, who are both deaf and who won the clogging contest last year.

7. The reason Marilyn moved to Augusta.

8. *Tiger at the Gates*, written by Jean Giraudoux and a play about the futility of war.

9. Our rock group which includes seven members: a singer, two guitarists, an organist, a trumpeter, a drummer, and an arranger.

10. The old man, reclining in a lounge chair while reading Richard Connell's "The Most Dangerous Game."

Verbals 4

Difficulty in recognizing verbs is often encountered because certain verb forms which function partly as verbs and partly as other parts of speech are confused with sentence verbs. (The *sentence verb* is the verb that states something about the subject, one capable of completing a statement.) These other verb forms are made from verbs but also perform the function of nouns, adjectives, or adverbs. In other words, they constitute a sort of half-verb. They are called **verbals**. The three verbals forms are the **gerund**, the **participle**, and the **infinitive**.

4a   Verbals and Sentence Verbs

It is important that you distinguish between the use of a particular verb form as a verbal and its use as a main verb in a sentence. An illustration of the different uses of the verb form *running* will help you to make this distinction:

> *Running* every day is good exercise. [*Running* is a **gerund** and is the subject of the verb *is.*]
>
> *Running* swiftly, he caught the bandit. [*Running* is a **participle** and modifies the pronoun *he.*]
>
> The boy *is running* down the street. [*Is running* is the **sentence verb**. It is formed by using the present participle with the auxiliary verb *is.*]

It must be emphasized that *a verbal cannot take the place of a sentence verb* and that *any group of words containing a verbal but no sentence verb is a sentence fragment:*

> The boy *running* [A sentence fragment.]
>
> *To face* an audience [A sentence fragment.]
>
> The boy *running* up the steps is Charles. [A complete sentence.]
>
> *To face* an audience was a great effort for me. [A complete sentence.]

The following table shows the tenses and voices in which verbals appear:

GERUNDS AND PARTICIPLES

Tense	*Active Voice*	*Passive Voice*
Present	doing	being done
Past		done (This form applies only to participles.)
Present Perfect	having done	having been done
Progressive Present Perfect	having been doing	

INFINITIVES

Tense	*Active Voice*	*Passive Voice*
Present	to do	to be done
Present Perfect	to have done	to have been done
Progressive Present	to be doing	
Progressive Present Perfect	to have been doing	

4b The Gerund

A **gerund** is a verbal used as a noun and in its present tense always ends in *-ing*. Like a noun, a gerund is used as a subject, a complement, an object of a preposition, or an appositive. Do not confuse the gerund with the present participle, which has the same form but is used as an adjective:

> *Planning* the work carefully required a great deal of time. [*Planning* is a gerund used as subject of the sentence.]

> She was not to blame for *breaking* the vase. [*Breaking* is a gerund used as object of the preposition *for.*]

> I appreciated your *taking* time to help me. [*Taking* is a gerund used as direct object of *appreciated.*]

> His unselfish act, *giving* Marty his coat, plainly showed Ed's generosity. [*Giving* is a gerund used as the appositive of *act.*]

In the sentences above you will note examples of gerunds functioning as nouns but also taking objects as verbs do. In the first sentence the gerund *planning* is used as the subject of the verb *required. Planning* itself, however, is completed by the object *work* and is modified by the adverb *carefully.* This dual functioning of the gerund is apparent in the other three sentences as well.

It is important to remember a rule concerning the modification of gerunds: Always use the possessive form of a noun or pronoun before a gerund. Because gerunds are nouns, their modifiers, other than the adverbial ones just mentioned, must be adjectival; therefore, the possessive form, which has adjectival function, is the correct modifier:

Mr. Bridges was surprised at *Doug's* offering him the motorboat.

NOT

Mr. Bridges was surprised at Doug offering him the motorboat.

4c The Participle

A **participle** is a verbal used as an adjective. The present participle is formed by adding *-ing* to the verb: *do – doing*. Again, remember not to confuse the gerund and the present participle, which have the same form but do not function similarly. The past participle is formed in various ways. It may end in *-ed, -d, -t,* or *-n: talk – talked, hear – heard, feel – felt, know – known.* It may also be formed by a change of vowel: *sing – sung.*

> The baby, *wailing* pitifully, refused to be comforted. [*Wailing* is a present participle. It modifies *baby*.]
>
> The *broken* doll can be mended. [*Broken* is a past participle, passive voice. It modifies *doll*.]
>
> An old coat, *faded* and *torn*, was her only possession. [*Faded* and *torn* are past participles, passive voice, modifying *coat*.]
>
> *Having been warned*, the man was sent on his way. [*Having been warned* is the present perfect participle, passive voice. It modifies *man*.]

Like the gerund, the participle may have a complement and adverbial modifiers. In the sentence *Wildly waving a red flag, he ran down the track,* the participle *waving* has the object *flag* and the adverbial modifier *wildly*.

4d The Infinitive

An **infinitive** is a verbal consisting of the simple form of the verb preceded by *to* and used as a noun, an adjective, or an adverb:

> *To err* is human. [*To err* is used as a noun, the subject of *is*.]
>
> He wanted *to go* tomorrow. [*To go* is used as a noun, the object of the verb *wanted*.]
>
> He had few books *to read*. [*To read* is used as an adjective to modify the noun *books*.]
>
> Frank seemed eager *to go*. [*To go* is used as an adverb to modify the adjective *eager*.]
>
> She rode fast *to escape* her pursuers. [*To escape* is used as an adverb to modify the verb *rode*.]

Sometimes the word *to* is omitted:

> Susan helped *carry* the packages. [*To* is understood before the verb *carry*. (*To*) *carry* is used as an adverb to modify the verb *helped*.]

NOTE: An adverbial infinitive can frequently be identified if the phrase "in order" can be placed before it, as in *Katy paid ten dollars* (in order) *to get good seats at the play.*

Like the gerund and the participle, the infinitive may have a complement and adverbial modifiers:

> He did not want *to cut the grass yesterday.* [The infinitive *to cut* has the object *grass* and the adverbial modifier *yesterday*.]

Exercise 17   VERBS AND VERBALS

In the following sentences identify each *italicized* expression by writing on the line at the right.

V if it is a verb,   *Part* if it is a participle,
Ger if it is a gerund,   *Inf* if it is an infinitive.

EXAMPLE: I refuse *to eat* snails.   *Inf*

1. My pet hates are *skiing* and *hiking*.   ....

2. He stood at the window, *watching* the Founders' Day parade.   ....

3. Hugh's first job *was* washing pots and pans in Peoria, Illinois.   ....

4. The lion kills its prey by *choking* it with a throat bite.   ....

5. The weather in Maine *was* predictably cold.   ....

6. What underdeveloped countries need is *to increase* their technological
   capacity.   ....

7. The decision *to issue* new guidelines was not an easy one.   ....

8. The panoramic view was *breathtaking*.   ....

9. All visitors to Skidaway Island have the opportunity *to see* dozens of sea
   creatures.   ....

10. *Facing* the crowd, John Denver began singing "Country Road."   ....

11. *To master* a foreign language takes time and intelligence.   ....

12. We are faced with the necessity of *forming* international ocean management
    policies.   ....

13. I wanted *to eat* supper at Deacon Burton's.   ....

14. She always *kept* her tank full of gas.   ....

15. They said that he died of a *broken* heart.   ....

16. We plan *to spend* the summer in London.   ....

17. The leader, *deceived* by his advisors, was doomed to fail.   ....

18. Jeff enjoyed both *camping* and mountain *climbing.*   ....

19. *Have* you *told* our secret?   ....

20. Moderation is a difficult word *to define.*   ....

21. You can expect the chorus *to play* an important role in the opera <u>Carmen</u>.   ....

22. The *opening* scene of <u>Star</u> <u>Wars</u> is overwhelming.   ....

23. *Learning* can be exciting.   ....

24. I *have known* him for many years.   ....

25. *Are* you willing to accept the responsibility?   ....

Exercise 18   GERUNDS

In the following sentences underline each gerund. Copy the gerund on the first line at the right. On the second line write

> S if the gerund is the subject of the verb,
> PN if the gerund is the predicate nominative,
> DO if the gerund is the direct object of the verb,
> OP if the gerund is the object of the preposition.

	GERUND	FUNCTION
EXAMPLE: The children enjoyed <u>playing</u> soccer.	*playing*	*DO*
1. Selecting a career is not easy.		
2. We heard about your winning first prize.		
3. Gathering blackberries was a family venture.		
4. To be successful requires planning.		
5. What are her chances of recovering her sight?		
6. His greatest weakness was wasting his time.		
7. After a week of dieting, I had lost three pounds.		
8. Reading a play well requires an active imagination.		
9. Intelligent questioning of cultural values is the hallmark of a scholar.		
10. His reason was overshadowed by the importance of winning.		
11. Angie's summer pastime was reading the poetry of Emily Dickinson.		
12. Mary Ann's responsibility included training all new cadets.		
13. The New York model discovered new ways of standing and moving.		

14. Can't you make a decision without asking for my opinion?   ....

15. Riding with Eric is never dull.   ....

16. This summer I am enjoying bird-watching.   ....

17. His job on the assembly line consists of tightening bolts.   ....

18. He continued experimenting with dangerous drugs.   ....

19. Living in the country offers new experiences daily.   ....

20. I heard the crying of a child.   ....

21. By working late, we finished the float on time.   ....

22. Jane's job was mowing the grass.   ....

23. Hunting down the criminal became an intriguing challenge.   ....

24. She began training for the Olympics when she was eight years old.   ....

25. Rushing through dinner was not my idea.   ....

26. Chris enjoyed masquerading as a secret agent.   ....

27. The Europeans understand the art of eating.   ....

28. Eating too fast is an American way of life.   ....

29. After years of testing, the product was approved.   ....

30. Government spending has reached the point of absurdity.   ....

Exercise 19   PARTICIPLES

Underline the participle(s) in each of the following sentences, and then write in the space at the right the word which the participle modifies.

EXAMPLE: I have always been afraid of <u>haunted</u> houses. ....*houses*............

1. The torn and uprooted trees showed the power of the wind. ....

2. The child was aware of the flashing lights. ....

3. Her wrecked car sat in the driveway for a week. ....

4. The text of the completed novel was never found. ....

5. An industrialized society has many problems to solve. ....

6. His declining popularity worried the senator. ....

7. A throbbing headache kept me from attending the Bluegrass Festival in Dodge City. ....

8. I could not sleep because of the screaming sirens and screeching tires. ....

9. Jerusalem is one of the most inspiring cities in the world. ....

10. Alice is looking for a furnished apartment. ....

11. The frightened puppy hid under the table. ....

12. Experienced writers know the need for conciseness. ....

13. Scott tried to protect his broken hand. ....

14. Christopher Smart is a forgotten eighteenth-century poet. ....

15. Her demanding attitude made me angry. ....

16. David's flight, arriving late, circled the airport. ....

17. The doctor left the room, followed by two nurses. ....

18. Can the mechanic repair my clogged carburetor? ....

19. As we entered the room, we sensed impending danger. ....

20. Having won the tournament, the team celebrated. ....

21. Dorothy prepared a written summary of her view of the meeting. ....

22. White-water canoeing is both exciting and dangerous. ....

23. Lois sprained her ankle playing tennis. ....

24. Do you enjoy eating dried apples? ....

25. All interested students will be given free tickets to the concert. ....

26. Her most recent book, developed from previous lectures, received excellent reviews. ....

27. The little boy, having arrived at camp, was immediately ready to go home. ....

28. The girl standing by the door is my sister. ....

29. Having washed the car, I expected it to rain. ....

30. She answered the want ad announcing the job. ....

Exercise 20   INFINITIVES

Underline the infinitive in each of the following sentences, and in the space at the right indicate its use in the sentence by writing *N* for noun, *Adj* for adjective, *Adv* for adverb.

EXAMPLE: To fail the Kansas Bar Examination would delay my graduation.   *N*
....

1. The purpose of life is to seek knowledge.   ....

2. Most political speeches try to affect an audience emotionally.   ....

3. No one wants to spend money on junk.   ....

4. It is difficult to direct you to my farm.   ....

5. We were all sorry to see Ralph go.   ....

6. The purpose of our meeting is to elect a president.   ....

7. Harold's party was an event to remember.   ....

8. Hermann Hesse's *Demian* is an intriguing book to read.   ....

9. Coretta was close enough to the speaker to ask a question.   ....

10. What did the man want to know?   ....

11. To write well requires frequent practice.   ....

12. I was eager to meet my blind date.   ....

13. Bob wants to cut down the trees and the shrubs in the front yard.   ....

14. I have always hoped to tour Australia.   ....

15. The committee was ready to recommend her for a distinguished-service award.   ....

16. The boy needs to regain his confidence.   ....

17. The city is planning to rebuild the inner city area.   ....

18. Todd was too sick to attend the dinner party.   ....

19. She has the right to refuse his request.   ....

20. We will want to discuss the matter further.   ....

21. Alexis has tried for years to lose weight. ....

22. Do you really expect to pass without studying? ....

23. He left college to find his place in society. ....

24. Being in a hurry to leave, I forgot my pocketbook. ....

25. Al expects to take a trip to Canada someday. ....

26. The coach did not try to win the game. ....

27. Plans to build a new coliseum are underway. ....

28. To argue with the umpire is a waste of time. ....

29. Ruth wanted to explain the problem briefly. ....

30. The speaker decided to talk informally. ....

Exercise 21   VERBALS

In the following sentences underline each verbal. On the first line at the right identify the type of verbal by writing

        Ger for gerund, *Part* for participle, *Inf* for infinitive.

On the second line at the right indicate the use of the verbal by writing

    Adj for adjective,   *PN* for predicate nominative,
    Adv for adverb,   *DO* for direct object,
    S for subject,   *OP* for object of a preposition.

	TYPE	USE
EXAMPLE: I objected to Jim's <u>playing</u> hockey.	*Ger*	*OP*
1. Before leaving Washington, please give me your new address.	....	....
2. He tried to make a cardboard box look like a suitcase.	....	....
3. We appreciate your accepting our invitation.	....	....
4. Many Americans spend too much time watching television.	....	....
5. Jogging around the pond is the way I begin my day.	....	....
6. The farmer enjoys working the land.	....	....
7. We decided not to buy new furniture until next year.	....	....
8. After knocking on several doors, I finally found my aunt's apartment.	....	....
9. The old man refused to accept the physicians' advice.	....	....
10. The child looked sad and dejected.	....	....
11. Ed resented Jan's driving his sports car.	....	....
12. Walking through the woods, I met a rattlesnake on my path.	....	....
13. Each girl should bring her own camping equipment.	....	....
14. To take your vacation next week, you must complete all your work.	....	....
15. Motorcycle racing is dangerous.	....	....

16. He had a moral obligation to publish his report. ....

17. A truck jackknifed on the turnpike, spilling a load of apples across the highway. ....

18. Marge was anxious to know the verdict. ....

19. They needed a place to practice. ....

20. The increasing popularity of country living poses many problems for big city officials. ....

21. Only you and Bill are able to help him. ....

22. Spinning around on the piano stool, the little boy howled. ....

23. After her Scandinavian tour, she had many experiences to tell. ....

24. The adventurer's only hope was to find a sunken treasure. ....

25. Jessie plans to buy a new Jeep truck next year. ....

Recognizing Phrases 5

A **phrase** is a group of related words, generally having neither subject nor predicate and used as though it were a single word. It cannot make a statement and is therefore not a clause.

A knowledge of the phrase and how it is used will suggest to you ways of diversifying and enlivening your sentences. Variety in using sentences will remedy the monotonous "subject first" habit. For instance, the use of the participial phrase will add life and movement to your style, because the participle is an action word, having the strength of its verbal nature in addition to its function as a modifier.

We classify phrases as **gerund, participial, infinitive, absolute, prepositional,** and **appositive.** The following sentences will show how the same idea may be expressed differently by the use of different kinds of phrases:

> Sue swam daily. She hoped to improve her backstroke. ["Subject first" sentences.]
>
> By *swimming daily*, Sue hoped to improve her backstroke. [Gerund phrase.]
>
> *Swimming daily*, Sue hoped to improve her backstroke. [Participial phrase.]
>
> Sue's only hope of improving her backstroke was *to swim daily*. [Infinitive phrase.]
>
> *With a daily swim* Sue hoped to improve her backstroke. [Prepositional phrase.]

5a The Gerund Phrase

A **gerund phrase** consists of a gerund and any complement or modifiers it may have. The function of the gerund phrase is always that of a noun:

> *Being late for breakfast* is Joe's worst fault. [The gerund phrase is used as the subject of the verb *is*.]
>
> She finally succeeded in *opening the camera*. [The gerund phrase is the object of the preposition *in*.]

Bill hated *driving his golf balls into the lake.* [The gerund phrase is the object of the verb *hated.*]

His hobby, *making furniture,* is enjoyable and useful. [The gerund phrase is an appositive.]

5b   The Participial Phrase

A **participial phrase** consists of a participle and any complement or modifiers it may have. It functions as an adjective:

Disappointed by his best friend, Roger refused to speak to him. [The participial phrase modifies the proper noun *Roger.*]

Having written the letter, Julie set out for the Post Office. [The participial phrase modifies the proper noun *Julie.*]

The boy *standing in the doorway* is the one who asked to borrow our rake. [The participial phrase modifies the noun *boy.*]

PUNCTUATION: Introductory participial phrases are set off by commas. Other participial phrases are also set off by commas unless they are essential to the meaning of the sentence. (See Chapter 19, Section b.)

5c   The Infinitive Phrase

An **infinitive phrase** consists of an infinitive and any complement or modifiers it may have. Infinitives function as adjectives, adverbs, or nouns:

She had a plane *to catch at eight o'clock.* [The infinitive phrase modifies the noun *plane.*]

To be in Mr. Foster's class was *to learn the meaning of discipline.* [The first infinitive phrase is the subject of the verb *was.* The second infinitive phrase is the predicate nominative after the verb *was.*]

Millie left early *to avoid the heavy traffic.* [The infinitive phrase modifies the verb *left.*]

After the night outdoors we were happy *to be warm and dry again.* [The infinitive phrase modifies the adjective *happy.*]

Ted has no plans except *to watch television.* [The infinitive phrase is the object of the preposition *except.*]

We decided *to go for a long walk.* [The infinitive phrase is the direct object of the verb *decided.*]

Her fiancé seems *to be very pleasant.* [The infinitive phrase is the predicate adjective after the verb *seems.*]

PUNCTUATION: Introductory infinitive phrases used as modifiers are set off by commas. (See Chapter 19, Section b.)

5d   The Absolute Phrase

A noun followed by a participle may form a construction grammatically independent of the rest of the sentence. This construction is called an **absolute phrase**. It is never a subject, nor does it modify any word in the sentence, but it is used *absolutely* or independently:

> *The bus having stopped,* the tourists filed out.
>
> *The theater being nearby,* I decided to walk.
>
> I shall do as I please, *all things considered.*

PUNCTUATION: An absolute phrase is always separated from the rest of the sentence by a comma. (See Chapter 19, Section b.)

5e The Prepositional Phrase

A **prepositional phrase** consists of a preposition followed by a noun or pronoun used as its object, together with any modifiers the noun or pronoun may have. The prepositional phrase functions usually as an adjective or an adverb:

> The plan *of the house* is very simple. [The prepositional phrase modifies the noun *plan.*]
>
> The river runs *through rich farmland.* [The prepositional phrase modifies the verb *runs.*]

PUNCTUATION: An introductory prepositional phrase, unless unusually long, is not set off by a comma. (See Chapter 19, Section b.)

5f The Appositive Phrase

An **appositive** is a word or phrase which follows another word and means the same thing. An appositive may be a noun phrase (that is, a noun and its modifiers), a gerund phrase, an infinitive phrase, or a prepositional phrase:

> This book, *a long novel about politics,* will never be a best seller. [Noun phrase used as an appositive.]
>
> Jean knew a way out of her difficulty: *telling the truth.* [Gerund phrase used as an appositive.]
>
> His greatest ambition, *to make a million dollars,* was doomed from the start. [Infinitive phrase used as an appositive.]
>
> The rustler's hideout, *in the old cave by the river,* was discovered by the posse. [Prepositional phrase used as an appositive.]

An appositive may be **essential** (sometimes called **fused**) or **nonessential**; it is essential if it positively identifies that which it renames, frequently by use of a proper noun. Examples of both essential and nonessential appositives occur in the sentences below:

> The Victorian poets *Tennyson and Browning* were outstanding literary spokesmen of their day. [The appositive, *Tennyson and Browning,* identifies *poets* and thus is essential.]
>
> Tennyson and Browning, *two Victorian poets,* were outstanding literary spokesmen of their day. [The appositive, *two Victorian poets,* is nonessential because the poets are already identified by their names.]

PUNCTUATION: An appositive phrase is enclosed with commas unless it is essential. (See Chapter 19, Section b.)

Exercise 22   PHRASES

In each of the sentences below identify the *italicized* phrase by writing in the space at the right

> *Prep* if it is a prepositional phrase,   *Inf* if it is an infinitive phrase,
> *Part* if it is a participial phrase,   *App* if it is an appositive phrase,
> *Ger* if it is a gerund phrase,   *Abs* if it is an absolute phrase.

EXAMPLE: *The rain having stopped,* I plowed the south forty.   *Abs*
....

1. The silence of the night was cut *by a woman's scream.*   ....

2. *All things considered,* the Dallas Cowboys played a good game.   ....

3. *To provide efficient service* requires tremendous staff effort.   ....

4. The man *standing on the corner* is a foreign agent.   ....

5. *Between these two covers* you will find a spellbinding book.   ....

6. By *establishing residency,* you will be allowed to vote in the next election.   ....

7. The veterans, *scarred by the war*, returned home.   ....

8. I think that *working crossword puzzles* is fun.   ....

9. The Romantic poets *Keats and Byron* lived tragic lives.   ....

10. All employees have been asked *to read the personnel handbook.*   ....

11. We hurried home, *the storm having started.*   ....

12. One night we camped on a sand dune *near the ocean.*   ....

13. My truck, *a 1972 Ford Courier,* has traveled over seventy thousand miles.   ....

14. *Rappelling down the cliff* frightened me my first time.   ....

15. Dr. Alexander, *a university professor,* has an almost unlimited knowledge of Greek literature.   ....

16. The man *wearing the bow tie* is the quarterback's father.   ....

17. The stadium became silent, *the crowd having gone.*   ....

18. *To write effectively* requires clear thinking.   ....

19. Henry had a habit of *locking his keys in the car.*   ....

20. My two hobbies, *fishing and mountain climbing,* take up all my leisure time.   ....

Exercise 23   PHRASES

The sentences in the following exercise contain prepositional, verbal, and appositive phrases. Underline each phrase, and in the space at the right of each sentence show how each phrase is used by writing *Adj* for adjective, *Adv* for adverb, and *N* for noun.

EXAMPLE: The snake moved gracefully <u>through the grass</u>.   *Adv*
....

1. Reid wanted to ride his new bicycle home.   ....

2. The young man driving the Mustang will probably win the race.   ....

3. To avoid the afternoon traffic, we left early.   ....

4. We decided to postpone our trip.   ....

5. Our speaker, a famous writer, will read various popular poems.   ....

6. The attorney for the defendant asked too many embarrassing questions.   ....

7. The two women, carrying their own golf bags, crossed the fairway.   ....

8. Ned tried to control his anger.   ....

9. I enjoy an early morning walk on the beach.   ....

10. Our flight was delayed by the storm.   ....

11. The enemy retreated shortly before dawn.   ....

12. He paused to admire the shiny new cabin cruiser.   ....

13. The man wearing the pinstripe suit is my favorite uncle.   ....

14. Lord Emsworth tried to find an answer which would satisfy his sister.   ....

15. The shy rabbit disappeared into the shrubbery.   ....

16. Making vacation plans is always fun.   ....

17. Constance began playing the piano when she was three years old.   ....

18. Today's assignment is to read Frank O'Connor's "First Confession." ....

19. Driving an old, fenderless truck did not bother Sally.   ....

20. Steve always did enjoy reading biographies. ....

21. Her failure to appear raised eyebrows. ....

22. Chris tore her dress on the barbed wire. ....

23. To make the table steady, we braced the legs. ....

24. When we visit Pawley's Island, I plan to buy a hammock. ....

25. The old coon dog was lying behind the kitchen stove. ....

PHRASES

In each of the following sentences underline the phrase. In the first space at the right identify
the type of phrase by writing

>   *Prep* for prepositional phrase,   *Inf* for infinitive phrase,
>   *Part* for participial phrase,   *App* for appositive phrase.
>   *Ger* for gerund phrase,

Then indicate in the second space its use by writing *Adj, Adv,* or *N.*

	TYPE	USE
EXAMPLE: Washing the car is not my responsibility.	*Ger*	*N*
1. Her library was filled with books, magazines, and papers.	....	....
2. The man wearing the dark glasses introduced the mysterious lady.	....	....
3. How many books did you read during the summer?	....	....
4. She does not like to be disturbed.	....	....
5. Almost anything would have tasted good to the lost campers.	....	....
6. Watching television is often a pleasant escape.	....	....
7. Having finished his research, Jeff left the library.	....	....
8. Dr. Davis, my mother's doctor, is a very humane woman.	....	....
9. Several new books about World War II have recently been published.	....	....
10. We plan to visit New Orleans this fall.	....	....
11. Our children enjoy gathering the pecans.	....	....
12. Have you read Eugene O'Neill's play *Emperor Jones?*	....	....
13. Giving advice is sometimes dangerous.	....	....
14. To become a college president has always been her goal.	....	....
15. Our visit to the Lake Country was an unforgettable experience.	....	....
16. The young lawyer increased his business by hard work.	....	....

17. Upon the door she hung her new evening dress. ....

18. Riding her horse is Jan's current pastime. ....

19. My neighbor plans to plant his fall garden next week. ....

20. The new player kicked a field goal of sixty yards. ....

Exercise 25 **PHRASES**

A. Combine the following pairs of sentences, making one sentence a participial phrase. Punctuate each sentence properly.

EXAMPLE: We sat around the campfire. We told tales of the old days.
Sitting around the campfire, we told tales of the old days.

1. The heirs listened to the reading of the will. Most of the heirs became angry.

2. Tom missed his flight. He spent the night in Chicago.

3. Carlos considered several alternatives. He decided to apply for admission to medical school.

4. The Nathaniel Russell House was built in 1809. It is noted for its floating staircase and grand oval rooms.

5. She completed her research paper early. She had time to proofread it and make corrections.

6. The witness attempted to avoid the attorney's questions. He hesitated frequently.

7. The bat was attracted by the campfire. It frightened all of us.

8. We heard Sue's boisterous laughter. We knew that it was she.

9. Elmer worked diligently. He surpassed those who competed against him.

10. *Shogun* was written by James Clavell. It is a novel about Japan.

B. Combine the following pairs of sentences, making one of the sentences an appositive phrase.

EXAMPLE: Angie is a first-year medical student. She wants to become a surgeon.
    Angie, a first-year medical student, wants to become a surgeon.

1. Bill thinks that regular study is important. He is a Baylor University student.

2. *My Fair Lady* is a musical version of *Pygmalion*. It is an adaptation of Shaw's play about an uneducated Cockney girl.

3. Woodrow Wilson was born December 28, 1856, in Virginia. He was one of our greatest presidents.

4. My brother-in-law is the oldest of the four sons. He is an attorney in Atlanta.

5. Sir Walter Scott's first novel was *Waverly*. It was published in 1814.

6. Adam Tanner is our hockey coach. He will award the Best Player Trophy at the banquet.

7. Charlotte Bronte's most famous novel is *Jane Eyre*. It was published under her pseudonym Currer Bell.

8. My father is a good fisherman. He taught me how to fly-cast.

9. Perseus was a Greek hero. He killed the monster Medusa and saved the life of Andromeda.

10. Cycling was a popular sport during the twenties. It is returning.

Exercise 26   PUNCTUATION OF PHRASES

In the following sentences insert all commas required by the rules stated in Chapter 5. In the blanks write the commas with the words which precede them. When the sentence requires no comma, write *C* in the space.

EXAMPLE: The whistle having been blown $_\wedge$ the race began.   .... *blown,* ....

1. "A Good Man Is Hard to Find" written by Flannery O'Connor is a story of desperate people.   ....

     ....

2. Frances born in Canada did not want to move to Texas.   ....

     ....

3. Driving across town takes at least an hour.   ....

4. Sophocles a Greek dramatist believed that we obtain wisdom through suffering.   ....

     ....

5. All things considered I think that the committee made the right decision.   ....

6. Alarmed by the ambassador's report the President called a meeting of his cabinet.   ....

7. Watching television will dull a person's imagination.   ....

8. The blind girl hearing the crash hesitated before crossing the street.   ....

     ....

9. Taking the doctor's advice we both stopped smoking.   ....

10. To reduce our grocery bill we bought less junk food.   ....

11. Conserving energy is everyone's responsibility.   ....

12. Being an interpreter for the deaf Jimmy has the opportunity to meet people from all walks of life.

....

13. Constantly finding fault is the mark of a little mind.

....

14. The boy in the motorcycle accident was traveling too fast.

....

15. Determined to catch enough fish for supper my brother and nephew set several lines.

....

16. Beryl having lost her money cut her vacation short.

....

....

17. *Thanksgiving* a work by Doris Lee is a primitive painting.

....

....

18. Responding to his young daughter's curiosity he took her for a walk in the woods.

....

19. Wandering up an unpaved road we found an old mill.

....

20. The young woman eating alone is a new vice president of the University.

....

Independent 6
Clauses

6a Independent Clauses

A group of words containing a subject and a verb and expressing a complete thought is called a sentence or an **independent clause.** Some groups of words which contain a subject and a verb, however, do not express a complete thought and therefore cannot stand alone as a sentence. Such word groups are dependent on other sentence elements and are called **dependent clauses.**

Sometimes an independent clause stands alone as a sentence. Sometimes two or more independent clauses are combined into one sentence without a connecting word. Then a semicolon is used to connect the independent clauses:

> The day is cold.
> The day is cold; the wind is howling.

Sometimes independent clauses are connected by one of the coordinating conjunctions, *and, but, for, or, nor, so,* and *yet.* As these conjunctions do not subordinate, an independent clause beginning with one of them may stand as a complete sentence. Independent clauses joined by a coordinating conjunction are separated by commas. Therefore, to punctuate correctly, you must distinguish between independent clauses and other kinds of sentence elements joined by coordinating conjunctions. In the following examples note that only independent clauses joined by coordinating conjunctions are separated by commas:

> The day was *dark* and *dreary.* [The conjunction *and* joins two adjectives, *dark* and *dreary.* No comma permitted.]
>
> The fallen tree *blocked* the highway and *delayed* travel. [The conjunction *and* joins the two verbs. No comma permitted.]
>
> She ran *up the steps* and *into the house.* [The conjunction *and* joints two phrases. No comma permitted.]

Mrs. Brown caught the fish, and *her husband cooked them.* [The conjunction *and* connects two independent clauses, and these are separted by a comma.]

Sometimes two independent clauses are connected by a **conjunctive**, or **transitional, adverb** such as one of the following:

however	moreover	nevertheless	therefore
then	accordingly	otherwise	thus
hence	besides	consequently	

A semicolon is necessary before any of these words beginning a second clause. After the longer *conjunctive adverbs* a comma is generally used:

We drove all day; *then* at sundown we began to look for a place to camp.

It rained during the afternoon; *consequently,* our trip to the mountains had to be postponed.

NOTE: Conjunctive adverbs can be distinguished from subordinating conjunctions by the fact that the *adverbs* can be shifted to a later position in the sentence, whereas the *conjunctions* cannot:

It rained during the afternoon; our trip to the mountains, *consequently,* had to be postponed.

SUMMARY OF PUNCTUATION: From the foregoing discussion and examples we can establish the following rules for the punctuation of independent clauses:

1. *Two independent clauses connected by a coordinating conjunction are separated by a comma:*

   Our goat chewed up the morning paper, *and* Father is angry.

   You should call Hank tonight, *for* he is all alone.

2. *Two independent clauses which are not connected by a coordinating conjunction are separated by a semicolon.* Remember that this rule also holds true when the second clause begins with a conjunctive adverb:

   Philip is quite strong; he is much stronger than I.

   We both wanted to go to the toboggan race; *however,* Mother had asked us to be home by six.

3. *A semicolon is used to separate independent clauses which are joined by a coordinating conjunction but which are heavily punctuated with commas internally:*

   Harry, George, and Kitty went to Sky Valley for skiing; but Tony and I were too tired to go.

4. *Short independent clauses, when used in a series with a coordinating conjunction preceding the final clause, may be separted by commas:*

   The audience was seated, the lights were dimmed, and the curtain was raised.

   NOTE: A series consists of at least three elements.

6b The Comma Splice

Use of a comma between two independent clauses not joined by a coordinating conjunction (Rule 2), is a major error called the **comma splice** (This term comes from the idea of splicing or "patching" together two clauses which should be more strongly separated.):

COMMA SPLICE: I enjoyed his company, I do not know that he enjoyed mine.

CORRECTION: I enjoyed his company, but I do not know that he enjoyed mine. (Using Rule 1)

I enjoyed his company; I do not know that he enjoyed mine. (Using Rule 2)

OR

I enjoyed his company; however, I do not know that he enjoyed mine. (Using Rule 2)

6c The Run-together Sentence

The **run-together sentence** results from omitting punctuation between two independent clauses not joined by a conjunction. Basically the error is the same as that of the comma splice: it shows ignorance of sentence structure:

Twilight had fallen it was dark under the old oak tree near the house.

When you read the sentence just given, you have difficulty in getting the meaning at first because the ideas are run together. Now consider the following sentence:

Twilight had fallen, it was dark under the old oak tree near the house.

The insertion of the comma is not a satisfactory remedy, for the sentence now contains a comma splice. There are, however, four approved devices for correcting the run-together sentence and the comma splice:

1. Connect two independent clauses by a comma and a coordinating conjunction if the two clauses are logically of equal importance:

   Twilight had fallen, and it was dark under the old oak tree near the house.

2. Connect two independent clauses by a semicolon if they are close enough in thought to make one sentence and you want to omit the conjunction:

   Twilight had fallen; it was dark under the old oak tree near the house.

3. Write the two independent clauses as separate sentences if they need separate emphasis:

   Twilight had fallen. It was dark under the old oak tree near the house.

4. Subordinate one of the independent clauses:

   When twilight had fallen, it was dark under the old oak tree near the house.

Exercise 27 THE COMMA SPLICE AND THE RUN-TOGETHER SENTENCE

Mark correct sentences with a *C*, run-together sentences with an *R*, and sentences containing a comma splice with *CS*.

EXAMPLE: The Studio Theater is small, consequently, we should arrive early.   *CS*

1. Norma's pet snake sneaked out of the house this morning it has not returned.   ....

2. The schooner was crushed by the force of the wave, all aboard were miraculously saved.   ....

3. Although I enjoy shopping for Christmas presents, buying each relative a gift is expensive.   ....

4. The artist had spent the entire day with a collector, therefore, he wanted to spend the evening alone.   ....

5. Scuba diving is his favorite sport each year he takes a Caribbean vacation.   ....

6. We ate our meals in the pine-walled dining room, which was noisy with the chatter of hungry guests.   ....

7. The tide is in, now we have a comfortable breeze.   ....

8. We spent the day sunbathing on the beach I got sunburned.   ....

9. She wanted to major in electrical engineering, accordingly, she applied to Georgia Tech.   ....

10. Although bears are numerous in Smoky Mountain Park, they seldom attack people.   ....

11. Many of the barns of Lancaster County are disappearing, new agricultural methods no longer require the old-fashioned barns.   ....

12. We are having dinner at Custy's restaurant, it is impossible to describe everything offered on his buffet.   ....

13. I enjoyed reading Schumacher's *Small Is Beautiful* because of the author's novel approach to economics.   ....

14. Sandra was sorry to see the short days of winter come she did not have time to work in her garden before dark.   ....

15. Chaucer is frequently called the father of English poetry; he is the author of *The Canterbury Tales.*   ....

16. In the story the hero successfully returns home, however, he soon yearns for new adventures.   ....

17. On rainy days we play dominoes I always lose.   ....

18. Every fruit grower fears a late spring frost which would destroy his crop.   ....

19. Heavy snows prevented our hike, hence, we spent the evening telling stories of our children.   ....

20. The College of William and Mary was founded in 1693, it is recognized for its academic excellence.   ....

Exercise 28   THE COMMA SPLICE AND THE RUN-TOGETHER SENTENCE

Mark correct sentences with a *C*, run-together sentences with an *R*, and sentences containing a comma splice with *CS*.

EXAMPLE: Ireland loves folklore, for this reason many popular festivals are held.   *CS*

1. *The End of the Dream* is a thought-provoking novel by Philip Wylie.   ....

2. Mrs. Smith made me a birdhouse, she also made me a feeder.   ....

3. I decided in August to attend college therefore, I encountered several obstacles.   ....

4. The White House is an American showplace; it contains beautiful antiques and gifts from foreign dignitaries.   ....

5. The bank agreed to our paying the note late, thus we received an extension of time.   ....

6. There are many ways to solve a problem everyone thinks his way is the only one.   ....

7. The ambassador's plane landed at the airport on time, she was met by the British Embassy's limousine.   ....

8. You are philosophical about your failures, so you will be able to learn from them.   ....

9. Ronnie has invited his roommates to the country for the weekend they plan to fish and to hunt.   ....

10. Howard knows the fine points of the game, he, therefore, rarely loses.   ....

11. After his speech the Dean received a standing ovation.   ....

12. It looked like rain this morning, so I took my umbrella.   ....

13. Bring your tentative schedule to me I am your advisor.   ....

14. News concerning violent crimes always makes the headlines, however, stories of quiet courage seldom make news.   ....

15. The Industrial Revolution enabled most people to enjoy comforts and conveniences which were only dreamed of by previous generations.   ....

16. Jerry's speech was not particularly convincing, however, it did last an hour and a half. ....

17. Mt. Everest is the world's highest mountain, it is located in Tibet. ....

18. Harvey looked inquiringly at the stranger and waited for him to say something. ....

19. The old mountaineer sat fiddling softly it was past time for him to go to bed. ....

20. The professor paused a moment for comments from the class none of the students responded. ....

Exercise 29   PUNCTUATION OF INDEPENDENT CLAUSES

In the following sentences insert all necessary commas and semicolons. In the space at the right write the correct punctuation mark with the word which precedes it. If the sentence is correct, write *C* in the space.

EXAMPLE: We discovered the entrance to the cave‸ but Tim and Mary were afraid to explore it.   ....*cave,*........

1. Politicians spend their time getting votes statesmen spend their time determining the will of the people.   ....

2. I am sorry that I disagree with your interpretation of the story however, I am the author.   ....

3. To participate in the Honors Day program, a student must be in the upper ten percent of her class you are not eligible.   ....

4. It was nearly dark when we got home and we were too exhausted to cut the grass.   ....

5. Carol has finished her year of internship but she has four more years of specialization.   ....

6. The judge was not satisfied with the testimony of the witnesses he called each of them back for further questioning.   ....

7. The house that Nevin built is beautiful but small.   ....

8. Jimmy and Angie get up early and dress quickly they catch the first school bus.   ....

9. We were required to take a physical examination before we could join the biking club.   ....

10. Jessica's children have frequently exposed her to measles but she has never had it.   ....

11. The professor contrasted the Greeks' praise of the individual with the Romans' praise of accomplishments.   ....

12. The afternoon passed rapidly and all too soon it was time to go back to the hotel.   ....

13. We are leaving for Washington tomorrow morning therefore, I will be unable to see you before I leave. ....

14. The price of each dinner included a soup, salad, entree, and dessert we decided not to think about calories. ....

15. Bradford Academy was incorporated in 1820, it was one of the first tuition-free coeducational schools in Vermont. ....

16. The weather is very cold in the mountains, so we will need to take our blankets. ....

17. The tide is out we can walk along the shore. ....

18. Too many people confuse a college degree with a college education. ....

19. Juanita has the highest grade point average in her class in spite of being blind. ....

20. I realize that each of you has a busy schedule, nevertheless, I hope you will come to the county fair. ....

Dependent Clauses

7

Any clause beginning with a subordinating word like *what, that, who, which, when, since, before, after,* or *if* is a **dependent clause**. Dependent clauses, like phrases, function as grammatical units in a sentence—that is, as nouns, adjectives, and adverbs:

I went to school.
Too much time had elapsed. } [Both clauses are independent.]

When I went to school, I studied my lessons. [The first clause is subordinate.]

Since too much time had elapsed, she remained at home. [The first clause is subordinate.]

In the last two sentences *I studied my lessons* and *she remained at home* are complete statements. But the clauses *When I went to school* and *Since too much time had elapsed* do not express complete thoughts. They depend upon the independent statements to complete their meanings. Both of these dependent clauses function as adverbs.

7a Noun Clauses

A **noun clause** is a dependent clause used as a noun, that is, as a subject, complement, object of a preposition, or appositive. Noun clauses are usually introduced by *that, what, why, whether, who, which,* or *how.* Some of these introductory words can introduce both noun and adjective clauses, since the function of the whole clause in the sentence, and not its introductory word, determines its classification. Most sentences containing noun clauses differ from those containing adjective and adverbial clauses in that with the clause removed they are no longer complete sentences:

Your *plan* is interesting. [The subject is the noun *plan.*]

What you intend to do [your plan] is interesting. [The italicized noun clause is the subject of the verb *is.* Notice that the noun *plan* can be substituted for the clause.]

Tell me *what you intend to do* [your plan]. [The italicized noun clause is the direct object of the verb *tell*.]

That is *what you intend to do* [your plan]. [The italicized noun clause is a predicate nominative.]

I am interested in *what you intend to do* [your plan]. [The italicized noun clause is the object of the preposition *in*.]

The fact *that he had not told the truth soon became apparent.* [The italicized noun clause is in apposition with the noun *fact*.]

PUNCTUATION: Noun clauses used as non-essential appositives are set off by commas.

7b Adjective Clauses

An **adjective clause** is a dependent clause which modifies a noun or pronoun. The common connective words used to introduce adjective clauses are the relative pronouns *who* (and its inflected forms *whom* and *whose*), *which, that*, and relative adverbs like *where, when,* and *why*. (*Where* and *when* can introduce all three kinds of clauses.)

The italicized clauses in the following sentences are all adjective clauses:

She is a woman *who is respected by everyone.*

Mr. Johnson, *whose son attends the University,* is our friend.

He saw the place *where he was born.*

It was a time *when money did not count.*

I know the reason *why I failed the course.*

Adjective clauses are classified as **essential** (restrictive) and **nonessential** (non-restrictive).

An *essential* clause, as its name indicates, is necessary in a sentence, for it identifies or points out a certain person or thing; a *nonessential* clause adds information about the word it modifies, but it is not essential in pointing out or identifying a certain person or thing:

Thomas Jefferson, *who was born on the frontier,* became President. [The name *Thomas Jefferson* has identified the person, and the italicized clause is not essential.]

A person *who loves to read* will never be lonely. [The italicized adjective clause is essential in identifying a particular kind of person.]

My father, *who was a country boy,* has lived in the city for years. [Since a person has only one father, an identifying clause is not essential.]

The girl *by whom I sat in class* is an honor student. [The italicized adjective clause is essential to the identification of *girl*.]

To determine whether an adjective clause is essential. you may apply this test: read the sentence leaving out the adjective clause and see whether the removal omits necessary identification. Try this test on the following sentence:

Jet pilots, *who work under a great deal of stress,* must stay in excellent physical condition.

You will see that the removal of the adjective clause does not change the basic meaning of the sentence. The italicized adjective clause is, therefore, nonessential.

Now read the following sentence, leaving out the italicized adjective clause:

Jet pilots *who are not in excellent physical condition* should not be allowed to fly.

If the adjective clause of this sentence is removed, the statement is not at all what the writer meant to say. The adjective clause is, therefore, essential.

PUNCTUATION: Nonessential adjective clauses are set off from the rest of the sentence by commas. (See Chapter 19, Section b.)

7c Adverbial Clauses

An **adverbial clause** is a dependent clause that functions exactly as if it were an adverb. Like an adverb it modifies a verb, an adjective, an adverb, or the whole idea expressed in the sentence's independent clause; e.g., *As luck would have it,* we missed his telephone call.

An adverbial clause is used to show *time, place, cause, purpose, result, condition, concession, manner,* or *comparison.* Its first word is a subordinating conjunction. Common subordinating conjunctions and their uses are listed below:

1. Time (*when, before, since, as, while, until, after, whenever*)

   I will stay *until you come.*
   When the whistle blew, the laborer stopped.

2. Place (*where, wherever, whence, whither*)

   He went *where no one had ever set foot before.*
   Wherever you go, I will go too.

3. Cause (*because, since, as*)

   Since I had no classes on Saturday, I went home.
   Because he was afraid of being late, Bob ran all the way.

4. Purpose (*in order that, so that, that*)

   My family made many sacrifices *so that I could have an education.*
   Men work *that they may eat.*

5. Result (*so . . . that, such . . . that*)

   The weather was *so* cold *that I decided not to walk to school.*

6. Condition (*if, unless*)

   You will hurt your hand *if you are not careful.*
   Unless you apply at once, your name will not be considered.

7. Concession (*though, although*)

   Although she had no money, she was determined to go to college.

8. Manner (*as, as if, as though*)

   She looked *as though she wanted to laugh.*
   Do *as you like,* but take the consequences.

9. Comparison (*as, than*)

   He is older *than his brother.*
   He is as tall *as his brother.*

PUNCTUATION: Introductory adverbial clauses are always set off by commas:

> *Although he had tests to take and a term paper to write,* he went home for the weekend.
>
> *While I was eating lunch,* I had a phone call from my brother.

7d Kinds of Sentences

For the purpose of varying style and avoiding monotony, you may need to be able to distinguish the four basic types of sentences. According to the number and kind of clauses (phrases do not affect sentence type), sentences may be grouped into four types: **simple, compound, complex,** and **compound-complex.**

1. A **simple** sentence is a single independent clause; it has one subject and one predicate. But it may have as a subject more than one noun or pronoun and as a predicate more than one verb:

> Robert has a new car. [Single subject and single predicate.]
>
> *Robert* and his *brother* have a new car. [There is one verb, *have,* but the subject consists of two nouns.]
>
> Robert *washed* and *polished* his new car on Sunday. [There is one subject, *Robert,* but two verbs.]
>
> *Robert* and his *brother washed* and *polished* their new car. [The subject consists of two nouns, *Robert* and *brother*; and the predicate consists of two verbs, *washed* and *polished.*]

2. **A compound** sentence contains at least two independent clauses and no dependent clause:

> Mary likes the mountains, but Jackie prefers the seashore.
>
> A lamp was lighted in the house, the happy family was talking together, and supper was waiting.

3. **A complex** sentence contains only one independent clause and one or more dependent clauses (the dependent clauses are in italics):

> The toy truck *that you gave Molly for her birthday* is broken.
>
> *Why he refused to contribute to the fund* we do not know.

4. **A compound-complex** sentence has at least two independent clauses and one or more dependent clauses (the independent clauses are in italics):

> *My friend was offended by my attitude,* and *I was sorry* that she was hurt.
>
> *We spent the morning looking for the home of the woman* who paints landscapes, but *we were unable to find it.*

Exercise 30 CLAUSES

In the following sentences underline each dependent clause. In the space at the right, write *Adj* if the clause is an adjective clause, *Adv* if it is an adverbial clause, and *N* if it is a noun clause. If the sentence contains no dependent clause, leave the space blank.

EXAMPLE: Will those students <u>who are candidates for the Bachelor of Arts degree</u> please rise. *Adj*

1. My father insisted that David complete his secondary education in England. ....

2. What I have read on his application form is all that I know about him. ....

3. If I had time to read a book, I would reread Tolstoy's *War and Peace.* ....

4. Dean did not share the easygoing attitude of the sportsmen who romanticized the hunt. ....

5. An analysis was made of the information furnished by the agent before it was sent to headquarters. ....

6. Wanda wished desperately that she had not asked the question. ....

7. After fifty hours of instruction she was a full-fledged pilot. ....

8. As she ended her speech, she was almost confident again. ....

9. The man with the mustache pressed Adam for an answer. ....

10. Although I never knew much about my father, I think of him often. ....

11. Life is never simple for anyone except those who refuse to face it. ....

12. If I had worked all day in the factory, I could not have been more exhausted. ....

13. Sheila is older than her sister. ....

14. Mr. Hoffer, whose family lives in Germany, will be our guest this weekend. ....

15. Unless you leave immediately, you will miss your train. ....

16. You will be surprised at how simply one can live. ....

17. He watched her thoughtfully as she walked across the room. ....

18. When we were seniors in high school, we read *As You Like It* and *Macbeth*.   ....

19. As soon as the poet walked in, the audience stood.   ....

20. During the first months of World War II, secrecy was our only defense.   ....

21. What seems most evident to me is Richard's failure to understand the problem.   ....

22. A strange bird call echoed through the trees.   ....

23. Once in the woods, she stopped and listened again.   ....

24. When the door opened, a white-haired woman entered the room carrying a gun in her hand.   ....

25. The explanation which she had given them seemed too horrible to be true.   ....

CLAUSES

Give the function of each of the *italicized* clauses by writing the proper abbreviation in the space at the right:

> S for subject of a verb,   OP for object of a preposition,
> DO for direct object,   Adj for adjective modifier,
> PN for predicate nominative,   Adv for adverbial modifier.

EXAMPLE: Hermann Hesse, *who was awarded both the Goethe Prize and the Nobel Prize,* was a writer with a pronounced sense of justice.   *Adj*

1. The truth is *that I have lost interest in the course.*   ....

2. *While he was searching the archives of the village,* Alex found a forgotten letter written by Napoleon.   ....

3. *That our environment cannot bear unlimited burdens* is a fact which we cannot escape.   ....

4. Visitors to the museum see the technological changes *which have taken place in the field of transportation.*   ....

5. The senator did not have the slightest idea of *how the poor lived or suffered.*   ....

6. We did not know *what the test was going to cover.*   ....

7. *Because the microphone was not working,* the audience had difficulty hearing the speaker.   ....

8. Did you ever dream *that you would live in Sydney?*   ....

9. The rocket was thoroughly tested *before it was launched.*   ....

10. *What one desires* is sometimes hard to get.   ....

11. That model is *what we plan to build next year.*   ....

12. My neighbors suggested *how I should plant my garden.*   ....

13. Agnes is two years younger *than Hugh.*   ....

14. Well, because of *what you said* a discussion will be unnecessary.   ....

15. The photographer *who was hired to take our wedding pictures* forgot to put film in the camera.   ....

16. *That Jeff had neglected studying his calculus* was obvious to everyone in his class. ....

17. *If you are going to be browsing in a bookstore,* please buy me *Bramble Bush* by Karl N. Llewellyn. ....

18. *After Juliet had apparently died,* Romeo took his own life. ....

19. I suppose *that we cannot change your mind.* ....

20. His being admitted to college depended on *how well he did on the Scholastic Aptitude Test.* ....

21. My father, *who loves to cook,* bakes bread every Saturday. ....

22. *If you are not here on time,* we will leave you. ....

23. Most of the paintings *which are now on exhibit* represent the Hudson River school of art. ....

24. *Because I enjoy living close to nature,* I bought a farm last year. ....

25. Ted said *that his sister is planning to work in Dallas this summer.* ....

26. The wind was blowing so hard *that I had to move inside to finish my letters.* ....

Exercise 32   REVIEW OF CLAUSES

In the following sentences enclose the dependent clauses in parentheses. In the space at the right indicate the number of independent and dependent clauses in each sentence. Be able to tell the function of each of the dependent clauses. (Note that some sentences may not contain a dependent clause.)

	IND.	DEP.
EXAMPLE: Finally, Albert confessed (that he did not remember) (where Nancy lived.)	1	2

1. I wish that I could go with you.   ....

2. If I should hem my slacks which I bought on sale, I would have three new outfits.   ....

3. When she was a little girl in Los Angeles, she wanted to become an archaeologist who would travel to ancient lands.   ....

4. Charlotte was twelve years old when her parents moved to America.   ....

5. If Don, who is the team's captain, cannot inspire the team, perhaps the coach can.   ....

6. I was surprised to learn that Della is not coming.   ....

7. In the doorway appeared Haskins, his hair soaking wet, his clothes dirty and torn.   ....

8. To understand a work of literature, one must study the times in which it was written and the author who wrote it.   ....

9. The names of those who have passed the final examination will be posted on the bulletin board in the Dean's office.   ....

10. Gary, who is a university student, is interested in electronics, because the field offers excellent opportunities.   ....

11. Whoever was questioned appeared cautious and gave vague responses.   ....

12. That is the young man who I think won the contest.   ....

13. On the way home Roy punctured both of his tires, and we had to pick him up.   ....

14. After listening to both speakers, I tried to decide which had presented the better argument.   ....

15. That Al was not given a fair trial is his attorney's main basis for appeal.   ....

16. Jane wanted to be a physician, but her parents wanted her to be a teacher.   ....

17. Devil's Island, which is eight miles off the coast of French Guiana, is the site of a former French penal colony.   ....

18. Whose music do you like better, Bach's or Mozart's?   ....

19. The department head wanted to know how many students are in each class.   ....

20. If we win this game, we will go to the Sugar Bowl.   ....

21. Eugene O'Neill, a famous American playwright, wrote *Long Day's Journey Into Night.*   ....

22. I wish that I had time for a nap.   ....

23. Jeff did not know how he should answer the question.   ....

24. Because the woman had a criminal record, she had difficulty getting a job.   ....

25. If the book were mine, I would make notes in the margin, but it belongs to my roommate, who does not write in her books.   ....

Exercise 33   CLAUSES

Complete each of the sentences below by writing in the spaces an *adjective clause,* an *adverbial clause,* or a *noun clause* as indicated above each space.

(adverbial clause)

EXAMPLE: We must leave at once ....*if we are going to catch the train.*...................

(adverbial clause)

1. I could see the small boat ....

....

(adjective clause)

2. Have you seen the cherry trees ....

....

(noun clause)

3. The country singer knew ....

....

(adverbial clause)

4. Mother had begun mixing the waffle batter ....

....

(noun clause)

5. This map does not show ....

....

(adjective clause)

6. These are my friends ....

....

(adjective clause)

7. Sandra took from her golf bag the club ....

....

(adverbial clause)

8. His father awoke suddenly ....

....

(noun clause)

9. The jury's decision is ....

....

(adverbial clause)

10. We are happy ....

....

Exercise 34   PUNCTUATION OF CLAUSES

In the following sentences supply commas and semicolons where they are needed. In the spaces at the right, write the marks of punctuation with the words that precede them. Write *C* if the sentence is correct.

EXAMPLE: As the car swerved, the packages tumbled from the seat.

.... *swerved,* ....

1. Although the mall is open all night the shops close at six.

....

....

2. That he works as a steeplejack does not worry his family.

....

....

3. She opened the small velvet box the ring was not there.

....

....

4. My father who enjoys crossword puzzles usually works the one in the Sunday paper.

....

....

5. The woman who drives the bus is from Minnesota.

....

....

6. I am not going to breakfast furthermore I may not get up for lunch.

....

....

7. We followed the path across the field and then climbed slowly to the top of the hill.

....

....

8. Marilyn as we all know will probably be late.

....

....

9. The problem is not that Sarah is undecided about her major it is that she decides upon a new one every quarter.

....

....

10. The Senator does not know whether the Congress will vote on that bill before Easter.

....

....

11. The robins have returned but patches of snow are still on the ground.

....

....

12. The sun rose the ice melted and last night's storm was forgotten.

....

....

13. When the essays are completed they should be given to the student assistant.

....

....

14. Some climbed to the top of the falls others waded in the cold stream.

....

....

15. The one who gets my vote for MVP is Marjorie Latimer.

....

....

16. Had you rather watch the Tarzan movie or switch to the baseball game?

....

....

17. We got up early to put on the roast then we left for a day of shopping.

....

....

18. Call me when you reach the airport.

....

....

19. If you have time call me from the airport.

....

....

20. I have recently read *The Adventures of Augie March* which Saul Bellow wrote in the 1950's.

....

....

21. Where has Susan gone for the weekend and when does she plan to be back?

....

....

22. Write me what you plan to do this summer.

....

....

23. Because roses are her favorite flower she planted several vines along the fence.

....

....

24. The visiting professor finished her remarks concerning DNA nevertheless I still had questions that remained unanswered.

....

....

25. The train struggled up the steep grade but then sped down into the valley.

....

....

Exercise 35   KINDS OF SENTENCES

Identify the type of sentence by writing one of the following abbreviations in the space at the right:

> S if the sentence is simple,   Cx if the sentence is complex,
> Cp if the sentence is compound,   Cp-Cx if the sentence is compound-complex.

EXAMPLE: We hope that she does not serve her tuna casserole.   ......*Cx*......

1. Margaret, who had curled up on the top bunk, was reading a biography of Amelia Earhart.   ....

2. Our cat, a curious creature, explored the darkest corners of the attic.   ....

3. I had hoped to go to Daytona for spring vacation; I wrote a paper instead.   ....

4. She hurried into the house and turned off the stove.   ....

5. I suppose that most of us enjoy the study of parapsychology.   ....

6. When I first met Dean Graham, I was surprised that he also was interested in ice hockey.   ....

7. Reaching a decision about his future was difficult for Abe.   ....

8. The visitor from England does not understand why we have few passenger trains.   ....

9. I understand why Olivia charms him; she charms me.   ....

10. His keen interest in whales began when he was only a child.   ....

11. The first warm day brought out every bicyclist in the neighborhood.   ....

12. Neither the rocky beach nor the heavy waves kept my brothers from swimming.   ....

13. Have you read the article in the current *Newsweek* which describes the President's trip abroad?   ....

14. We hurried to reach the airport but missed our plane anyway.   ....

15. We hurried to reach the airport, but we missed our plane anyway.   ....

16. Spring is meant for sunbathing, and Minnie will not take afternoon classes this quarter if she can possibly avoid them. ....

17. Mother says that she does not know who will be here for supper. ....

18. How do you explain your fascination with astrology? ....

19. She saw a bright flash of lightning; then the electricity went off. ....

20. He grew up in the mountains, and he returned to them whenever he grew tired of New York. ....

21. The Orient Express, which ran from Istanbul to Paris, was the setting of the book. ....

22. As I was driving home, I listened to the baseball game, which was broadcast from Houston. ....

23. Walking to the drugstore, I saw Margaret sitting on her front steps. ....

24. We do not want to study, nor do we want to clean the room. ....

25. Singapore, which has a population of more than two million, has done much to solve its traffic problems. ....

Agreement of Subject and Verb

8

The verb in every independent or dependent clause must agree with its subject in person and number. (There are **three persons**: the **first person** is the speaker, the **second person** is the person spoken to, and the **third person** is the person or thing spoken about. There are **two numbers**: the **singular**, denoting one person or thing, and the **plural**, denoting more than one person or thing.) A careful study of the conjugation of the verb in Chapter 1 will show you that a verb can change form not only in *tense* but also in *person* and *number.* If you can recognize the subject and the verb, you should have no trouble making the two agree. Although there is ordinarily no problem in doing so, certain difficulties need special attention.

8a Intervening Expressions

The number of the verb in a sentence is not affected by any modifying phrases or clauses standing between the subject and the verb but is determined entirely by the number of the subject:

> The *evidence* which they submitted to the judges *was* [not *were*] convincing. [*Evidence* is the subject of the verb *was.*]

> The new *library* with its many books and its quiet reading rooms *fills* [not *fill*] a long-felt need. [*Library* is the subject of the verb *fills;* the phrase *with its many books. . .* has nothing to do with the verb.]

8b Verb Preceding the Subject

In some sentences the verb precedes the subject. This reversal of common order frequently leads to error in agreement:

> There *is* [not *are*] in many countries much *unrest* today. [*Unrest* is the subject of the verb *is.*]

There *are* [not *is*] a *table*, two *couches*, four *chairs*, and a *desk* in the living room. [*Table, couches, chairs,* and *desk* are the subjects of the verb *are.*]

Where *are* [not *is*] *Bob* and his *friends going*? [*Bob* and *friends* are subjects of the verb *are going.*]

8c   Indefinite Pronouns

The indefinite pronouns or adjectives *either, neither,* and *each,* as well as such compounds as *everybody, anybody, everyone, anyone,* are always singular. *None* may be singular or plural. The plural usage is commoner:

Each of the plans *has* [not *have*] its advantages.

Everyone who heard the speech *was* [not *were*] impressed by it.

Every bud, stalk, flower, and seed *reveals* [not *reveal*] a workmanship beyond the power of man.

Is [not *Are*] *either* of you ready for a walk?

None of the men *have* brought their wives.

None of the three *is* [*are*] interested.

None—no, not one—*is* prepared.

8d   Compound Subjects

Compound subjects joined by *and* normally require a plural verb:

Correctness and *precision are* required in all good writing.

Where *are* the *bracelets* and *beads*?

NOTE: When nouns joined by *and* are thought of as a unit, the verb is normally singular:

The *sum* and *substance* of the matter *is* [not *are*] hardly worth considering.

My *friend* and *coworker* Mr. Jones *has* [not *have*] gone abroad.

8e   Subjects Joined by *Or* and *Nor*

Singular subjects joined by *or* or *nor* take a singular verb. If one subject, however, is singular and one plural, the verb agrees in number and person with the nearer one:

Either the *coach* or the *player was* [not *were*] at fault.

Neither the *cat* nor the *kittens have* been fed. [The plural word *kittens* in the compound subject stands next to the verb *have been fed.*]

Neither the *kittens* nor the *cat has* been fed. [The singular subject *cat* stands next to the verb, which is therefore singular.]

Neither my *brothers* nor *I am* going. [Note that the verb agrees with the nearer subject in person as well as in number.]

8f   Nouns Plural in Form

As a general rule use a singular verb with nouns that are plural in form but singular in meaning. The following nouns are usually singular in meaning: *news, economics, ethics, physics, mathematics, gallows, mumps, measles, shambles, whereabouts:*

> The *news is* reported at eleven o'clock.
>
> *Measles is* a contagious disease.

The following nouns are usually plural: *gymnastics, tactics, trousers, scissors, athletics, tidings, acoustics, riches, barracks:*

> *Athletics attract* him.
>
> The *scissors are* sharp.
>
> *Riches* often *take* wing and fly away.

Plural nouns denoting a mass, a quantity, or a number require a singular verb when the subject is regarded as a unit.

> Five *dollars is* too much for her to pay.
>
> Fifty *bushels was* all the bin would hold.

Though usage is mixed, phrases involving addition, multiplication, subtraction, and division of numbers preferably take the singular:

> *Two and two is* [are] four.
>
> *Two times three is* six.
>
> *Twelve divided by six is* two.

In expressions like *part of the apple, some of the pie, all of the money,* the number of *part, some,* and *all* is determined by the number of the noun in the prepositional phrase:

> *Some* of the pie *is* missing.
>
> *Some* of the pies *are* missing.

8g   The Subject of Some Form of *To Be*

When one noun precedes and another follows some form of the verb *to be,* the first noun is the subject, and the verb agrees with it and not with the complement even if the complement is different in number:

> The only *fruit* on the market now *is* peaches.
>
> *Peaches are* the only fruit on the market now. [In the first sentence *fruit* is the subject; in the second, *peaches.*]

8h   Relative Pronoun as Subject

When a relative pronoun (*who, which,* or *that*) is used as the subject of a clause, the number and person of the verb are determined by the antecedent of the pronoun, the word to which the pronoun refers:

This is the student *who is* to be promoted. [The antecedent of *who* is the singular noun *student;* therefore, *who* is singular.]

These are the students *who are* to be promoted. [The antecedent of *who* is the plural noun *students.*]

Should I, *who am* a stranger, be allowed to enter the contest? [*Who* refers to *I; I* is first person, singular number.]

She is one of those irresponsible persons *who are* always late. [The antecedent of *who* is *persons.*]

If sentences such as the last one give you trouble, try beginning the sentence with the "of" phrase, and you will readily see that the antecedent of *who* is *persons* and not *one*:

Of those irresponsible *persons who are* always late she is one.

8i Collective Nouns

Some nouns are singular in form but plural in meaning. They are called **collective nouns** and include such words as *team, class, committee, crowd,* and *crew.* These nouns may take either a singular or a plural verb: if you are thinking of the group as a unit, use a singular verb; if you are thinking of the individual members of the group, use a plural verb:

The *crew is* striking for higher pay. [The crew is acting as a unit.]

The *crew are* writing reports of the wreck. [The members of the crew are acting as individuals.]

8j Nouns with Foreign Plurals

Some nouns retain the plural forms peculiar to the languages from which they have been borrowed: *alumni, media, crises.* Still other nouns occur with either their original plural forms or plural forms typical of English: *aquaria* or *aquariums, criteria* or *criterions.* If you are in doubt as to the correct or preferred plural form of a noun, consult a good dictionary.

NOTE: Be careful not to use a plural form when you refer to a singular idea. For instance, write *He is an alumnus of Harvard,* not *He is an alumni of Harvard.*

Exercise 36   SUBJECT-VERB AGREEMENT

Write the correct form of the *italicized* verb in the space at the right.

EXAMPLE: Leaning against the shed (*were, was*) a hoe and two rakes.   ....*were*........

1. Each of the freshmen on the tennis team (*hope, hopes*) to make the
   trip to Texas.   ....

2. Now that the Olympic games are being televised, everyone (*have, has*)
   a front-row seat.   ....

3. The United States often (*send, sends*) artists as good-will ambassadors
   to other countries.   ....

4. Neither the barn nor the fences (*are, is*) in need of paint this spring.   ....

5. It was one of those sultry summer nights that (*cause, causes*) us
   to long for an air conditioner.   ....

6. The Secretary of State along with members of his staff (*are, is*)
   boarding the plane for Tokyo.   ....

7. My friend and teammate (*is, are*) going to share a room with me
   on the next road trip.   ....

8. Athletics (*are, is*) Mary Sue's first and last interest.   ....

9. Do you know whether the Ways and Means Committee (*have, has*)
   adjourned for the day?   ....

10. I am afraid that the trousers that match this coat (*are, is*) hanging
    in my closet back home.   ....

11. The only fruit that Uncle Luke likes with cornflakes (*are, is*) strawberries.   ....

12. There (*are, is*) a drugstore, a toy shop, and a bank at this end of
    the mall.   ....

13. Everybody in the cast (*were, was*) impressed by Sidney's performance.   ....

14. "The Jumblies" (*are, is*) the title of one of Edward Lear's
    nonsense poems.   ....

15. Vanilla ice cream topped with peaches and strawberry jam (*are, is*)
    called Peach Melba.   ....

16. Economics (*were, was*) called the "Dismal Science" by Thomas
    Carlyle, the Scottish writer.   ....

17. My sister and my coach (*have, has*) helped me with the
    backstroke.   ....

18. China is one of those countries that (*have, has*) a history longer
    than human memory.   ....

19. (*Have, Has*) the news of Foster's appointment appeared in the *Times*?   ....

20. All afternoon the garden club (*were, was*) discussing their opinions of
    the flower show.   ....

Exercise 37   SUBJECT-VERB AGREEMENT

Write the correct form of the *italicized* verb in the space at the right.

EXAMPLE: Each of the suitcases (*bear, bears*) a name tag.   *bears*
....

1. At the heart of all the troubles that they have (*are, is*) their attitude.   ....

2. (*Don't, Doesn't*) everyone want to turn to another channel?   ....

3. Vincent claims that neither my pizza nor my spaghetti (*are, is*) like that his mother used to make.   ....

4. The Scout leader along with her troop (*plan, plans*) a canoe trip down the Chattooga River.   ....

5. Is it I who (*is, am*) to gather the holly for the wreath?   ....

6. None of the skaters (*think, thinks*) the ice is safe.   ....

7. Every man, woman, and child (*were, was*) at the airport to see the Concorde land.   ....

8. Their favorite pastime (*are, is*) bridge or scrabble.   ....

9. Neither our pines nor our pear trees (*have, has*) escaped the tornado.   ....

10. On the book shelf by my desk (*are, is*) my dictionary and my thesaurus.   ....

11. Lunceford and Company (*have, has*) a shoe store in town and at the new mall.   ....

12. No matter what you may think, fourteen gallons (*are, is*) all this gas tank will hold.   ....

13. Both the *National Geographic* and the *Smithsonian* (*are, is*) frequently read in our library.   ....

14. Each of the short stories in this collection (*treat, treats*) a different theme.   ....

15. (*Are, Is*) Marian or Carol responsible for the music at the convocation?   ....

16. Ham and eggs (*is, are*) my idea of a good breakfast.   ....

119

17. The police officer reminded me that thirty-five miles per hour (*are, is*) the speed limit on North Green Street. ....

18. Bruce is one of those nationalists who (*support, supports*) Scottish independence year in and year out. ....

19. Edith as well as a number of her friends (*are, is*) going to the concert at the Coliseum tomorrow night. ....

20. We have no shortage of milk at our house: four quarts (*are, is*) lined up in the refrigerator. ....

Exercise 38   SUBJECT-VERB AGREEMENT

Write the correct form of the *italicized* verb in the space at the right.

EXAMPLE: These scissors (*need, needs*) sharpening.   *need*
....

1. Have you noticed that gymnastics (*are, is*) a sport in which many Russians excel?   ....

2. The librarian said that only half of the overdue books (*have, has*) been returned to the library.   ....

3. You will find that *Letters of E. B. White* (*are, is*) reviewed in the *Atlantic Monthly*   ....

4. Either of these films (*deserve, deserves*) an Academy Award.   ....

5. The basis for the problems at the local pickle factory (*are, is*) a fuel shortage.   ....

6. Neither of the Witherby sisters (*have, has*) traveled in the United States.   ....

7. High above the earth (*circle, circles*) the hawks, watching for their prey.   ....

8. Every nook and cranny of the apartment (*are, is*) filled with his belongings.   ....

9. (*Are, Is*) either of you going to the carnival on Saturday?   ....

10. Reading my history assignments (*require, requires*) much of my time every night.   ....

11. Neither this shade of lipstick nor the pale rose one (*suit, suits*) her coloring.   ....

12. Every spring measles (*make, makes*) an appearance at kindergarten.   ....

13. Ten dollars (*are, is*) enough to pay for this secondhand rug.   ....

14. (*Are, Is*) seven times eight *54* or *56*?   ....

15. According to Will Rogers, "all politics (*are, is*) applesauce."   ....

16. Chester, one of the chessmen (*are, is*) under your chair.   ....

17. The recently built barracks (*are, is*) supposed to house recruits.   ....

18. Although it is September, some of the magnolia trees (*are, is*) still blooming.   ....

19. Those small green grapes (*are, is*) a delicious fruit.   ....

20. The media (*are, is*) frequently discussed in communications class.   ....

Exercise 39   SUBJECT-VERB AGREEMENT

Write the correct form of the *italicized* verb in the space at the right.

EXAMPLE: (*Have, Has*) each of the students brought pencil and paper?   *Has*
....

1. Who said that mathematics (*are, is*) the "queen of sciences"?   ....

2. Neither of the movies on television tonight (*appeal, appeals*) to me.   ....

3. There on the bench (*were, was*) Tim, Hank, and Dave.   ....

4. Some of the passengers (*plan, plans*) to remain aboard ship.   ....

5. The shambles left by the hurricane (*were, was*) visible all along the coast.   ....

6. A great deal of thought and energy (*have, has*) gone into plans for our new uniforms.   ....

7. Half of the swimmers (*have, has*) lined up at the pool side.   ....

8. Only one quarter of the watermelon (*have, has*) been eaten.   ....

9. The criteria used for grading our speeches (*were, was*) posted the first day of class.   ....

10. Two liters of cider (*are, is*) all this jug will hold.   ....

11. The whereabouts of the mountain climbers (*were, was*) announced on the six o'clock news.   ....

12. (*Do, Does*) the teacher or his aide grade the vocabulary tests?   ....

13. Ethics (*have, has*) always been a concern of the local bar association.   ....

14. Canoeing across lakes and down rivers (*occupy, occupies*) much of his time in the summer.   ....

15. Either of the artists (*appear, appears*) capable of painting the mural for the court house.   ....

16. When (*are, is*) Richard and his family moving to Hackensack?   ....

17. Everyone who had played on the team (*were, was*) invited to the banquet.   ....

18. Neither my roommate nor I (*are, am*) going to the political rally.   ....

19. The alumni of the Class of '45 (*are, is*) having a reunion this spring.   ....

20. Did you know that riches (*are, is*) what Croesus had?   ....

Exercise 40   SUBJECT-VERB AGREEMENT

In each of the following sentences fill in the blank with the correct form of the verb *to be* in the present tense. Then write the correct form again in the space at the right.

EXAMPLE: At the top of the menu ...*are*... listed the appetizers.   *are*
....

1. I believe that the acoustics in the old auditorium .... better than those in the new one.   ....

2. The only green vegetable on the menu .... snap beans.   ....

3. The crew .... coming on board today and tomorrow.   ....

4. Did you know that the Eagles .... the group that cut this record?   ....

5. Every morning two quarts of milk .... delivered to our house.   ....

6. Two quarts .... all the ice cream I can make in our churn.   ....

7. Mother thinks that the kitchen scissors .... in the top drawer of the cabinet.   ....

8. Either my brother or I .... responsible for distributing the circulars.   ....

9. The long and short of the matter .... that I cannot work this Saturday.   ....

10. Neither the instructor nor his students .... able to recognize the source of the quotation.   ....

11. "Delta Air Lines .... paging Ms. Frances Stuart."   ....

12. His former student and friend .... presenting a paper on Jack London.   ....

13. Nine miles to the gallon .... all the sheik's Rolls-Royce can manage.   ....

14. Unfortunately, the whereabouts of my philosophy notes .... unknown.   ....

15. I, who .... fond of all winter sports, especially enjoy cross-country skiing.   ....

16. A willow is one of those trees that .... often found by rivers.   ....

17. The alumnae of the College .... represented on the Board of Trustees by your friend Maria Holmes.   ....

18. The great crowd .... cheering as the Pope appears at the window.   ....

19. Three dollars .... your share of the supper check.   ....

20. Some of the sparrows .... already fussing over the birdseed you put in the feeder.   ....

Agreement of Pronoun and Antecedent 9

Pronouns, as we saw in Chapter 1, are words that are used in the place of nouns when repetition of a noun would be awkward. *The dog hurt the dog's foot* is clearly an unnatural expression. Usually a pronoun has a definite, easily recognized *antecedent* (the noun or pronoun to which it refers), with which it agrees in *person, number,* and *gender.* The *case* of a pronoun, however, is not dependent on the case of its antecedent.

9a Certain Singular Antecedents

Use singular pronouns to refer to singular antecedents. *Each, either, neither, anyone, anybody, everyone, everybody, someone, somebody, no one, nobody* are singular, and pronouns referring to them should be singular:

> *Each* of the girls has *her* own car.
>
> *Neither* of the boys remembered *his* poncho.
>
> Does *everyone* have *his* ticket?

NOTE: In the last of the preceding examples *his* is used even though its antecedent may be either male or female. You should be aware of and sensitive to objections to this traditional practice, but you should also recognize that no completely satisfactory solution exists, inasmuch as our language has no singular form that refers to persons of either sex. Because the expressions *he or she, his or her, his or hers,* and *him and her* are awkward, you are justified in using the masculine pronouns (or possessive adjectives) in a universal sense. It is often possible, however, to avoid the problem by rephrasing the sentence:

> Does *everyone* have *a* ticket?
>
> Do *we* all have *our* tickets?
>
> *Who* doesn't have *a* ticket? etc.

127

9b   Collective Nouns as Antecedents

With *collective nouns* use either a singular or a plural pronoun according to the meaning of the sentence. Since collective nouns may be either singular or plural, their correct usage depends upon (1) a decision as to meaning (See Chapter 8, Section 8i) and (2) consistency:

> The *team* has elected Jan as *its* captain. [The team is acting as a unit and therefore requires the singular pronoun *its*.]

> The *team* quickly took *their* positions on the field. [Here each member of the team is acting individually.]

Exercise 41   AGREEMENT OF PRONOUN AND ANTECEDENT

From the forms in parentheses choose the correct pronoun for each sentence, and write it in the space at the right.

EXAMPLE: Each of the contestants brought (*their, his*) own instrument. ....*his*...........

1. Someone has left (*their, her*) glasses at the box office. ....

2. I am sure that neither of the hounds has had (*their, its*) breakfast. ....

3. You can be sure that not every one of the students is satisfied with (*their, his*) grade. ....

4. Each of the perfumes had an appeal of (*their, its*) own. ....

5. The jeweler said that one should wind (*their, his*) watch at the same time every day. ....

6. That library's collection of books is noted for (*their, its*) appeal to young people. ....

7. According to the magazine article, the media want to set (*their, its*) own code of conduct. ....

8. It is remarkable that nobody lost (*their, his*) head when the fire broke out. ....

9. Everyone had (*their, his*) own idea of how the story should end. ....

10. When I was a child, bad news always found (*their, its*) way home quickly. ....

11. In preparing my report, I discovered that last year's criteria had lost (*their, its*) usefulness. ....

12. Either Millie or Louise will have to lend me (*their, her*) psychology notes. ....

13. Each of the dancers took (*their, her*) costume home after the performance. ....

14. Before practice the band must try on (*their, its*) new uniforms. ....

15. The United Nations expressed (*their, its*) disapproval of the aggression in the Near East. ....

16. How can anyone enjoy (*themselves, herself*) in this disagreeable weather?

    ....

17. Everybody should order (*their, his*) tickets for the play-off game by Friday.

    ....

18. Each of the automobiles had (*their, its*) final inspection before being sent to a dealer.

    ....

19. Excitement mounted as the oarsmen took (*their, his*) positions in the shell.

    ....

20. Every golfer in the tournament played (*their, her*) best game on the back nine.

    ....

Exercise 42 AGREEMENT OF PRONOUN AND ANTECEDENT

In the following sentences underline each pronoun or pronominal adjective incorrectly used; then write the correct form and, if necessary, the correct form of the verb in the space at the right. Write *C* if the sentence is correct.

EXAMPLE: Surprisingly, everybody remembered <u>their</u> sneakers. ....*his*...........

1. Not one of the hikers could turn their back on the small, wet puppy. ....

2. The grand jury will report their findings to the court. ....

3. Neither author clearly explained their attitude toward slang. ....

4. My scissors, with their dull blades, would scarcely cut paper. ....

5. The old barracks with its sagging walls had sat empty for years. ....

6. I wish that I could help you, but everyone has to apply for their own parking sticker. ....

7. As the ferry moved from the dock, every man, woman, and child were ordered to put on their life jacket. ....

8. Each of the routes to Bar Harbor had their advantages. ....

9. As a matter of fact, neither my father nor my brother take their fishing seriously. ....

10. The audience gave their undivided attention to the young man reading poetry. ....

11. I believe that someone is trying out her vocal cords in the shower. ....

12. Does anybody know their French well enough to translate this recipe? ....

13. Not one of the delegates know where they should register for the convention. ....

14. The legislature delayed their vote until after the public hearing. ....

15. At Class Day the alumni returned to admire its recent gift to the College. ....

16. I am sure that athletics themselves attract a large number of students to the school.

....

17. Of course, nobody would agree to lend those two clowns their car for the weekend.

....

18. Any one of us would be more than willing to share their book with Sue Ellen.

....

19. Some absent-minded professor has left their keys in the door to the biology lab.

....

20. Every one of the contestants in the Miss America pageant were in the process of deciding upon their acceptance speech.

....

Reference 10
of Pronouns

The word to which a pronoun refers should always be clear to the reader; that is, a **pronoun** and the **antecedent** to which it refers must be instantly identified as belonging together. A pronoun may be used with grammatical correctness and still be confusing or misleading. Therefore, it is sometimes necessary to repeat the antecedent or to reword the whole sentence for the sake of clearness.

10a Ambiguous Reference

Sometimes a sentence contains more than one word to which a pronoun may grammatically refer (the term *ambiguous* means "capable of more than one interpretation"). The sentence should be written in such a way that the reader has no doubt which word is the antecedent:

> Albert told his uncle that his money had been stolen. [The first *his* is clear, but the second *his* could refer to either *Albert* or *uncle*.]
>
> Albert told his uncle that Albert's money money had been stolen. [The meaning is clear, but the sentence is unnatural and awkward.]

To avoid the ambiguous reference of the first sentence and the awkward repetition of the second, reword the sentence:

> Albert said to his uncle, "My money has been stolen."

Another kind of ambiguous reference (sometimes called *divided* or *remote* reference) occurs when a modifying clause is misplaced in a sentence:

> INCORRECT: The colt was almost hit by a car which jumped over the pasture fence.
>
> CORRECT: The colt which jumped over the pasture fence was almost hit by a car.

NOTE: A relative pronoun should always be placed as near as possible to its antecedent. (See Chapter 15.)

10b   Broad Reference

Usually a pronoun should not refer broadly to the whole idea of the preceding clause:

> She avoided using slang, which greatly improved her speech. [*Which* has no clearly apparent antecedent but refers broadly to the whole idea in the first clause.]
>
> She talked incessantly about her operation, and this talkativeness was distressing.

A method often used to improve such sentences is to supply a definite antecedent or to substitute a noun for the pronoun:

> She avoid using slang, a practice which greatly improved her speech.
>
> She talked incessantly about her operation, and this talkativeness was distressing.

As you can see, these sentences are awkward, adding unnecessary words. A better method is to get rid of the pronoun and make a concise, informative sentence that says everything in one clause:

> Her avoidance of slang greatly improved her speech.
>
> Her incessant talking about her operation was distressing.

10c   Weak Reference

A pronoun should not refer to a word which is merely implied by the context. Nor, as a common practice, should the pronoun refer to a word used as a modifier:

> INCORRECT: My father is a chemist. *This* is a profession I intend to follow. [The antecedent of *This* should be *chemistry,* which is implied in *chemist* but is not actually stated.]
>
> CORRECT: My father is a chemist. Chemistry is the profession I intend to follow.
>
> ALSO CORRECT: My father's profession of chemistry is the one I intend to follow.
>
> INCORRECT: When she thrust a stick into the rat hole, it ran out and bit her. [*Rat* in this sentence is the modifier of *hole*.]
>
> CORRECT: When she thrust a stick into the rat hole, a rat ran out and bit her.

10d   Impersonal Use of the Personal Pronoun

Remember that pronouns are frequently used impersonally and when so used do not have antecedents. Notice the correct impersonal use of *it* in statements about *weather, time,* and *distance*:

> *It* looks like rain. [Reference to weather.]
>
> *It* is now twelve o'clock. [Reference to time.]
>
> How far is *it* to the nearest town? [Reference to distance.]

Avoid the use of *you* and *your* unless you are directing your statement specifically to the reader. Instead, use an impersonal word like *one* or *person*. Also note that the pronoun *you* can never refer to an antecedent in the third person:

> INCORRECT: If *you* want to excel in athletics, *you* should watch your diet. [Incorrect when referring to athletes in general.]

CORRECT: If *one* wants to excel in athletics, *he* should watch his diet.

INCORRECT: When a person gets married, *you* take on new responsibilities. [Here *you* refers incorrectly to *person*, an antecedent in the third person.]

CORRECT: When a person gets married, *he* takes on new responsibilities.

INCORRECT: One must always remember to lock *your* doors before leaving home.

CORRECT: One must always remember to lock *his* doors before leaving home.

Exercise 43   REFERENCE OF PRONOUNS

Write *R* after each sentence which contains an error in the reference of a pronoun. Then rewrite the sentence correctly. Write *C* if the sentence is correct.

EXAMPLE: The library was closed for the holidays, which inconvenienced the students.   *R*

   Closing the library for the holidays inconvenienced the students.

1. My neighbor often works in her vegetable garden, which is obvious.   ....

2. Julia told Virginia that she needed to repair her eye shadow.   ....

3. The groom disliked cooking; this was certainly unfortunate.   ....

4. The weatherman said that it was four degrees Celsius at seven o'clock this morning.   ....

5. If a person has a talent, you should develop it.   ....

6. Dorothy is a happy person, whose smile reveals it.   ....

7. Martin went bass fishing Wednesday and caught a string of them.   ....

8. Although Agnes is majoring in banking, she does not want to work in one.   ....

9. The golf course is about a mile from town where we play.   ....

10. The balloon rose slowly into the air, which was a thrilling sight. ....

11. Since Rachel's sister has moved away, she rides with me to work. ....

12. Because Tim practices his diving regularly, I believe that someday he will be an excellent one. ....

Exercise 44 REFERENCE OF PRONOUNS

Write *R* after each sentence which contains an error in the reference of a pronoun. Then rewrite the sentence correctly. Write *C* if the sentence is correct.

EXAMPLE: She frequently called long distance, which annoyed her father.   *R*
....

Her frequent long distance calls annoyed her father.

1. Hugh told his brother that he should make his own decisions about investments.   ....

2. The angry child was taken out of the swing by his mother, who was crying and kicking.   ....

3. The group sponsoring the book fair hopes to collect thousands of them.   ....

4. Her books and papers were strewn all over the den floor, which made my job of cleaning up harder than ever.   ....

5. The tourists discovered that it is farther from Cairo to Athens than they had realized.   ....

6. When one begins eating Hazel's doughnuts, you find it almost impossible to stop.   ....

7. As the child stared intently at the ant hill, they continued to hurry back and forth.   ....

8. I saw a story in the newspaper about the discovery of a Hawthorne notebook, which made interesting reading.   ....

9. *Horizon* contains an article on the theater in America, which is always a fascinating subject.   ....

10. The book includes reproductions of Michelangelo's paintings and photographs of his sculpture, which made an ideal gift for Augusta.   ....

11. If one is addicted to detective novels, he often becomes quite good at solving them.   ....

12. The poet Randall Jarrell wrote a number of books for children, which I did not know.   ....

Exercise 45   REFERENCE OF PRONOUNS

Write *R* after each sentence which contains an error in the reference of a pronoun. Then rewrite the sentence correctly. Write *C* if the sentence is correct.

EXAMPLE: The oyster stew contained very few of them.   *R*

The oyster stew contained very few oysters.

1. On the way to the starting gate the horse was led past the interested crowd, which was handsome and high strung.   ....

2. Now that Sheila has a tennis racket and shoes, she is ready to take it up.   ....

3. The tea cups sat in a row on the shelf which had been a gift from a German cousin.   ....

4. One must be honest about his likes and dislikes if you expect them to be respected.   ....

5. At the last minute the game between the Reds and the Braves was rained out, which disappointed Bo and me.   ....

6. Will the almanac tell me what time it is in Tokyo when it is noon in San Francisco?   ....

7. I told the employment agency that I did not want to be a typist because I do not enjoy it.   ....

8. The summer rains came often in the mountains; this made it difficult for the campers to keep their equipment dry.   ....

9. I mailed the box of pralines to my friends in Boston which I had bought in Mobile.   ....

10. Mary Jane has studied French for a number of years but has yet to visit it.   ....

11. My father decided to leave his job at the assembly plant and to buy a farm, which certainly pleased my mother.   ....

12. It is drizzling now; furthermore, the forecast says that it is to rain all day.   ....

Case 11
of Pronouns

Nouns and pronouns have three case functions: the **nominative**, the **objective**, and the **possessive**. Except in the possessive, nouns do not show case by change of form and consequently do not present any problems of case. The chief difficulties are in the correct use of pronouns.

11a The Nominative Case

The **nominative case** is used (1) as the subject of a verb (*I* shall come); (2) as the complement after *is, are,* and the other forms of the verb *to be* (It is *I*); or (3) as an appositive of the subject or of the complement after forms of the verb *to be* (Two of us—*he* and *I*—called). Ordinarily the case of a pronoun which comes before a verb presents no difficulties, for we naturally write "I am going," not "Me am going." But all constructions requiring the nominative case are not so simple as this one. Study carefully the following more difficult constructions:

1. A clause of comparison introduced by *as* or *than* is often not written out in full. The verb is then understood. The subject of this understood verb is in the nominative case:

No one can do the work as well as *he* (can).

He knows more about the subject than *she* (does).

2. After forms of the linking verb *to be*, nouns and pronouns used to identify the subject agree in case with the subject. Nouns and pronouns used in this way are called **predicate nominatives** and are in the nominative case:

It was *they* [not *them*].

The persons referred to were her sister and *she* [not *her*].

He answered, "It could not have been *I* [not *me*]."

3. Pronouns are frequently combined with a noun or used in apposition with a noun. If they are thus used with the subject of the sentence or with a predicate nominative, they are in the nominative case:

> *We* boys will be responsible for the equipment.
>
> Two photographers—*you* and *he*—must attend the convention.

If you read these sentences omitting the nouns, the correct form of the pronoun will at once be clear.

4. The position of the relative pronoun *who* often causes confusion, especially if it follows a verb or a preposition. The role of the relative pronoun within the dependent clause determines its case. Thus if *who* is the subject of the verb in the dependent clause, it is in the nominative case:

> You know *who* sent the money. [Since *who* is the subject of the verb *sent* and not the object of *know*, it must be in the nominative case. The whole clause *who sent the money* is the object of *know*.]
>
> Give the praise to *whoever* deserves it. [*Whoever* is the subject of *deserves*. The whole clause *whoever deserves it* is the object of the preposition *to*.]

5. Parenthetical expressions such as *you think, I believe, I suppose,* and *he says* often stand between a verb and the pronoun which is the subject. The pronoun must still be in the nominative case:

> *Who* do you think called me last night? [The expression *do you think* has nothing to do with the case of *who*. Leave it out, or place it elsewhere in the sentence, and you will see that *who* is the subject of *called*.]
>
> The man *who Jim* says will be our next governor is in the room. [Leave out or place elsewhere *Jim says,* and you will see that *who* is the subject of *will be*.].

11b The Objective Case

The **objective case** of a pronoun is used when the pronoun is the direct or indirect object of a verb, the object of a preposition, or an appositive of an object:

1. Compound subjects present a special difficulty:

> He wrote a letter to Mary and *me*. [Both words *Mary* and *me* are objects of the preposition *to* and therefore in the objective case. Omit *Mary and* or shift *me* to the position of *Mary*, and the correct form is at once apparent.]
>
> She gave George and *him* the address. [*Him* is part of the compound indirect object.]
>
> They invited William and *me* to the barbecue. [*Me* is part of the compound direct object.]

2. You will also have to watch the case of a pronoun combined with a noun in apposition with an object:

> She spoke cordially to *us* boys.
>
> They told three of us girls—Mary, Sue, and *me*—to go.

3. *Whom*, the objective case of *who*, deserves special consideration:

Whom were you talking to? [To *whom* were you talking?]

He is the boy *whom* we met on the plane. [*Whom* is the object of the verb *met*. The subject of *met* is *we*. Remember that the case of the relative pronoun is determined by its role within the dependent clause.]

Whom do you think we saw last night? [The parenthetical expression does not change the fact that *whom* is the object of *saw*.]

11c   Case of Pronouns Used with Infinitives

An infinitive phrase, as you have learned already, can have both an object and adverbial modifiers. In addition, an **infinitive** may have a subject. There are rules governing the case of pronouns when they are subjects or complements of infinitives:

1. When a pronoun is the subject of an infinitive, it will be in the objective case:

We want *him* to be elected.

2. If the infinitive is a form of the verb *to be* and if it has a subject, its complement will also be in the objective case:

She took him to be *me*.

3. If the infinitive *to be* does not have a subject, its complement will be in the nominative case:

The best player was thought to be *he*.

11d   The Possessive Case

Personal pronouns and the relative pronoun *who* have **possessive case** forms, which may be used with a noun or a gerund.

1. When the possessive forms *my, our, your, her, his, its,* and *their* modify nouns or gerunds, they are classified as **possessive adjectives**:

My book is on the table. [*My* is a possessive adjective, modifying *book*.]

We appreciate *your* giving to the Community Chest. [Not *you giving*. The object of the verb *appreciate* is the gerund *giving*; therefore, *your* is merely the possessive adjective modifying the gerund.]

2. Personal and relative pronouns form their possessives without the apostrophe:

The boy *whose* car is in the driveway works here.

The dog chewed *its* bone.

NOTE: Notice the difference between *its*, the possessive form, and *it's*, the contraction of *it is*:

It's time for your car to have *its* oil changed.

Exercise 46   CASE OF PRONOUNS

In the following sentences underline each pronoun which is used incorrectly, and then write
the correct form in the space at the right. Write *C* if the sentence is correct.

EXAMPLE: For who should he ask?   *whom*
....

1. Whom did you say caught the sailfish yesterday?   ....

2. Us children think that our allowances should be raised.   ....

3. Did he know that Virginia and me ate at Mrs. Burton's?   ....

4. Between you and I, I need another day to study for this test.   ....

5. Mary Alice wants him to be the one to light the candles.   ....

6. No one could be as tired of English peas as me.   ....

7. The basketball coach has already decided who he wants for center.   ....

8. In the late afternoons Barbara often took my sister and I for walks.   ....

9. The students appreciated him postponing the deadline for the research
papers.   ....

10. The three of us—Jim, Roger, and I—are going out for the tennis team.   ....

11. My father writes frequently to both of us, Emma and I.   ....

12. Everybody except you and I must have already heard of Charlie's
engagement to Beth.   ....

13. Eloise does not know who has borrowed the tape player.   ....

14. The least you can do is to send Mother and I a post card from London.   ....

15. Dr. Morgan was annoyed by them whispering throughout her lecture.   ....

16. Whom do you think should be in charge of the clean-up committee?   ....

17. The boy in the striped shirt has asked Clarence and I to the cookout.   ....

18. The executive committee will decide who to send to the conference in
Chicago.   ....

19. The music dictionary states that the composer of this waltz is thought to be her. ....

20. My passing this course is no foregone conclusion. ....

21. In spite of he and Arthur, the bus left for the races on time. ....

22. No one can loaf as successfully as him. ....

23. The captains of the team, Rufus and him, will accept the award at the banquet. ....

24. Mr. Parker offered she and Polly a ride to the fairground. ....

25. Not one of Mrs. Montgomery's daughters is as attractive as her. ....

Exercise 47   CASE OF PRONOUNS

In the following sentences underline each pronoun which is used incorrectly, and then write
the correct form in the space at the right. Write *C* if the sentence is correct.

EXAMPLE: None of my brothers is as tall as me.   ....*I*.......

1. The reporter asked Fred and I our opinion of the mayor's decision.   ....

2. We have to acknowledge that the winners of the raft race are them.   ....

3. After we go to school, my mother wants either Freeman or I to call home
every week.   ....

4. Will you ever forget me calling him Theodore instead of Franklin?   ....

5. Miss Marple considered him to be the prime suspect.   ....

6. Whom do you believe will be Julia's next fiancé?   ....

7. Uncle Herbert says that us boys must paint the fence on Monday.   ....

8. The sea fascinates me; its forever changing form and color.   ....

9. The proposals of the union leaders suit both they and management.   ....

10. Whom was Ferguson planning to dance with?   ....

11. Surely you can guess whom she is.   ....

12. My dog loses it's courage when confronted with your cat Harry.   ....

13. Whose that skating on the pond back of the school?   ....

14. Us riding the roller coaster is out of the question.   ....

15. Because it was dark in the alley, I took Joe to be he.   ....

16. No one but she and his mother thinks that Angus can sing.   ....

17. Could it have been them who stole the team's mascot?   ....

18. I am pleased to report that Aunt Annie is fond of Gilbert and I.   ....

19. I have no idea who's pen I am using.   ....

20. Last night at the masquerade the mystery guest was thought to be him.   ....

Exercise 48   CASE OF PRONOUNS

In the space at the right, write the correct form of the pronoun *who* (*whoever*).

EXAMPLE: Kennedy is the man (*who, whom*) she voted for.   *whom*
....

1. (*Who, Whom*) should I address this letter to?   ....

2. Did he say (*who, whom*) he would like as president of the student body?   ....

3. Report the robbery to (*whoever, whomever*) answers the telephone at the police station.   ....

4. Alice Jacobs is the person (*who, whom*) I hear will head the delegation to Washington.   ....

5. (*Who, Whom*) is Sylvia touring New England with?   ....

6. Do you know (*who, whom*) to ask about the plane schedules to St. Louis?   ....

7. The boy (*who, whom*) she introduced to Father plans to be an engineer.   ....

8. (*Whoever, Whomever*) designed this jacket did not have me in mind.   ....

9. You'll have to introduce me; I don't know (*who, whom*) is (*who, whom*).   ....

10. I cannot imagine (*who's, whose*) clubs these are lying on the green.   ....

11. (*Whomever, Whoever*) concocted such a recipe for fruit cake?   ....

12. (*Who's, Whose*) going skating on the Norton's pond Saturday afternoon?   ....

13. The man (*who, whom*) is reporting the game played baseball years ago.   ....

14. The old reactionary was opposed to (*whoever, whomever*) had a new idea.   ....

15. I have not heard (*who, whom*) is speaking at the political rally.   ....

16. I believe that Anderson is the person (*who, whom*) illustrated the cover of the literary magazine.   ....

17. (*Who, Whom*) does the dictionary say first used the expression "straight ticket"?   ....

18. Have they announced (*who, whom*) was the winner of the relay?   ....

19. Give these daisies to (*whoever, whomever*) answers the door.   ....

20. (*Who, Whom*) do you attribute this quotation to?   ....

Exercise 49   REVIEW OF AGREEMENT AND CASE

Underline each word that is incorrectly used. Then write the correct word in the space at the right. Write *C* if the sentence is correct.

EXAMPLE: The telephone call was for either my brother or <u>I</u>.   *me*
....

1. Because Mr. Edwards is nearsighted, he thought Morris to be I.   ....

2. On the back seat, between she and Callaway, sat a large sheep dog.   ....

3. According to this article, there remains widespread instances of drug abuse.   ....

4. The vocalist as well as members of the band were running for cover as the rain began.   ....

5. A number of we hikers want to try Mt. Mitchell.   ....

6. I believe that the boy driving the yellow Honda is him.   ....

7. Lining his book shelves are the works of Samuel Clemens, who the professor frequently quotes in class.   ....

8. Each individual will have to look after their own luggage.   ....

9. Whose son was John Barrymore?   ....

10. On the far side of the lawn was a bright umbrella and several canvas chairs.   ....

11. The student body rose as one to express its respect for the old teacher.   ....

12. Me trying to understand why you prefer pistachio ice cream is pointless.   ....

13. The editor of the annual along with the business manager plan to attend a workshop this spring.   ....

14. There are a number of questions for we on the program committee to discuss.   ....

15. The person in charge of the lighting for the dance recital was her.   ....

16. I do not believe that either of you have read the paper recently.   ....

17. The media continues to report news of the drought in the Midwest.   ....

18. Josephine and him are to give the first report in our German class.   ....

19. Belle had three puppies, all of which were marked exactly like she.   ....

20. Him telling his father about last quarter's grades took nerve.   ....

21. His father is every bit as tall as him.   ....

22. The alumnae is asked to attend the opening of the College's art gallery.   ....

23. Neither the campers nor the counselor were prepared for the onslaught of mosquitoes.   ....

24. I am weary of our discussing questions without answers.   ....

25. No one can make a blackberry cobbler as well as her.   ....

26. Its always later than you think.   ....

27. The two of us, Albert and me, plan to work at Democratic headquarters this summer.   ....

28. Either mowing the law or clipping the hedges are my task for the afternoon.   ....

29. Our parents appreciated Al coaching the soccer team.   ....

30. I hope that us two can take the horseback trip Mr. Holmes mentioned at the Scout meeting.   ....

31. All across the library table are scattered books and magazines.   ....

32. Just between we two I think that this teacher has ESP.   ....

33. The last one down to breakfast always seemed to be him.   ....

34. I am proud of him making a hole in one.   ....

35. Could it have been them who were singing "Auld Lang Syne"?   ....

Adjectives and Adverbs 12

Adjectives and adverbs, as you saw in Chapter One, are words which modify, describe, or add to the meaning of other words in a sentence. It is important to remember the special and differing functions of these two kinds of modifier; *adjectives* modify only nouns and other substantives; *adverbs* modify verbs, adjectives, adverbs, and certain phrases and clauses.

12a Adjective and Adverb Forms

An adverb is frequently formed by adding *-ly* to the adjective form of a word: for example, the adjectives *rapid, sure,* and *considerate* are converted into the adverbs *rapidly, surely,* and *considerately* by this method. But there are numerous exceptions to this general rule. Many common adverbs, like *well, then,* and *quite,* do not end in *-ly*; moreover, there are many *adjectives* that do end in *-ly,* like *manly, stately, lonely,* or *unsightly.*

Sometimes the same form is used for both adjective and adverbial forms: *fast, long,* and *much,* for example. (There are no such words as *fastly, longly,* or *muchly.*) Certain adverbs have two forms, one being the same as the adjective and the other ending in *-ly*: *slow, slowly; quick, quickly; loud, loudly;* etc. The first form is often employed in short commands, as in the sentences *Drive slow* and *Speak loud.*

12b Predicate Adjectives

In any sentence which follows a "subject-verb-modifier" pattern, you must be especially careful to determine whether the modifier is describing the subject or the verb:

> John talks *intelligently.*
>
> John is *intelligent.*

In the first sentence the modifier clearly describes how John talks — that is, it modifies the verb *talks;* consequently, the adverb *intelligently* is needed. But in the second sentence the modifier describes the subject *John*; therefore, an adjective is used. In this construction the adjective following the linking verb *is* is called the **predicate adjective.**

The term **linking verb**, as you learned from Chapter One, refers to certain intransitive verbs which make a statement not by expressing action but by expressing a condition or state of being. These verbs "link" the subject of the sentence with some other substantive that re-names or identifies it or with an adjective that describes it. Any adjective that appears after a subject-linking verb construction is called the **predicate adjective.** The verbs most commonly used as linking verbs are the following:

appear	become	remain	stay
be	grow	seem	feel (as an emotion)

Along with these are the five "sense" verbs, which are usually linking verbs:

look	feel	smell	taste	sound

The following sentences illustrate the use of predicate adjectives:

The little dog was *glad* to be out of his pen. [*Glad*, a predicate adjective, follows the linking verb *was* and describes *dog*.]

Father appeared *eager* to drive his new car.

Laurie became *angry* at being put to bed.

Jackie seems *happy* in her new job.

Please remain *quiet*, and I will give you your seat assignments. [*Quiet*, the predicate adjective, describes the subject, *you*, understood.]

The day grew *dark* as the clouds gathered.

Peggy looks *sporty* in her new tennis outfit.

I fell *confident* that Ty will win his case.

That cinnamon bread smells *delicious*.

The rain sounds *dismal* beating on the roof.

Almond toffee ice cream tastes *marvelous*.

This warm robe feels *comfortable*.

A practical test to follow in determining whether to use an adjective or an adverb is to try to substitute some form of the verb *to be* for the verb in the sentence. If the substitution does not substantially change the meaning of the sentence, then the verb should be followed by an adjective. For instance, *She is smart in her new uniform* has essentially the same meaning as *She looks smart in her new uniform*; therefore, the adjective *smart* is the correct modifier.

Occasionally, one of the "sense" verbs is followed by an adverb because the verb is being used not as a *linking* verb but as an *action* verb: *He looked nervously for his keys. Nervously* describes the act of looking, so the adverb is used to express how the looking was done. The substitution test would show immediately that an adjective would be incorrect in the sentence.

12c Misuse of Adjectives

Using an adjective to modify a verb is a common error but a serious one. The sentence *The doctor spoke to the sick child very kind* illustrates this error. *Kind* is an adjective and cannot be used to modify the verb *spoke*; the adverb *kindly* must be used.

Four adjectives which are frequently misused as adverbs are *real, good, sure,* and *some.* When the adverbial form of these words is needed, the correct forms are *really, well, surely,* and *somewhat:*

> The mountain laurel is *really* (or *very,* not *real*) colorful.
> You did *well* (not *good*) to stop smoking so quickly.
> I *surely* (not *sure*) hope to see him before he leaves.
> I feel *somewhat* (not *some*) better today.

NOTE: Remember that *well* can also be an adjective, referring to a state of health, as in *I feel well now, after my long illness.*

12d Comparison of Adjectives and Adverbs

When you wish to indicate to what extent one noun has a certain quality in comparison with that of another noun, you change the form of the modifying adjective that describes the quality: My dog is *bigger* than your dog. My dog is the *biggest* dog in town.

Descriptive adverbs, like adjectives, may be compared in the same way:

> We awaited the holidays *more eagerly* than our parents did.
> The shrimp and the oysters were the foods *most rapidly* eaten at the party.

Adjectives and adverbs show or imply comparison by the use of three forms, called **degrees**: the **positive, comparative,** and **superlative degrees.**

POSITIVE DEGREE

The **positive degree** of an adjective or adverb is its regular form:

> He is a *fine* man.
> John took notes *carefully.*

COMPARATIVE DEGREE

The **comparative degree** of an adjective or adverb compares two things, persons, or actions:

> He is a *finer* man than his brother.
> John took notes *more carefully* than Bob did.

SUPERLATIVE DEGREE

The **superlative degree** compares three or more persons, things, or actions:

> He is the *finest* man I know.
> John took notes *most carefully* of all the boys in his class.

The comparative degree is regularly formed by adding *-er* to the positive form of an adjective or adverb or by using *more* or *less* before the positive form. The superlative degree is formed either by adding *-est* to the positive or by using *most* or *least* before the positive. The number of syllables in the word determines which of these forms must be used:

	Positive	*Comparative*	*Superlative*
Adj.	strong	stronger	strongest
	pretty	prettier	prettiest
	difficult	more difficult	most difficult
Adv.	quietly	more quietly	most quietly
	easily	more easily	most easily
	fast	faster	fastest

The comparison of some words is irregular, as of *good* (*good, better, best*) and *bad* (*bad, worse, worst*).

Be careful not to use the superlative form when only two persons, groups, objects, or ideas are involved:

Tom is the *healthier* (not *healthiest*) of the two brothers.

Certain adjectives and adverbs such as *perfect* and *unique* cannot logically be used in the comparative or superlative degree; such words represent the superlative in their simple forms, incapable of being added to or detracted from:

ILLOGICAL: Samuel is the *most unique* person I know.

LOGICAL: Samuel is a *unique* person.

Exercise 50   ADJECTIVES AND ADVERBS

Underline the word which is modified by the *italicized* adjective or adverb. Then in the space at the right, write *Adj* if the italicized word is an adjective, *Adv* if it is an adverb.

EXAMPLE: The truck <u>drove</u> *slowly* along the narrow road.   *Adv*
....

1. Did you notice that the air became *cool* after the rain began?   ....

2. *Slowly* the old dog stretched himself in the winter sun.   ....

3. Herman is *especially* glad to finish his courses this quarter.   ....

4. The boy hurried home as the shadows grew *long*.   ....

5. The swimmer dived *deep* into the dark pool of water.   ....

6. The squirrel jumped from limb to limb in the great *sycamore* tree.   ....

7. *Each* one of these horses has won at least one race this spring.   ....

8. Gayle, you *surely* can play a good hand of bridge.   ....

9. The guide says that he is *sure* of the way out of the canyon.   ....

10. A line of tall fir trees broke the *wind's* force.   ....

11. As we hurried from the beach, the thunder crashed *loudly*.   ....

12. The large tiger jumped *down* and disappeared into the brush.   ....

13. *Never* have I taken a riverboat down the Mississippi.   ....

14. Surprisingly, the lilies do *not* appear wilted this morning.   ....

15. *Not* one of the newspapers mentions the story of the helicoper crash.   ....

16. Don't you agree that Imogene has a *unique* philosophy of life?   ....

17. The sign clearly says, "Drive *Slow*."   ....

18. It is *really* a long way to Goose Bay, Labrador, from here.   ....

19. Anyone would call this party a *real* success.   ....

20. Norman *often* had difficulty balancing his checkbook.   ....

159

21. The blue jay quarreled *continually* with the other birds at the feeder.   ....

22. Father says that the coffee cake is *ready* at last.   ....

23. The instructor's explanation of the unification of Germany is *quite* clear.   ....

24. Finally the train crowded with skiers pulled *away* from the platform.   ....

25. The bacon smells *delicious* cooking over the open fire.   ....

26. I agree that nothing smells *more* delicious.   ....

27. The car skidded *wildly* across the wet pavement.   ....

28. Have you grown *too* tall to wear these jeans another year?   ....

29. My broker feels *good* about the news in today's *Wall Street Journal.*   ....

30. Mrs. Harper has felt good since the doctor told her that she was *well.*   ....

Exercise 51   ADJECTIVES AND ADVERBS

Underline any adjective or adverb which is incorrectly used. Then write the correct form in the space at the right. Write *C* if a sentence is correct.

EXAMPLE: Every one of us had a <u>real</u> good time.   ....*really*............

1. Appearing as handsomely as ever, Walter seated the wedding guests.   ....

2. Her string of pearls is the most perfect one I have ever seen.   ....

3. Jay feels badly about losing his class ring down at Holden's Beach.   ....

4. She seems some better since having a good night's sleep.   ....

5. All night the highway crew worked steady to clear away the snow.   ....

6. The window panes shone bright in the morning sun.   ....

7. You have certainly done good to finish your psychology paper this early in the quarter.   ....

8. My cousin sure has enjoyed working in Colorado this summer.   ....

9. Please be careful with those goblets; they shatter easy.   ....

10. These cookies taste so well that I know Mrs. Martin made them.   ....

11. Everett is real disappointed that you cannot go sailing this weekend.   ....

12. Her offer of a ride to the clambake is muchly appreciated.   ....

13. Despite the lack of rain the roses in his garden bloomed profuse.   ....

14. Of all the cakes I have ever baked this is the worse one.   ....

15. Dr. Steiner says that you should feel well in no time.   ....

16. This morning in church Aunt Pauline looked sharp at the squirming child.   ....

17. Which of these two tables is the broadest?   ....

18. The lights grew dimly as we sailed out of the small harbor.   ....

19. Walking cautious, the small boy made his way across the log.   ....

20. Philmont, you have not done satisfactory in this course.   ....

21. My sister is an optimist, always speaking positive about the future.   ....

22. Please do not mumble; answer distinct when I ask you a question.   ....

23. I don't know who first advised, "Work hard and save your money."   ....

24. Is it your sunburn that has caused you to feel uncomfortably?   ....

25. Your speech this morning is the best of the two you have made.   ....

26. Each flower bed is the most perfect square imaginable.   ....

27. I do not suppose anyone feels good about the possibility of higher taxes.   ....

28. Although the old sergeant spoke curt, he was a kind man.   ....

29. Do not think that knowledge comes easy.   ....

30. Morton has a most unique way of waking his roommate.   ....

31. We had to run fast to catch the last ferry to the island.   ....

32. Which of the two paths to the lake is the shortest?   ....

33. Though always on a diet, Becky certainly does eat hearty.   ....

34. I sure do agree with those critics who like the novels of Graham Greene.   ....

35. The pavement felt hot to the child's bare feet.   ....

Exercise 52   ADJECTIVES AND ADVERBS

Select the correct form of the words in parentheses, and write it in the space at the right.

EXAMPLE: The breeze coming in the kitchen window felt (*cool, coolly*). ....*cool*...........

1. Appearing (*pale, palely*) after the steep climb, the hiker rested by the trail. ....

2. Which of our three dictionaries do you use (*more, most*) often? ....

3. As Miss Aiken walked along the path, her dog tugged (*impatient, impatiently*) at its leash. ....

4. The day was gray, and the wind felt (*bitter, bitterly*) as I stepped off the bus. ....

5. Steve threw the life preserver to the girl floundering (*helpless, helplessly*) in the lake. ....

6. Persuade Louis to sing "Old Man River"; he sings it (*mighty, mightily*). ....

7. The green apples that we picked from Mr. Hardman's tree tasted (*sour, sourly*). ....

8. The leaves piled (*high, highly*) in the doorways along the alley. ....

9. The shortstop looked (*alert, alertly*), waiting for Beasley's next pitch. ....

10. The plane skimmed the water but then climbed (*rapid, rapidly*) toward the sun. ....

11. Although the dancer is a prima ballerina, she always seems (*gracious, graciously*) and friendly. ....

12. The plot of *Treasure Island* is (*real, really*) interesting to children and adults alike. ....

13. The motor in his old car whirred (*confident, confidently*) as Edward drove toward Key West. ....

14. Several children watched (*close, closely*) as the small crab skittered across the sand. ....

15. Because the books had been stored in the basement, they had become (*damp, damply*) and moldy.   ....

16. The sailors appeared (*regular, regularly*) at Marlowe's when their ship was in port.   ....

17. Beowulf appeared (*courageous, courageously*) even as the dragon dealt him a death blow.   ....

18. Mr. Crump's voice sounded unusually (*harsh, harshly*) as he questioned the boys about the missing watermelons.   ....

19. The children whispered (*mysterious, mysteriously*) about their plans for the Christmas party.   ....

20. From the top of the bluff, the visitors stared (*curious, curiously*) at the activities below.   ....

21. I believe that Odysseus' experiences on his journey home were (*unique, most unique*).   ....

22. As the season progressed, our football team's record became the (*worse, worst*) in the league.   ....

23. I like this perfume because it has a light scent that smells (*spicy, spicily*).   ....

24. In spite of the weatherman's predictions, the sky turned (*clear, clearly*) around noon.   ....

25. Do you agree with Chaucer that no one "may work well and (*hasty, hastily*)"?   ....

26. Topped with chocolate sauce, the vanilla ice cream tasted especially (*good, well*).   ....

27. Although Maria wore bright colors, her clothes never seemed (*gaudy, gaudily*).   ....

28. The tires squealed (*loud, loudly*) as the police car rounded the corner.   ....

29. Once little more than twigs, the maple trees in front of the town hall have grown (*rapid, rapidly*).   ....

30. Surely today will be (*some, somewhat*) cooler than yesterday.   ....

31. The lawyer searched (*careful, carefully*) through the safe for the deed
to the gold mine.   ....

32. The rose that won the blue ribbon was the (*most perfect, most nearly
perfect*) one that Mr. Merton had ever shown.   ....

33. The tigers in the wallpaper stared (*fierce, fiercely*) at him as he tried
to eat his breakfast.   ....

34. John Milton is the (*younger, youngest*) of the Dean's two sons.   ....

35. The structure of Paris's new cultural center is (*unique, very unique*). ....

Tense, Voice, Mood 13

In Chapter 1 we found that a single verb may be classified according to **tense, voice,** and **mood**; therefore, it is not surprising that choosing the appropriate verb form occasionally presents difficulty.

13a Principal Parts of Verbs

We know that there are three **principal parts** of a verb. These are (1) **the first person singular, present indicative**; (2) **the first person singular, past indicative**; (3) **the past participle**. The first two of these provide the basic forms of the present, past, and future tenses; the third is used as the basis for the three perfect tenses:

PRINCIPAL PARTS:
begin, began, begun

Present:	I begin	
Past:	I began	
Future:	I shall (will) begin ————	(This form based on present tense *begin*)
Present Perfect:	I have begun	
Past Perfect:	I had begun	(These forms based on past participle *begun*)
Future Perfect:	I shall (will) have begun	

If you know the principal parts of a verb and the way to form the various tenses from them, you should never make a mistake such as the one contained in the following sentence: "The play had already began when I arrived." If the speaker had known that the principal parts of *begin* are *begin, began, begun* and that the past perfect tense is formed by using *had* with the past participle, he would have known that the correct form is *had begun.*

Regular verbs—that is, those verbs which form their past tense and past participle by adding -d or -ed to the present tense—rarely cause difficulty. It is the **irregular verbs** that are most frequently used incorrectly. When necessary, consult a dictionary for their principal parts. The following list contains the principal parts of certain especially troublesome verbs. Learn these forms:

Present	Past	Past Participle	Present	Past	Past Participle
ask	asked	asked	know	knew	known
bite	bit	bitten	lead	led	led
blow	blew	blown	ride	rode	ridden
break	broke	broken	ring	rang (rung)	rung
burst	burst	burst	run	ran	run
choose	chose	chosen	see	saw	seen
come	came	come	shake	shook	shaken
dive	dived (dove)	dived	sing	sang (sung)	sung
do	did	done	speak	spoke	spoken
drag	dragged	dragged	steal	stole	stolen
draw	drew	drawn	sting	stung	stung
drink	drank	drunk	suppose	supposed	supposed
drown	drowned	drowned	swim	swam	swum
eat	ate	eaten	swing	swung	swung
fall	fell	fallen	take	took	taken
fly	flew	flown	tear	tore	torn
freeze	froze	frozen	throw	threw	thrown
give	gave	given	use	used	used
go	went	gone	wear	wore	worn
grow	grew	grown	write	wrote	written

Note that the past tense and the past participle of the verbs *ask, suppose* and *use* are regularly formed by the addition of *-ed* (or *-d*) to the present tense. Possibly because the *d* is not always clearly sounded in the pronunciation of the past tense and the past participle of these verbs, people frequently make the mistake of writing the present-tense form when one of the other forms is required:

> I have *asked* (not *ask*) him to go with me.
>
> I was *supposed* (not *suppose*) to do that job.
>
> He *used* (not *use*) to be my best friend.

13b   Two Troublesome Pairs of Verbs

Lie and *lay* and *sit* and *set* are frequent stumbling blocks to correct writing. These verbs need not be confusing, however, if the following points are remembered:

1. Each verb has a distinguishing meaning. *Lay* and *set*, for instance, are clearly distinguished from *lie* and *sit* by their meanings: both *lay* and *set* usually mean *place* and are correctly used when the verb *place* can be substituted for them.

2. *Lay* and *set* are always transitive verbs; that is, they require an object to complete their meaning when they are used in the active voice. *Lie* and *sit* are intransitive verbs and hence do not take an object.

3. Although *lay* and *lie* share the form *lay*, they use it in different tenses. The remaining principal parts are clearly distinguishable.

These three points may be graphically shown:

PRINCIPAL PARTS	
Intransitive (takes no object)	*Transitive (takes an object)*
lie lay lain, *recline, remain in position*	lay laid laid, *place*
sit sat sat, *be in a sitting position*	set set set, *place*

Let us look at a few sentences which illustrate these distinguishing characteristics. Should we say *I set the box on the table* or *I sat the box on the table*? To answer the question, we should try substituting *placed* for *set* and should also see whether there is a direct object following the verb. We can say *I placed the box on the table*; also, *box* is clearly the direct object of the verb. Therefore, the first sentence, employing *set*, is the correct one. But in the sentence *I left the box sitting on the table*, the correct form is *sitting*, not *setting*, since *placing* cannot be substituted for *sitting* and since there is no direct object after *sitting*:

I *laid* (that is, *placed*) the book by the bed and *lay* (past tense of *lie*) down to rest.

Do not fall into the error of thinking that only animate things can stand as subjects of intransitive verbs. Note the following sentences in which inanimate objects are used as subjects of the intransitive verbs:

The book *lies* on the table.

The house *sits* near the road.

13c Tense Sequence

Tense sequence demands that a logical time relationship be shown by the verbs in a sentence. Through force of habit we generally indicate accurate time relationships. A few cautions, however, should be stressed:

1. Use the present tense in the statement of a timeless universal truth or a customary happening:

   I wonder who first discovered that the sun *rises* (not *rose*) in the east. [The fact that the sun rises in the east is a universal truth.]

   Joe said that the class *begins* (not *began*) at 10:30. [The clause *that the class begins at 10:30* states a customary happening.]

2. Use the present tense of an infinitive or the present participle if the action it expresses occurs at the same time as that of the governing verb:

Yesterday I really wanted *to go*. [Not *to have gone*. The governing verb *wanted* indicates a past time. At that past time I wanted to do something *then* — that is, yesterday — not at a time prior to yesterday.]

Skipping along, she hummed a merry tune. The skipping and the humming occur at the same time.)

3. When necessary for clarity, indicate time differences by using different tenses:

INCORRECT: I told him that I *finished* the work just an hour before.

CORRECT: I told him that I *had finished* the work just an hour before. [The verb *told* indicates a past time. Since the work was finished before the time indicated by *told*, the past perfect tense *had finished* must be used.]

INCORRECT: *Making* my reservations, I am packing to go to Cape Cod.

CORRECT: *Having made* my reservations, I am packing to go to Cape Cod. [The perfect participle *having made* must be used to denote an action before the time indicated by the governing verb *am packing*.]

13d Voice

Transitive verbs always indicate whether the subject is acting or is being acted upon. When the subject is doing the acting, the verb is said to be in the **active voice**:

I *laid* the book on the table. [*Laid* is in the active voice because the subject *I* is doing the acting.]

When the subject is being acted upon or receiving the action, the verb is in the **passive voice**:

The book *was laid* on the table. [*Was laid* is in the passive voice because the subject *book* is being acted upon.]

NOTE: The passive voice verb always consists of some form of the verb *to be* plus a past participle: *is seen, was laid, have been taken.*

In general, the active voice is more emphatic than the passive and therefore should normally be used in preference to the passive voice:

WEAK: The automobile *was driven* into the garage.

MORE EMPHATIC: She *drove* the automobile into the garage.

When, however, the receiver of the action should be stressed rather than the doer, or when the doer is unknown, the passive voice is appropriate:

Class officers *will be elected* next Thursday. [The receiver of the action should be stressed.]

The dog *was found* last night. [The doer is unknown.]

Generally speaking, one should not shift from one voice to the other in the same sentence:

AWKWARD: John *is* the best athlete on the team, and the most points *are scored* by him.

BETTER: John *is* the best athlete on the team and also *scores* the most points.

AWKWARD: After Dr. Lovett *was conferred* with, I *understood* the assignment.

BETTER: After I *conferred* with Dr. Lovell (OR After *conferring* with Dr. Lovett), I *understood* the assignment.

13e   The Subjunctive Mood

The **subjunctive mood** is most frequently used today to express a wish or to state a condition contrary to fact. In both types of statement the subjunctive *were* is used instead of the indicative *was*. Tenses in the subjunctive do not have the same meaning as they do in the indicative mood. For example, the past subjunctive form points toward the present or future, as seen in the sentence *If I WERE you, I would give his suggestion strong consideration.* The present subjunctive form usually points toward the future with a stronger suggestion of hopefulness than does the past subjunctive. (*I move that John Marshall BE named chairman of our committee.*) The present subjunctive form of the verb *to be* is invariably *be* for all persons, and the past subjunctive form of the verb *to be* is invariably *were*. In all other verbs the subjunctive form varies from the indicative only in that in the present tense the third person singular ending is lost, as in *I suggest that he TAKE the subway to his friend's house.* Note the following examples of verbs in the subjunctive mood:

I wish that I *were* (not *was*) going with you to Hawaii this summer.

If I *were* (not *was*) king, I couldn't be happier.

The subjunctive mood may also be used in the following instances:

If the report *be* true, we will have to modify our plans. [To express a doubt or uncertainty.]

She commanded that the rule *be* enforced. [To express a command.]

Even though he *disagree* with me, I will still admire him. [To express a concession.]

It is necessary that he *see* his parents at once. [To express a necessity.]

I move that the proposal *be* adopted. [To express a parliamentary motion.]

Exercise 53   TWO TROUBLESOME PAIRS OF VERBS

Select the correct form of the verbs in parentheses, and write it in the space at the right.

EXAMPLE: Mrs. O'Neill (*lain, laid*) her packages on the counter. ....*laid*........

1. We cannot continue to (*lie, lay*) under these trees with the hay (*lying, laying*) in the field. ....

2. Judith (*lain, laid*) the baby doll in the cradle and then (*lain, laid*) the blanket over her. ....

3. The giant oak was (*lying, laying*) across the highway and had (*lain, laid*) there since yesterday's storm. ....

4. Let's find a sheltered spot to (*lie, lay*) the sleeping bags and then (*lie, lay*) down for a nap. ....

5. After (*lying, laying*) the bright yellow cloth on the rock, she opened the picnic basket which (*lay, laid*) beside her. ....

6. My father has (*lain, laid*) his plans to begin (*lying, laying*) a flagstone walk on the next warm day. ....

7. Please (*lie. lay*) more wood on the fire so that the room will be warm when we (*lie, lay*) down to sleep. ....

8. As he (*lay, laid*) on the sand, he watched the sun (*lying, laying*) low on the horizon. ....

9. Once again the yellow brick road (*lay, laid*) before Dorothy, and I (*laid, lain*) aside my Sunday paper to watch the film. ....

10. As the story opens, the sailor is (*lying, laying*) in his hammock, thinking of the long voyage that (*lies, lays*) ahead. ....

11. Often, after I have (*lain, laid*) down to read, I cannot remember where I have (*lain, laid*) my glasses. ....

12. Having (*lain, laid*) the beach towel on the sun deck, Eloise (*lay, laid*) down for her daily sunbath. ....

13. Once she had (*lain, laid*) the tea table, she (*lay, lain*) on the lounge to wait for her guests. ....

14. The heat (*lay, laid*) heavy over the fields; the boy (*sat, set*) for a time in the shade of the old truck. ....

15. After Snuffy Smith (*sat, set*) his jug next to a log, he (*lay, laid*) down
    for a brief snooze. ....

16. The mockingbird (*sitting, setting*) in the birdbath lives dangerously
    as long as the cat (*sits, sets*) under the nearby bush. ....

17. Before the two of them (*sat, set*) out the tulip bulbs, they (*sat, set*)
    for a while over a cup of coffee. ....

18. Please (*sit, set*) the books from the bindery on the cart, and then
    (*sit, set*) here to check them in. ....

19. The four of us (*sat, set*) around the campfire, listening to the owl
    (*sitting, setting*) somewhere in the trees. ....

20. (*Sitting, Setting*) atop the ferris wheel is no place to (*sit, set*)
    Lucy Lee's mind at ease. ....

21. She (*sat, set*) the crying baby in his arms and then commanded
    him to (*sit, set*) in the rocking chair. ....

22. After (*sitting, setting*) the bowl of pink asters on the chest, Carrie
    (*sat, set*) down to admire them. ....

23. Have you (*sat, set*) enough chairs at the table so that everyone
    will have a place to (*sit, set*)? ....

24. Margie (*sat, set*) her straw hat on her head and (*sat, set*) down in the
    beach chair to await further developments. ....

25. Having (*sat, set*) the last crate of apples in the truck, the boys
    (*sat, set*) on the platform to wait for Mr. Sparks. ....

26. Once the old woman (*sits, sets*) the pot of coffee on the stove, she
    (*sits, sets*) on the porch to watch the sunrise. ....

27. After we have (*sat, set*) the plans for the new constitution before
    the club, then we need to (*sit, set*) down for a conference. ....

28. (*Sit, Set*) the music on the piano so that Mrs. Brown will be certain
    to see it when she (*sits, sets*) down to play. ....

29. After (*sitting, setting*) the sherbert in the freezer, I (*sat, set*) down
    for a chat with my visitors. ....

30. The girl has (*sat, set*) the bucket of blackberries beside her while she
    (*sits, sets*) waiting at the top of the hill. ....

Exercise 54   TWO TROUBLESOME PAIRS OF VERBS

Underline any form of *lie, lay, sit, set* which is incorrectly used. Then write the correct form in the space at the right. Write *C* if a sentence is correct.

EXAMPLE: The farmer left his hoe <u>laying</u> in the field.   ....*lying*........

1. During the morning the highway crew lain a long ribbon of asphalt.   ....

2. The small statue of Hiawatha had set on the mantel for years.   ....

3. I think that you will find that the directory is laying by the telephone.   ....

4. The coals lay in the grate, burning lower and lower.   ....

5. The hitchhiker set by the roadside, holding a sign which read, "California or bust."   ....

6. The Baileys have already lain out their plans for a trip to the Canadian Rockies.   ....

7. Please set this bowl of walnuts on the table by your father's chair.   ....

8. The waiter sat the plate of snails before the astonished customer.   ....

9. Hoping the school bus had not left her, Mary continued to set on the school steps.   ....

10. At the fair the prize pigs have laid for hours dozing in the sun.   ....

11. Be sure to lie the keys on the table by the door.   ....

12. She was ready to come down the stairs only after each red curl was set in place.   ....

13. The bookkeeper was setting on the tall stool as he carefully figured the company's accounts.   ....

14. Don knew that he was laying in the sun longer than he should.   ....

15. Was it Shakespeare who said, "Uneasy lies the head that wears the crown"?   ....

16. Carol was setting on her motorcycle before she realized that she had left her helmet in the restaurant.   ....

17. Sit the tapes you want to hear on the front seat of the car.   ....

18. All day a thin coat of ice had laid on the marble steps into the
museum.   ....

19. Once the crew had sat the chairs on the stage, the curtain went up.   ....

20. The rocks had been lain carefully around the edge of the flower bed.   ....

21. Aunt Lily could seldom find her glasses because she was forever
laying them first one place and then another.   ....

22. When Schroder sets at the piano, can Lucy be far behind?   ....

23. Lying the receiver down, Joseph called his sister to the telephone.   ....

24. The boys lain the logs for the fire on the back porch of the cabin.   ....

25. In the foyer of the library you will find a stand in which to sit your
umbrella.   ....

26. She bought the old highchair which had been setting in front of the
antique shop.   ....

27. According to the fable, the ant sits aside food for the winter, but
the grasshopper fiddles the summer away.   ....

28. As Kathleen unpacked, she carefully lain her blouse in the second
drawer of the chest.   ....

29. Just after sitting the ball on the tee, the golfer heard the heavy
rumble of thunder.   ....

30. I did not know that Dickens is credited with the expression "Let
sleeping dogs lie."   ....

Exercise 55   TENSE AND MOOD

A. In the space at the right write the correct form of the verb in parentheses.

EXAMPLE: Someone has (*take*) the phone off the hook. ....*taken*............

1. The very foundation of the old house seemed to be (*shake*) by the heavy thunder. ....

2. Last summer while working at the park, Leah (*wear*) a uniform. ....

3. The wind (*sting*) my checks as I rounded the corner of Cain Street. ....

4. A small balding man (*lead*) the way as the family filed into the restaurant. ....

5. With every pitch the batter has (*swing*) at the ball. ....

6. Is there milk in the refrigerator, or has Simon (*drink*) it all? ....

7. When we were children, we (*use*) to ride the ferris wheel at the county fair. ....

8. Last Christmas the young people (*sing*) carols throughout the neighborhood. ....

9. Yesterday my brother (*drag*) some driftwood from the beach for the bonfire tonight. ....

10. Pictures of all the family were (*hang*) over her small maple table. ....

11. The boys (*dive*) again and again as the tourists threw pennies into the harbor. ....

12. Did you know that Sloan is (*suppose*) to wear his glasses when he drives? ....

13. Almost as quickly as the child blew a bubble, it (*burst*) before his eyes. ....

14. My grandmother often has (*choose*) to take a nap after lunch. ....

15. The telephone (*ring*) often at our house when Ruby came home for a holiday. ....

B. Underline all verbs in the following sentences. Then write the past tense of the underlined verbs in the space at the right.

EXAMPLE: The children <u>draw</u> the sled back up the steep slope.   ......*drew*......

1. The sun rises out of the Atlantic and sinks behind the forest of pines and scrub oaks.

   ....

   ....

2. The fan whirs continuously overhead as the couple eat breakfast in the small café.

   ....

   ....

3. While we swing away from the dock, the ship's fog horn blows repeatedly.

   ....

   ....

4. She always asks to see *Harper's* because a friend of hers writes for the magazine.

   ....

   ....

5. The leaves of the sycamore tree fall in October and soon gather in heaps in the corners of the yard.

   ....

   ....

C. Select the correct form of the verb in parentheses, and write it in the space at the right.

EXAMPLE: If I (*was, were*) you, I would rent an unfurnished apartment. ......*were*......

1. The young woman at the welcome center said that it (*was, is*) about forty-five miles to Greenville.

   ....

2. All that summer Mother insisted that we (*were, be*) home by midnight.

   ....

3. (*Reaching, Having reached*) the far side of the island, we stopped to buy some cheese and fruit.

   ....

4. Tell Homer that it is necessary that he (*calls, call*) Joan at once.

   ....

5. I wish that I (*was, were*) going with you on your trip to Peru.

   ....

Exercise 56   TENSE AND MOOD

Underline any verb form which is incorrect. Then write the correct form in the space at the right. Write *C* if a sentence is correct.

EXAMPLE: He has <u>tore</u> a hole in the bottom of his boat.   ....*torn*............

1. Last night we ask to see the collection of rare coins, but the museum was closed.   ....

2. If he was ten years younger, I believe that he would run for Congress.   ....

3. Our guide lead us through the old house, pointing out possessions prized by Mr. Emerson.   ....

4. My father will never believe that I have wore out my shoes walking to the library.   ....

5. The girls sat on the dormitory steps and sang all the old favorites.   ....

6. Walking along the beach, we seen a dozen or more people looking for shells.   ....

7. She done the weeding in the garden early in the morning before the sun grew hot.   ....

8. Do I hear a motion that this meeting is adjourned?   ....

9. Chandler knows that he should have took mathematics his freshman year.   ....

10. Rain or shine, he has swam every morning this summer.   ....

11. Tarzan grabbed the heavy vine and swang across the treacherous rapids.   ....

12. Virginia torn off a slip of paper and jotted down his telephone number.   ....

13. No sooner had the clown given the child a balloon than it busted.   ....

14. Completing his broadcast, the announcer hurriedly left the studio.   ....

15. The mosquitoes bitten Ophelia as she gathered the beans.   ....

16. It is essential that the passengers be back on board by noon.   ....

17. When she went to New York, she planned to have studied music. ....

18. Exhausted after the free-style race, Horace dragged himself onto the raft. ....

19. Although the child was disobedient, you should not have shooken him. ....

20. The governing boards simultaneously announced that the corporations merged. ....

21. I am afraid that Aunt Lulu has came down with rheumatism again. ....

22. Our Canadian visitor said that the St. Lawrence Seaway has froze over during the winter. ....

23. The new short-order cook is suppose to know how to make an omelet. ....

24. Margie has rode the Great Scream Machine at least three times today. ....

25. Franklin wishes that he was eligible to play in the golf tournament. ....

26. Has the second game of the double-header began? ....

27. Julius has gave any number of excuses for not writing home. ....

28. When I first woke up this morning, I planned to have spent today painting the porch swing. ....

29. As the old man walked along the beach, his small terrier run in and out of the waves. ....

30. Down at the newspaper office they hanged Father's portrait above his roll-top desk. ....

31. Standing in the hotel lobby, Jack suddenly caught sight of his college roommate. ....

32. No one can count the number of times I have fell while learning to ski. ....

33. I have heard that a woman from the southern part of the state is suppose to run for governor. ....

34. The radio announcer told me that his station signed on the air every morning at six o'clock. ....

35. While traveling in Europe this summer, Wilbur growed a beard.   ....

36. The corner of the barn caught the kite just before it flown away.   ....

37. If the truth is told, none of us should drive to work alone.   ....

38. Every Sunday afternoon the children use to enjoy watching the five o'clock train arrive from Washington.   ....

39. Whom has the mayor chose to represent the city at the conference?   ....

40. The lifeguard did not hesitate but immediately dove into the murky pond.   ....

41. Once the officer blown his familiar whistle, the school children scurried across the street.   ....

42. We are not accustom to eating at midday and napping away the afternoon.   ....

43. Watching one soap opera after another, Kitty managed to finish making the cheese straws.   ....

44. The reporters standing on the cold platform wished that the President was through with his remarks.   ....

45. Paul bent over and drunk some of the cold water spewing from the rocks.   ....

46. The almanac stated that Easter was never earlier than March 22.   ....

47. We were suppose to leave right after breakfast, but of course we had to wait for Annabelle Wiggins.   ....

48. On the walls of the old building the boys drawn an absurd picture of the team's mascot.   ....

49. I think that the rustler should have been hung for horse stealing by now.   ....

50. If I was your mother, I would retire as your cook and laundress.   ....

Exercise 57   VOICE

Revise the following sentences, using verbs in the active voice and eliminating unnecessary verbs.

EXAMPLE: The letter to the editor was written by Rosa.

Rosa wrote the letter to the editor.

1. The Sisters' Chapel was designed by Neel Reid and is located on the campus of Spellman College.

2. The article which was written by Dr. Stuart was concerned with the novels of John Cheever.

3. It was announced in the Sunday paper by our neighbors the Watsons that Mary and John would be married in May.

4. The music for *The Mikado* was composed by Arthur Sullivan and the libretto was written by W. S. Gilbert.

5. The pot roast which was prepared Sunday by Grandmother was considered by the family to be one of her best.

6. The portrait which was painted by Picasso is entitled *Seated Woman* and is hung in the Tate Gallery in London.

7. The six o'clock news was announced by a different team of reporters when an assignment in Japan was given the regular pair.

8. Early each morning the car was driven to the country store by Norman in order that a newspaper might be bought.

9. The canoe was paddled most of the afternoon by my two cousins who had been asked by my mother to visit our moutain cottage.

10. The award was won by a guitar player for a song which had been recorded by her earlier in the year in Nashville.

12. After the guest list for the tea was decided upon, the menu was planned by the two sister

13. The walls of the store-front church were painted by the young people with the help of Phil Talbot, who had been selected by them to be their advisor.

14. The sailboat which had been launched in the pond by Alan was enjoyed by him all summer long.

15. There was a party planned by Louis for New Year's Eve at which egg nog and fruit cake would be served.

Dangling Modifiers 14

A **modifier** must always have a word to modify. This fact seems almost too obvious to warrant discussion. And yet we frequently see sentences similar in construction to this one: "Hearing a number of entertaining stories, our visit was thoroughly enjoyable." *Hearing a number of entertaining stories* is a modifying phrase. But where in the sentence is there a word for it to modify? Certainly the phrase cannot logically modify *visit*: it was not our visit that heard a number of entertaining stories. Who did hear the stories? *We* did. Since, however, the word *we* does not appear in the sentence for the phrase to modify, the phrase is said to "dangle." Any modifier dangles, or hangs unattached, when there is no obvious word to which it is clearly and logically related. (Note the similarity of this problem of modifiers and the problem of pronouns and their antecedents.)

14a Recognizing Dangling Modifiers

It is important that you recognize dangling modifiers when you see them. Such modifiers usually appear as two types of constructions—as *verbal phrases* and as *elliptical clauses*. (An elliptical clause, as applicable to this lesson, is a dependent clause in which the subject and/or verb are omitted.)

> *Hearing a number of entertaining stories,* our visit was thoroughly enjoyable. [Dangling participial phrase.]
>
> *On entering the room,* refreshments were being served. [Dangling gerund phrase.]
>
> *To play tennis well,* the racket must be held properly. [Dangling infinitive phrase.]
>
> *When only three years old,* my father took me to a circus. [Dangling elliptical clause.]

In each of the examples given above, the dangling modifier stands at the beginning of the sentence. If the modifier were *not* dangling—that is, if it were correctly used—it would be related to the subject of the sentence. In none of these sentences, however, can the introductory modifier logically refer to the subject. If the error is not immediately apparent, try placing the modifier just after the subject. The dangling nature of the modifier becomes easily recognizable because of the illogical meaning which results when you say, "Our visit, *hearing a number of entertaining stories, . . "* or "Refreshments, *on entering the room, . . .*"

Dangling modifiers frequently appear at the end as well as at the beginning of sentences. The participial phrase dangles in the sentence "The dog had only one eye, *caused by an accident."*

At this point an exception to the rules governing the recognition of dangling modifiers should be noted: some introductory verbal phrases are general or summarizing expressions and therefore need not refer to the subject which follows:

CORRECT: *Generally speaking,* the boys' themes were more interesting than the girls'.

CORRECT: *To sum up,* our vacation was a disaster from start to finish.

14b   Correcting Dangling Modifiers

Sentences containing dangling modifiers are usually corrected in one of two ways. One way is to leave the modifier as it is and to recast the remainder of the sentence so that the word to which the modifier should refer becomes the subject of the sentence. Remember that when modifiers such as those discussed in this lesson stand at the beginning of the sentence, they must always clearly and logically modify or be related to the subject of the sentence:

Hearing a number of entertaining stories, *we* thoroughly enjoyed our visit.

On entering the room, *I* found that refreshments were being served.

To play tennis well, *one* must hold the racket properly.

When only three years old, *I* was taken to a circus by my father.

You may test the correctness of these sentences, as you tested the incorrectness of the others, by placing the modifier just after the subject. Then see whether the sentence reads logically; if it does, the modifier has been correctly used. The following sentence, though awkward, is clear and logical: "We, hearing a number of entertaining stories, thoroughly enjoyed our visit."

The other way to correct sentences containing dangling modifiers is to expand the modifiers into dependent clauses:

Since we heard a number of entertaining stories, our visit was thoroughly enjoyable.

When I entered the room, refreshments were being served.

If one wishes to play tennis well, he must hold the racket properly.

When I was only three years old, my father took me to a circus.

Exercise 58 DANGLING MODIFIERS

Rewrite in correct form all sentences which contain dangling modifiers. Write *C* if a sentence is correct.

EXAMPLE: To receive the recordings, a check must accompany your order.

To receive the recordings, you must enclose a check with your order.

1. Having finished the first chapter of his autobiography, it was forwarded by the colonel to the publisher.

2. After drinking my cup of coffee and reading "Blondie," my day begins in earnest.

3. To understand James Joyce's *Finnegans Wake*, a key is needed by most readers.

4. Generally speaking, height is an advantage for a basketball player.

5. The bridges began freezing over just after setting out for Montreal.

6. While curled up on the windowsill, I noticed that my cat Rameses kept a close watch on the bird feeder.

7. Although looking forward to his job in Dallas, there remained the necessity of finding an apartment.

8. Flying low over the heavily wooded mountains, the lost prospectors were finally spotted.

9. While investigating the burglary, a number of clues were found by the detective.

10. To understand the use of the computer terminal, carefully written directions were given us by our instructor.

11. Hurrying to catch the last train, Stuart's cap flew off his head and onto the tracks.

12. Having told our guests goodbye, the next task was to gather up the glasses and empty the ashtrays.

13. When finished with the evening paper, please leave it as you found it.

14. The snow began to fall just after waking up.

15. To cook bacon well, starting with a cold skillet is recommended.

16. Before cleaning the closet, the prospects of locating the ice cream freezer seemed dim.

17. Having heard the siren, the car swerved to the curb.

18. Rushing up and down again on the roller coaster, my hands gripped the steel bar in front of me.

19. Carefully focusing his camera, the photographer took a picture of the prize-winning hog.

Exercise 59   DANGLING MODIFIERS

Using the following phrases and elliptical clauses as introductory modifiers, write complete sentences.

EXAMPLE: When watching the late show, ... *I often fall asleep.* ....

1. Having raked the leaves into great piles, ...

   ....

2. Before reshelving the law books, ...

   ....

3. To arrive at the church by noon, ...

   ....

4. Dressed in a white linen suit and a panama hat, ...

   ....

5. While attending her class reunion, ...

   ....

6. Hearing the long wail of the train whistle, ...

   ....

7. Once having begun his painting, ...

   ....

8. When confronted with an algebra problem, ...

   ....

9. To appreciate my father's attitude toward money, ...

   ....

10. Tied tightly beneath her chin, ...

   ....

11. Standing in front of Tiffany's window, ...

....

12. To sum up, ...

....

13. Instead of waiting for the bus on this windy corner, ...

....

14. Having banished the villain from Dodge City, ...

....

15. When not seen together, ...

....

16. Being optimisic about most matters, ...

....

17. While trying to read the map, ...

....

18. To make the brass candlesticks shine, ...

....

19. After hanging the curtains, ...

....

20. Once surrounded by the entire family, ...

....

21. Rapidly descending from the plane, ...

....

22. Without apologizing for the interruption, ...

....

Misplaced Modifiers 15

Modifiers must always be so placed that there will be no uncertainty about the words they modify. A modifier should, in general, stand as close as possible to the word that it modifies. This does not mean, however, that in every sentence there is only one correct position for a modifier. The following sentence, in which the adverb *today* is shifted from one position to another, is equally clear in any one of these three versions:

Today she arrived in Chicago.

She arrived *today* in Chicago.

She arrived in Chicago *today*.

The position of the modifier *today* can be shifted because, no matter where it is placed, it clearly modifies the verb *arrived*.

15a Misplaced Phrases and Clauses

When, however, a modifier can attach itself to two different words in the sentence, the writer must be careful to place it in a position which will indicate the meaning intended:

They argued the subject while I tried to study *at fever pitch*.

This sentence is illogical as long as the phrase *at fever pitch* seems to modify *to study*. The phrase must be placed where it will unmistakably modify *argued*:

CORRECT: They argued the subject *at fever pitch* while I tried to study.

ALSO CORRECT: *At fever pitch* they argued the subject while I tried to study.

A relative clause—that is, a clause introduced by a relative pronoun—should normally follow the word which it modifies:

ILLOGICAL: A piece was played at the dance *which was composed of dissonant chords.*

CORRECT: A piece *which was composed of dissonant chords* was played at the dance.

15b Ambiguous Modifiers

When a modifier is placed between two elements so that it may be taken to modify either element, it is **ambiguous.** These ambiguous modifiers are sometimes called **squinting modifiers:**

The girl who had been dancing *gracefully* entered the room.

Does the speaker mean that the girl had been dancing gracefully or that she entered the room gracefully? Either of these meanings may be expressed with clarity if the adverb *gracefully* is properly placed:

The girl who had been *gracefully* dancing entered the room. [*Gracefully* modifies *had been dancing.*]

The girl who had been dancing entered the room *gracefully*. [Here *gracefully* modifies *entered.*]

15c Misplaced Words Like *Only, Nearly,* and *Almost*

Words such as *only, nearly,* and *almost* are frequently misplaced. Normally these modifying words should immediately precede the word they modify. To understand the importance of properly placing these modifiers, consider in the following sentences the different meanings which result when *only* is shifted:

Only I heard John shouting at the boys. [*Only* modifies *I.* Meaning: I was the only one who heard John shouting.]

I *only* heard John shouting at the boys. [*Only* modifies *heard.* Implied meaning: I heard but didn't see John shouting.]

I heard *only* John shouting at the boys. [*Only* modifies *John.* Meaning: John was the only one whom I heard shouting.]

I heard John *only* shouting at the boys. [*Only* modified *shouting.* Possible implied meaning: I didn't hear John hitting the boys—I heard him only shouting at them.]

I heard John shouting at the boys *only*. [*Only* modifies *boys.* Possible implied meaning: The boys were the ones I heard John shouting at—not the girls.]

Misplacing *only, nearly,* or *almost* will frequently result in an illogical statement:

ILLOGICAL: The baby *only* cried until he was six months old.

CORRECT: The baby cried *only* until he was six months old.

ILLOGICAL: Since his earnings amounted to $97.15, he *nearly* made a hundred dollars.

CORRECT: Since his earnings amounted to $97.15, he made *nearly* a hundred dollars.

ILLOGICAL: At the recent track meet Ralph *almost* jumped six feet.

CORRECT: At the recent track meet Ralph jumped *almost* six feet.

15d   Split Infinitives

A **split infinitive** is a construction in which the sign of the infinitive *to* has been separated from the verb with which it is associated. *To vigorously deny* and *to instantly be killed* are split infinitives. Unless emphasis or clarity demands its use, such a construction should be avoided:

AWKWARD: He always tries *to efficiently and promptly do* his work.

CORRECT: He always tries *to do* his work *efficiently and promptly.*

CORRECT: We expect *to more than double* our sales in April. [Placing the modifiers *more than* anywhere else in this sentence would result in ambiguity or changed meaning.]

Exercise 60   MISPLACED MODIFIERS

Place *M* or *C* in the space at the right to indicate whether the sentence contains a misplaced modifier or is correct. Underline the misplaced words, and indicate their proper position by means of a caret. Use additional carets if there are additional correct positions.

EXAMPLE: The hurricane <u>only</u> hit ∧ an unpopulated area.   *M*

1. That winter we rode to school in a sleigh bundled up in our wraps.   ....

2. Even though it had grown dark, he continued to slowly trudge home.   ....

3. The boy who had been jogging steadily gained on the two of us.   ....

4. The rain swept across the highway which came in torrents.   ....

5. He only came to see the family at Thanksgiving.   ....

6. Summer after summer the dog returned to the lake cottage which had grown up with us.   ....

7. She wrote a children's story based on life in colonial America in 1970.   ....

8. We hardly saw any fiddlers we knew at the mountain fair.   ....

9. I was urged to carefully read the instructions on the can of insect repellent.   ....

10. Only I am flying to the game in New Orleans; my roommates are going by car.   ....

11. The outfielder who caught the ball easily threw it to first base.   ....

12. Just put the correct change in the coffee machine if you expect it to work.   ....

13. The room is especially inviting to Mother overlooking the garden.   ....

14. The small car struck the utility pole which had been speeding down the street.   ....

15. My old mule's muzzle has nearly turned gray.   ....

16. The child who skipped along happily dropped all her school books.   ....

17. He finished almost all the apple pie before going to bed.   ....

18. Even though the day was bitter, she only wore her light suit.   ....

19. The psychologist wrote the report on violence in his basement study.   ....

20. The bridge was designed by a local firm of engineers which everyone considers unusual.

....

Exercise 61   MISPLACED MODIFIERS

Place an *M* or a *C* in the space at the right to indicate whether the sentence contains a misplaced modifier or is correct. Underline the misplaced word or words, and indicate their proper position by means of a caret. Use additional carets if there are additional correct positions.

EXAMPLE: The quarterback for the Lions <u>nearly</u> gained˄ ten yards.   *M*
....

1. The old hound bayed at the moon sitting on the back steps.   ....

2. To merely pass the course should not be your aim, Jesse.   ....

3. The horse had been brought out of the stable which she hoped to ride.   ....

4. She almost drove to the end of the lane before finding the house.   ....

5. The beach which had eroded gradually disappeared into the sea.   ....

6. He hopes to finally finish printing the handbills this week.   ....

7. The holly tree is covered with green berries standing by the window.   ....

8. Jill received the clippings about the wedding from her roommate in the morning mail.   ....

9. Her finger nails called attention to her hands painted in bright red.   ....

10. The ivy which Roger was trimming continually crept along the stone wall.   ....

11. Claire has written barely a paragraph of her essay that is due tomorrow.   ....

12. The boy watched the passing crowd leaning against the wall of the pavilion.   ....

13. The crop duster's plane only flew a few feet from the ground.   ....

14. The wind pushed the clouds across the sun from the northeast.   ....

15. With his brother's help Hugh had hoped to quickly wax his car.   ....

16. To avoid the van, he swerved the motorcycle into the ditch which he had bought the day before.   ....

17. The young artist painted the portrait of King Solomon in his garret.   ....

18. The politician invited almost the entire county to her fish fry.   ....

19. The historian published a detailed account of the Battle of Waterloo in 1975.   ....

20. The cat belonged to the Cleghorn family which appeared one night at our back door.   ....

Parallelism 16

Frequently in our writing and speaking we need to indicate equality of ideas. To show this equality, we should employ **parallel** grammatical constructions. In other words, we should convey parallel thought in parallel language; and conversely, we should use parallel language only when we are conveying parallel thoughts.

16a Coordinate Elements

In employing parallelism, we should balance nouns against nouns, infinitives against infinitives, prepositional phrases against prepositional phrases, adjective clauses against adjective clauses, etc. We should never make the mistake of saying, "I have always liked *swimming* and *to fish*." Since the object of *have liked* is two parallel ideas, we should say:

> I have always liked *swimming* and *fishing*. (*And* joins two gerunds.)

OR

> I have always liked *to swim* and *to fish*. (*And* joins two infinitives.)

Parallel prepositional phrases are illustrated in the following sentence. The parallel elements appear immediately after the double bar:

Government ‖ of the people,
            ‖ by the people,
    and ‖ for the people   shall not perish from the earth.

Next we see an illustration of parallel noun clauses:

He said ‖ that he would remain in the East,
        ‖ that his wife would travel through the Northwest,
   and ‖ that his son would attend summer school in the South.

The following sentence contains parallel independent clauses:

‖ I came;
‖ I saw;
‖ I conquered.

Parallel elements are usually joined either by simple coordinating conjunctions or by correlative conjunctions. The most common coordinating conjunctions used with parallel constructions are *and, but, or.* Whenever one of these connectives is used, you must be careful to see that the elements which are being joined are coordinate or parallel in construction:

FAULTY: Ann is a girl with executive ability and who therefore should be elected class president.

This sentence contains faulty parallelism, since *and* is used to join a phrase (*with executive ability*) and a dependent clause (*who therefore should be elected class president*). To correct the sentence, (1) expand the phrase into a *who* clause, or (2) make an independent clause of the *who* clause:

CORRECT: Ann is a girl ‖ who has executive ability
               and ‖ who therefore should be elected class president.

NOTE: A safe rule to follow is this: *And who* or *and which* should never be used unless preceded by another *who-* or *which-*clause.

ALSO CORRECT: ‖ Ann is a girl with executive ability;
                  ‖ she therefore should be elected class president.

A common error results from making a construction appear to be parallel when actually it is not:

Mr. Lee is honest, intelligent, and works hard.

The structure of the sentence suggests an *a, b,* and *c* series; yet what we have is not three parallel elements but two adjectives (*honest, intelligent*) and a verb (*works*). The sentence can be corrected in two ways: we can use three adjectives in a series or two independent clauses in parallel construction, thus:

CORRECT: Mr. Lee is ‖ honest,
                        ‖ intelligent,
               and ‖ industrious.
ALSO CORRECT: ‖ Mr. Lee is honest and intelligent,
                  and ‖ he works hard.

16b   Use of Correlative Conjunctions

Correlative conjunctions are used in pairs: *either . . . or . . . ; neither . . . nor . . . ; both . . . and . . . ; not only . . . but also . . . .* When these conjunctions are employed in a sentence, they must be followed by parallel constructions:

INCORRECT: I hope *either* to spend my vacation in Mexico *or* Cuba. [In this sentence *either* is followed by an infinitive, *or* by a noun.]

CORRECT: I hope to spend my vacation either ‖ in Mexico
or ‖ in Cuba.

ALSO CORRECT: I hope to spend my vacation in either ‖ Mexico
or ‖ Cuba.

INCORRECT: She knew *not only* what to say, *but also* she knew when to say it.

CORRECT: She knew not only ‖ what to say
but also ‖ when to say it.

16c   Repetition of Certain Words

In order to make parallel constructions clear, you must sometimes repeat an article, a preposition, an auxiliary verb, the sign of the infinitive (*to*), or the introductory word of a dependent clause. Three of these types of necessary repetition are illustrated in the sentences which follow:

OBSCURE: He must counsel all employees who participate in sports and also go on recruiting trips throughout the Southwest.

CLEAR: He must counsel all employees who participate in sports and *must* also go on recruiting trips throughout the Southwest.

OBSCURE: The instructor wants to meet those students who enjoy barber-shop harmony and organize several quartets.

CLEAR: The instructor wants to meet those students who enjoy barber-shop harmony and *to* organize several quartets.

OBSCURE: He thought that economic conditions were improving and the company was planning to increase its dividend rate.

CLEAR: He thought that economic conditions were improving and *that* the company was planning to increase its dividend rate.

16d   *Than* and *As* in Parallel Constructions

Than and *as* are frequently used to join parallel constructions. When these two connectives introduce comparisons, you must be sure that the things compared are similar. Don't compare, for instance, a janitor's salary with a teacher. Compare a janitor's salary with a teacher's salary:

INCORRECT: A janitor's salary is frequently larger than a teacher.

CORRECT: ‖ A janitor's salary is frequently larger
than ‖ a teacher's (salary).

16e   Incorrect Omission of Necessary Words

A very common kind of faulty parallelism is seen in the following sentence:

I always have and always will *remember* to send my first-grade teacher a Christmas card.

In this sentence *remember* is correctly used after *will*, but after *have* the form needed is *remembered*. Consequently, *remember* cannot serve as the understood participle after *have*:

CORRECT: I ‖ always have *remembered*
    and ‖ always will remember   to send my first-grade teacher
    a Christmas card.

Other sentences containing similar errors are given below:

INCORRECT: I *was* mildly surprised, but all of my friends gravely shocked. [After *all of my friends* the incorrect verb form *was* seems to be understood.]

CORRECT: I was mildly surprised, but all of my friends *were* gravely shocked.

INCORRECT: He gave me an apple and pear. [Before *pear* the incorrect form *an* seems to be understood.]

CORRECT: He gave me an apple and *a* pear.

INCORRECT: I was interested and astounded *by* the story of his latest adventure.

CORRECT: I was ‖ interested *in*
    and ‖ astounded by   the story of his latest adventure

INCORRECT: She is as tall if not taller *than* her sister.

CORRECT: She is as tall *as* her sister, if not taller. [The reader understands *than her sister*.]

ALSO CORRECT: She is as tall *as*, if not taller than, her sister.

16f Correct Use of "Unparallel" Constructions

A caution should be added to this lesson. Parallelism of phraseology is not always possible. When it is not, do not hesitate to use natural, "unparallel" constructions:

CORRECT THOUGH "UNPARALLEL":   He spoke *slowly* and *with dignity*.

Here *slowly* and *with dignity* are parallel in a sense: they are both adverbial modifiers.

Exercise 62   PARALLELISM

Rewrite in correct form all sentences which contain faulty parallelism. Write *C* if a sentence is correct.

EXAMPLE: Tonight I plan to study, write a letter, and to do the laundry.

Tonight I plan to study, write a letter, and do the laundry.

1. The soldier had a heavy beard, deeply set eyes, and wore his hair cropped short.

2. The students were Americans and who wanted a room for the night.

3. At the foot of the bed lay an afghan, book, and a pair of glasses.

4. Tony decided that he would accept the job in Boston and to rent an apartment as near his work as possible.

5. My bedroom is not as large as my sister.

6. This course in Mexican history is as good if not better than any other course that Dr. Southerland has taught.

7. The small girl was bewildered, confused, and she could not find her way home.

8. My brother has resolved to exercise every morning, eat three well-balanced meals a day, and to be in bed by midnight.

9. I fear that I will continue to fill my time with watching television, eating snacks, and reading gothic novels half the night.

10. They not only worried about their plane reservations, but also they wondered whether the cable had reached their family.

11. I find my major in interior design more interesting than Bertha.

12. Duncan is a golfer with a powerful swing but who also tops the ball.

13. She was an energetic young woman, interested and excited about the future.

14. Hastings will wash and wax his car sometime this morning and pack it for the trip back to school early in the afternoon.

15. The old fisherman had bright blue eyes, a great shock of white hair, and his face was tanned from long days in the sun.

16. My father's idea of a vacation was to sit on the front porch and reading detective stories by Erle Stanley Gardner.

17. He was not disturbed by nor concerned with the noise of the children playing in the street.

18. Grandfather's day is not complete unless he either walks through the park or to the Post Office.

Exercise 63   PARALLELISM

Complete each of the following sentences by adding a construction which is parallel to the *italicized* construction.

EXAMPLE: She hurried *out of the building* and .... *into the waiting cab.* ....

1. Because gasoline is expensive, Americans are *riding buses more often* or ....

....

2. The owner of the gift shop either *will have to hire an additional sales person* or ....

....

3. The road to the top of the mountain was *narrow* but ....

....

4. In their basement one could find anything: *empty paint buckets,* ....

....

5. The morning paper reported *that the damage to the corn crop is severe* and ....

....

6. Boris wrote his mother that the trip to Manila was *long,* ....

....

7. My father insists on either *my working during the summer* or ....

....

8. The day *began with thick, dark clouds in the west* but ....

....

9. Maud plans *to work at Yellowstone National Park most of the summer* and then ....

....

10. Either *we will have to rent a car,* or ....

....

Subordination 17

Parallelism enables you to indicate equality of ideas. More often, however, your writing will include sentences in which some ideas are more important than others. The main device for showing the difference between major and minor emphasis is **subordination**: we reserve the independent clause for the main idea and use dependent clauses, phrases, and single words to convey subordinate ideas:

In our garden there is a birdbath *which is carved from marble.* [Subordinate idea placed in a dependent clause.]

In our garden there is a birdbath *carved from marble.* [Subordinate idea reduced to a participial phrase.]

In our garden there is a *marble* birdbath. [Subordinate idea reduced to a one-word modifier.]

17a Primer Style

It is necessary to understand the principle of subordination, for without subordination you would be unable to indicate the relative importance of ideas or their various shades of meaning in your thinking. The following group of sentences is both childish and monotonous because six dissimilar ideas have been presented in six simple sentences and thus appear to be of equal importance:

A pep meeting was held last Friday night. Memorial Stadium was the scene of the meeting. The meeting was attended by thousands of students. Over a hundred faculty members were there too. It rained Friday night. There was also some sleet.

As you know, coordinating conjunctions are used to join ideas of equal importance. Consequently, the six sentences given above would not be improved if they were joined by such conjunctions. As a matter of fact, a type of sentence which you should avoid is the long, stringy one which is tied together by *and, but, so,* or *and so.* Instead of using this kind of sentence, weigh the relative importance of your several ideas, and show their importance by the use of main and subordinate sentence elements. Notice how the six ideas can be merged into one clear sentence:

> Despite rain and some sleet the pep meeting held last Friday night at Memorial Stadium was attended by thousands of students and over a hundred faculty members.

In combining the six sentences, the writer has chosen to use the fact about student and faculty attendance as the main idea. Another writer might have chosen otherwise, for there will not always be complete agreement as to which idea can be singled out and considered the most important. You may be sure, however, that if your sentence reads with emphasis and effectiveness you have chosen a correct idea as the main one.

17b Upside-down Subordination

When there are only two ideas of unequal rank to be considered, you should have no difficulty in selecting the more important one:

1. He showed some signs of fatigue.
2. He easily won the National Open Golf Tournament.

Of these two sentences the second is undoubtedly the more important. Hence, when the two sentences are combined, the second should stand as the independent clause, and the first should be reduced to a dependent clause or even a phrase. If you made an independent clause of the first sentence and a subordinate element of the second, your sentence would contain upside-down subordination:

> FAULTY (upside-down subordination): Though he easily won the National Open Golf Tournament, he showed some signs of fatigue.

> CORRECT: Though he showed some signs of fatigue, he easily won the National Open Golf Tournament.

17c Choice of Subordinating Conjunctions

In introducing a subordinate element, be sure that you choose the right subordinating conjunction. The following sentences illustrate the correct use of certain conjunctions:

> I don't know *whether* (or *that*; not *as* nor *if*) I can see you tomorrow.

> *Although* (not *while*) she isn't a genius, she has undeniable talent.

> I saw in the autobiography of the actor *that* (not *where*) there is a question about the exact date of his birth.

(See Chapter 22, Glossary of Faulty Diction, for further discussion of accurate word choice.)

Exercise 64   SUBORDINATION

Combine the ideas of each of the following sentences into one effective simple or complex sentence.

EXAMPLE: The boys went swimming at Capri.
              Capri is an island located off southern Italy.
              It is near Naples.

            The boys went swimming at Capri, an island off southern Italy near Naples.

1. The Hudson River originates in the Adirondacks.
   It empties into the Atlantic Ocean.
   It is named for Henry Hudson.
   He was an English explorer.

2. Phillis Wheatley was an eighteenth-century American poet.
   She grew up as a slave in Boston.
   Her book of poetry was first published in England.

3. Our tour bus stopped at Loch Ness.
   It is a lake in Scotland.
   It is more than twenty miles long.
   A legendary monster makes its home there.

4. The Greater Snow Goose is white with black-tipped wings.
   It breeds in the Arctic.
   It migrates in winter to the coast of the Middle Atlantic states.

5. H. L. Mencken was a journalist.
He wrote a book entitled *The American Language.*
It was first published in 1919.
It reflects his interest in American English.

6. Children enjoy Halloween.
It is celebrated on the night of October 31.
It evolved from ancient fall festivals.
The Irish and Scots brought it to this country.

7. Nicolaus Copernicus was an astronomer.
He was born in Poland on February 19, 1473.
He perceived that the earth revolves around the sun.
Thus the earth is not the center of the universe.

8. Runes are symbols of an ancient alphabet.
They were brought to England by Germanic tribes.
Some persons thought that they had magical powers.
They were replaced by the letters of the Roman alphabet.

9. Dante Gabriel Rossetti was an English painter.
He married Elizabeth Siddal.
She was his model as well as his wife.
His father was a political exile from Italy.

Exercise 65	SUBORDINATION

Combine the ideas in each of the following groups of sentences into one effective simple or complex sentence.

EXAMPLE: Our neighbors have a cat.
             His name is Willie Shakespeare.
             He is a Siamese.
             He is extremely intelligent.

             Our neighbors have an extremely intelligent Siamese cat named Willie Shakespeare.

1. Last summer we went to the mountains of North Carolina.
   We visited a restored Indian village.
   The Indians were Cherokees.
   The name of the village is Oconaluftee.

2. The Norse gods and goddesses were not eternally young.
   They preserved their youth by eating magical apples.
   The goddess Idun kept these apples.
   She was the goddess of spring and youth.

3. Juan Pablos was an Italian printer.
   He lived in Spain.
   He migrated to Mexico in 1539.
   He was probably the first printer in the Americas.
   I read this in *The Book* by Douglas McMurtrie.

4. The couple set out for Fairbanks on the Alcan Highway.
   They had two dogs.
   The dogs' names were Homer and Horace.
   The couple sent the two dogs by air to their new station.

5. The Gulf Stream is an ocean current.
   It originates in the Gulf of Mexico.
   It flows along the east coast of the United States.
   Near Nantucket it turns out into the North Atlantic.

6. Joseph Jefferson III was an American actor.
   Both his father and grandfather were also actors.
   One of his roles was that of Rip Van Winkle.
   The comedy was based on Washington Irving's story.

7. Henry Clay was an influential political figure.
   He lived in the nineteenth century.
   John C. Calhoun and Daniel Webster were his contemporaries.
   Historians remember his efforts to preserve the Union.

8. David was a shepherd boy from Israel.
   He played the lyre.
   His music comforted King Saul.
   King Saul suffered from dark moods.

Exercise 66   SUBORDINATION

The following sentences contain upside-down subordination or too much coordination.
Rewrite each sentence to make it an effective simple or complex sentence.

EXAMPLE: Agatha Christie wrote a play, and it is entitled *The Mousetrap*, and it has been
performed in London for more than a quarter of a century.

Agatha Christie's play The Mousetrap *has been performed in London for more
than a quarter of a century.*

1. I heard the weather forecast at noon, and the forecaster announced that a tropical disturbance had developed, and it was in the Gulf of Mexico.

2. My car having rolled down the driveway and into the street, I realized that I had left the gear in neutral.

3. She had a camel corduroy skirt, and she had bought a matching sweater, but she still needed a blouse to complete the outfit.

4. Looking for the diamond ring that he had dropped somewhere on the lawn, he retraced his steps.

5. Our hockey team was well-conditioned and ready to play, and we were going to play our arch rivals, and all of us were looking forward to the game.

6. The young actress tried out for part after part, finally capturing the lead in *Major Barbara.*

7. My mother does not often enjoy cooking, but she does like to make preserves, and she especially likes to make muscadine preserves.

8. Hoping to find the house they had always dreamed of, the couple read the want ads in the Sunday paper.

9. Anton Chekhov practiced medicine, and then he began to write, and his work continues to influence other authors of fiction and drama.

10. Dropping all her Christmas packages, she stumbled over the curb.

Illogical Comparisons and Mixed Constructions

18

Correctness and clarity are essential to good writing. To reach these goals, you must know the rules of grammar and punctuation. But further, you must think logically and find the exact words in which to express your thoughts. Nothing is more bothersome to a reader than inexact, illogical, or confusing sentences. Some of the lessons which we have already studied have stressed means of avoiding certain errors which produce vagueness or confusion in writing; among these errors are faulty reference of pronouns, dangling or misplaced modifiers, and upside-down subordination. This lesson will consider certain other errors which obstruct clarity of expression.

18a Illogical Comparisons

When you make comparisons, you must be sure not only that the things compared are similar (a matter considered in the lesson on parallelism) but that all necessary elements of the comparison are included.

Note the following sentence:

Harold is taller than any boy in his class.

Since *Harold*, the first term of the comparison, is included in the classification *any boy in his class*, the comparison is obviously illogical: the sentence might be interpreted to mean *Harold is taller than Harold*. Therefore, the first term of the comparison must be compared with a second term or classification which excludes the first term, thus:

CORRECT: Harold is taller than any *other* boy in his class.

ALSO CORRECT: Harold is taller than any *girl* in his class.

It should also be pointed out that when the superlative is followed by *of*, the object of *of* must be plural:

ILLOGICAL: Harold is the tallest of any other boy in his class.

CORRECT: Harold is the tallest of *all the boys* in his class.

ALSO CORRECT: Harold is the *tallest boy* in his class.

Ambiguity results from a comparison like this one:

I helped you more than Jim.

Does the sentence mean *I helped you more than I helped Jim* or *I helped you more than Jim did*? The writer should use one sentence or the other, according to whichever meaning is intended.

The type of incomplete comparison illustrated by the following vague sentences is particularly popular with writers of advertising copy and with careless speakers:

VAGUE: Eastern Rubber Company makes a tire which gives twenty percent more mileage.

CLEAR: Eastern Rubber Company makes a tire which gives twenty percent more mileage *than any tire it made ten years ago.*

ALSO CLEAR: Eastern Rubber Company makes a tire which gives twenty percent more mileage *than any other tire made in the United States.*

VAGUE: Litter is more of a problem in cities.

CLEAR: Litter is more of a problem in cities *than in small towns.*

ALSO CLEAR: Litter is more of a problem in cities *than it used to be.*

18b Mixed on Confused Constructions

Mixed constructions are frequently the result of some sort of shift in a sentence. Through ignorance or forgetfulness the writer starts a sentence with one type of construction and then switches to another. Notice the shift of construction in the following sentence:

She bought an old, dilapidated house which by having it extensively repaired converted it into a comfortable home.

The sentence reads correctly through the realtive pronoun *which*. The reader expects *which* to introduce an adjective clause; however, he is unable to find a verb for *which*. Instead, he finds that the sentence is completed by a construction in which a gerund phrase stands as the subject of the verb *converted*. The sentence may be corrected in various ways. Two correct versions are:

She bought an old, dilapidated house which after extensive repairs was converted into a comfortable home.

By means of extensive repairs she converted into a comfortable home an old, dilapidated house which she had bought.

Other examples of mixed constructions are given below:

MIXED: Bob realized that during the conference how inattentive he had been. [This sentence is confusing because *that* as used here is a subordinating conjunction and should introduce a noun clause. However, the *that*-construction is left incomplete. Futher on, *how* introduces a noun clause. What we find then is only one noun clause but two words, *that* and *how*, used to introduce noun clauses. Obviously, only one such word should introduce the one dependent clause.]

CORRECT: Bob realized that during the conference he had been inattentive.

ALSO CORRECT: Bob realized how inattentive he had been during the conference.

MIXED: Because she had to work in the library kept her from attending the party. [A dependent clause introduced by *because* is always adverbial; hence such a clause can never be used as the subject of a sentence.]

CORRECT: Having to work in the library kept her from attending the party.

ALSO CORRECT: Because she had to work in the library, she could not attend the party.

MIXED: He pulled a leg muscle was why he failed to place in the broad jump. [He *pulled a leg muscle* is an independent clause standing as the subject of *was*. An independent clause, unless it is a quotation, can never be used as the subject of a sentence.]

CORRECT: Because he pulled a leg muscle, he failed to place in the broad jump.

MIXED: By attending the reception as a guest rather than as a butler was a new experience for him. [The preposition *by* introduces a modifying phrase, and a modifying phrase can never be used as the subject of a sentence.]

CORRECT: Attending the reception as a guest rather than as a butler was a new experience for him.

ALSO CORRECT: By attending the reception as a guest rather than as a butler, he enjoyed a new experience.

MIXED: A pronoun is when a word is used in the place of a noun. [Never use *is when* or *is where* in defining a word. Remember that a *when*- or *where*-clause which is clearly adverbial cannot be used as a predicate nominative.]

CORRECT: A pronoun is a word used in the place of a noun.

MIXED: I was the one about whom she was whispering to my father about. [To correct this sentence, omit either *about*.]

MIXED: We know that if he were interested in our offer that he would come to see us. [To correct this sentence, omit the second *that*. The first *that* introduces the noun clause *that . . . he would come to see us. If he were interested in our offer* is an adverbial clause within the noun clause.]

Exercise 67   ILLOGICAL COMPARISONS AND MIXED CONSTRUCTIONS

The following sentences contain illogical comparisons and mixed constructions. Rewrite each sentence in a correct form. (Note that some sentences permit more than one "correct" interpretation.)

EXAMPLE: Tony was more susceptible to colds than anyone in his family.

     Tony was more susceptible to colds than anyone else in his family.

1. I feel like that I am a pessimist for always expecting the worst.

2. Ty explained to me that in baseball a balk is when the pitcher does not complete his pitch.

3. The reason Mona asked the question is because she missed our earlier discussion on how to raise begonias.

4. Lewis said that he has always respected his mother more than his sister.

5. I believe that Robbie must be the laziest of any boy in the fifth grade.

6. We found that by doing all our packing the night before was a good way to get an early start in the morning.

7. Caroline knew that when she tried to bathe the baby how loudly he would cry.

8. Mr. Meredith is the person with whom I want to talk with before I decide to enlist in the Marines.

9. Because I was nervous and tired was why I didn't want to go to the zoo with my four little nephews.

10. There is a diet soda whose makers say that it has fewer calories.

11. It is really hard to believe that you trust George more than Patricia.

12. She submitted her novel to a publisher who, after reading her manuscript, he decided that it was a literary masterpiece.

13. It is harder to attract qualified people to the teaching profession.

14. By adding chopped pecans to her chicken salad was a new way of dressing up an old favorite recipe.

15. It was only after listening to Dot's story of what had really happened before I understood what danger the girls had faced.

16. Sally Ann has the most beautiful gold bracelet; I wish I had one too.

17. George says that he thinks Sunburst Margarine is really tastier.

18. A symbol in literature is when an object or a person is used to represent an idea.

19. When Earl was out walking in the snow was the time when he slipped and hurt his elbow.

20. Larry was quite sure that he owed me more money than Florence.

21. An old stray dog which, in following Laurie home, he seemed to know that she would take him in.

22. We were convinced that if we were going to win our point with Mr. Pell, that we would have to stick together.

23. Tom remembered that as a medical student how sleepy he would get while studying anatomy.

24. Nick has always contended that Perry Mason's detective skill far exceeds Nero Wolfe.

25. By trying to avoid hitting the cow was the reason I ran into the tree, Officer.

Punctuation 19

Punctuation depends largely upon the grammatical structure of a sentence. In order to punctuate correctly, you must therefore have an understanding of grammatical elements. For this reason, rules of punctuation in this text have been correlated, whenever applicable, with your study of grammar and sentence structure. You learned, for instance, how to punctuate certain phrases when you studied the phrase as a sentence unit.

In order that this chapter may present a reasonably complete treatment of punctuation, you will find here, along with additional rules, a summary of the rules already studied and reference to the chapters in which they are discussed. The rules given below have become to a large extent standardized; hence they should be clearly understood and practiced. Following the principle of punctuating "by ear" or of using a comma wherever there is a vocal pause results in an arbitrary and frequently misleading use of punctuation.

19a Terminal Marks

The terminal marks of punctuation—that is, those marks used to end a sentence—are the period, the question mark, and the exclamation mark.

Use a period after a declarative sentence, an imperative sentence, or an indirect question:

DECLARATIVE: John answered the telephone.

IMPERATIVE: Answer the telephone.

INDIRECT QUESTION: She asked whether John had answered the telephone.

NOTE: A request which is stated as a polite question should be followed by a period. Such a request frequently occurs in business correspondence:

Will you please send me your special summer catalogue.

Use a period also after most abbreviations:

Mr., Ms., Dr., B.S., Jr., *i.e.*, viz., etc., A.D., B.C., A.M., P.M.

Use three periods to indicate an omission of a word or words within a quoted sentence, three periods plus a terminal mark to indicate an omission at the end of a quoted sentence:

"Fourscore and seven years ago our fathers brought forth . . . a new nation . . . ."

Use a question mark after a direct question:

Did John answer the telephone?

"Have you finished your work?" she asked.

Use an exclamation mark after an expression of strong feeling. This mark of punctuation should be used sparingly:

"Halt!" he shouted.

How disgusting!

There goes the fox!

19b   The Comma

1. Use a comma to separate independent clauses when they are joined by *and, but, or, nor, for, so,* and *yet.* (See Chapter 6.) If the clauses are long or are complicated by internal punctuation, a semicolon may be used instead of a comma:

The game was over, but the crowd refused to leave the park.

2. Use a comma to separate words, phrases, and clauses written as a series of three or more coordinate elements. This includes short independent clauses when used in a series, as shown in the third example sentence below:

A trio composed of Marie, Ellen, and Frances sang at the entertainment.

Jack walked into my office, took off his hat, and sat down.

I washed the dishes, I dried them, and I put them away.

3. Use a comma to separate two or more coordinate adjectives that modify the same noun:

The noisy, enthusiastic freshman class assembled in Section F of the stadium. [*Noisy* and *enthusiastic* are coordinate adjectives; therefore they are separated by a comma. But *freshman,* though an adjective, is not coordinate with *noisy* and *enthusiastic*; actually *noisy* and *enthusiastic* modify not just *class* but the word group *freshman class.* Hence no comma precedes *freshman.*]

To determine whether adjectives are coordinate, you may make two tests: if they are coordinate, you will be able (1) to join them with *and* or (2) to interchange their positions in the sentence. You can certainly say *the noisy and enthusiastic freshman class* or *the enthusiastic, noisy freshman class*; thus *noisy* and *enthusiastic* are clearly coordinate. However, to say *the noisy and freshman class* or *the freshman noisy class* would be absurd; thus *freshman* is not structurally parallel with *noisy*:

a blue wool suit [Adjectives not coordinate.]

an expensive, well-tailored suit [Adjectives coordinate.]

a new tennis court [Adjectives not coordinate.]

a muddy, rough court [Adjectives coordinate.]

4. Use a comma to separate sharply contrasted coordinate elements:

He was merely ignorant, not stupid.

5. Use commas to set off all nonessential modifiers. Do not set off essential modifiers. (See Chapter 7 for a discussion of essential and nonessential clauses.)

NONESSENTIAL CLAUSE: Sara Sessions, *who is wearing red shorts today,* was voted the most versatile girl in her class.

NONESSENTIAL PHRASE: Sara Sessions, *wearing red shorts today,* was voted the most versatile girl in her class.

ESSENTIAL CLAUSE: The girl *who is wearing red shorts today* is Sara Sessions.

6. Use a comma after an introductory adverbial clause, verbal phrase, or absolute phrase. (See Chapter 7 for a discussion of dependent clauses, Chapter 5 for a discussion of phrases).

INTRODUCTORY ADVERBIAL CLAUSE: *When he arose to give his speech,* he was greeted with thunderous applause.

INTRODUCTORY PARTICIPIAL PHRASE: *Being in a hurry,* I was able to see him only briefly.

INTRODUCTORY GERUND PHRASE: *On turning the corner,* Tom ran squarely into a a police officer.

INTRODUCTORY INFINITIVE PHRASE: *To get a seat,* we have to arrive by 7:30 P.M.

INTRODUCTORY ABSOLUTE PHRASE: *My schedule having been arranged,* I felt like a full-fledged college freshman.

7. Use commas to set off nonesssential appositives. (See Chapter 5.)

Tom, *the captain of the team,* was injured in the first game of the season.

Sometimes an appositive is so closely "fused" with the word which it follows that it constitutes an essential element in the sentence and thus is not set off by commas:

William *the Conqueror* died in 1087.

The poet *Keats* spent his last days in Italy.

The word *bonfire* has an interesting history.

8. Use commas to set off items in dates, geographical names, and addresses and to set off titles after names:

July 22, 1977, was a momentous day in his life.

Birmingham, Alabama, gets its name from Birmingham, England.

Do you know who lives at 1600 Pennsylvania Avenue, Washington, D.C.?

Alfred E. Timberlake, Ph.D., will be the principal speaker.

9. Use commas to set off words used in direct address:

It is up to you, *Dot,* to push the campaign.

I think, *sir,* that I am correct.

You, *my fellow Americans,* must aid in the fight against inflation.

10. Use a comma after a mild interjection and after *yes* and *no*:

Oh, I suppose you're right.

Yes, I will be glad to go.

11. Use a comma to separate an independent clause from a question dependent on the clause:

You will try to do the work, won't you?

12. Use commas to set off expressions like *he said* or *she replied* when they interrupt a sentence of direct quotation. (But see rule 1 under The Semicolon, below.)

"I was able," *she replied,* "to build the bookcase in less than an hour."

13. Use commas to set off certain parenthetic elements:

I was, *however,* too tired to make the trip.

My hopes, *to tell the truth,* had fallen to a low ebb.

14. Use a comma to prevent the misreading of a sentence:

Above, the mountains rose like purple shadows.

To John, Harrison had been a sort of idol.

19c The Semicolon

1. Use a semicolon to separate independent clauses when they are not joined by *and, but, or, nor, for, so,* or *yet.* (See Chapter 6.)

Wade held the ball for an instant; then he passed it to West.

"He is sick," she said; "therefore, he will not come."

2. Use a semicolon to separate coordinate elements which are joined by a coordinating conjunction but which are internally punctuated:

His tour included concert appearances in Austin, Texas; Little Rock, Arkansas; Tulsa, Oklahoma; and Kansas City, Kansas.

3. Use a semicolon to punctuate independent clauses which are joined by a coordinating conjunction in sentences which are heavily punctuated with commas internally:

I invited Sara, Susan, Leon, and John to the party; but Joe, Robert, and Charles also dropped in.

19d The Colon

1. Use a colon after a clause which introduces a formal list. Do not use a colon unless the words preceding the list form a complete statement:

INCORRECT: The poets I like best are: Housman, Yeats, and Eliot.

CORRECT: The poets I like best are these: Housman, Yeats, and Eliot.

ALSO CORRECT: The poets I like best are Housman, Yeats, and Eliot.

INCORRECT: The basket was filled with: apples, oranges, and bananas.

CORRECT: The basket was filled with the following fruits: apples, oranges, and bananas.

ALSO CORRECT: The basket was filled with apples, oranges, and bananas.

2. Use a colon after a statement which introduces an explanation or amplification of that statement:

One characteristic accounted for his success: complete honesty. [A dash, which is less formal than the colon, may be substituted for the colon in this sentence.]

There was only one way to solve the mystery: we had to find the missing letter.

3. Use a colon after expressions like *he said* when they introduce a long and formal quotation:

The speaker rose to his feet and said: "Students and teachers, I wish to call your attention to . . . ."

4. Use a colon after the formal salutation of a letter, between the hour and minute figures in time designations, between a chapter and verse reference from the Bible, and between a title and subtitle:

Dear Sir:

8:40 P.M.

John 3:16

Victorian England: Portrait of an Age

19e The Dash

1. Use a dash to indicate an abrupt shift or break in the thought of a sentence or to set off an informal or emphatic parenthesis:

Harvey decided to go to—but you wouldn't be interested in that story.

Mary told me—would you believe it?—that she preferred a quiet vacation at home.

At the age of three—such is the power of youth—Mary could stand on her head.

2. Use dashes to set off an appositive or a parenthetic element which is internally punctuated:

Her roommates—Jane, Laura, and Ruth—are spending the weekend with her.

19f Quotation Marks

1. Use quotation marks to enclose direct quotations, but do not use them to enclose indirect quotations:

INCORRECT: He said that "I was old enough to know better."

CORRECT: He said, "You are old enough to know better."

ALSO CORRECT: He said that I was old enough to know better.

If a direct quotation is interrupted by an expression like *he said*, use quotation marks to enclose only the quoted material. This necessitates the use of two sets of quotation marks:

INCORRECT: "It's just possible, Mary responded, that I'll get up before six in the morning."

CORRECT: "It's just possible," Mary responded, "that I'll get up before six in the morning."

If there are two or more consecutive sentences of quoted material, use only one set of quotations marks to enclose all the sentences, not one set for each sentence:

INCORRECT: Ruby shouted, "Wait for me." "I'll be ready in two minutes."

CORRECT: Ruby shouted, "Wait for me. I'll be ready in two minutes."

Use single marks to enclose a quotation with a quotation:

The instructor asked, "Who said, 'Change the name of Arkansas? Never!'?"

Place the comma and the period inside the quotation marks, the semicolon outside. Place the question mark and exclamation mark inside the quotation marks when they apply to the quoted material, outside when they apply to the entire sentence:

"Of course," he replied, "I remember you." [Comma and period inside the quotation marks.]

Her favorite poem was Kipling's "If."

Several times the witness said, "I swear to the truth of my statement"; yet the jury remained unconvinced. [Semicolon outside the quotation marks.]

He asked, "Where are you going?" [The question mark comes within the quotation marks because only the quoted material is a question.]

Did she definitely say, "I accept your invitation"? [The question mark comes outside the quotation marks because the entire sentence is a question.]

2. Use quotation marks to enclose the titles of short works (short stories, short poems, articles, one-act plays, songs, and speeches) and of smaller units of books. (See Rule 3 under Italics, Chapter 20, Section b.)

Benét's story "The Devil and Daniel Webster" was first published in the *Saturday Evening Post.*

The kindergarten children sang "America" for us.

"Who Will Be the New Bishop?" is the title of the first chapter of *Barchester Towers.*

3. Use quotation marks to enclose words taken from special vocabularies or used in a special sense:

All the money he had won on the quiz program was invested in "blue chips."

In certain sections of the United States a man who is both honest and good-natured is known as a "clever man."

19g Parentheses

Use parentheses to enclose certain parenthetic elements. From a study of the preceding marks of punctuation you will remember that commas and dashes are also used to set off parenthetic material. There are no clearly defined rules by which you can always determine which marks to use. In general, however, commas are used to set off a parenthetic element which is fairly closely connected with the thought of the sentence. Dashes are used to set off a loosely connected element such as an abrupt break in the thought of the sentence; they tend to emphasize the element set off. Parentheses are used to enclose (1) material that is supplementary or explanatory and (2) figures repeated to insure accuracy or used to designate an enumeration. An element enclosed by parentheses is usually even more loosely connected with the sentence than one set off by dashes; and parentheses, unlike dashes, tend to minimize the element set off:

> The *Ville de Nantes* (see Plate 5) is a large, semidouble, red and white camellia.
>
> I am enclosing a check for thirty-five dollars ($35.00).
>
> Please write on the card (1) your full name, (2) your home address, and (3) a parent's or guardian's full name.

19h Brackets

Use brackets to enclose any interpolation, or insertion, which you add to material that is being quoted. (You will note that in this text brackets are used to enclose explanations which follow illustrative sentences.)

> In September, 1793, Robert Burns wrote a letter which included this sentence: "So may God ever defend the cause of truth and liberty as he did that day [the day of Bruce's victory over Edward II at Bannockburn]."

Exercise 68   THE COMMA

In the following sentences insert commas wherever they are needed. If a sentence is correctly punctuated, mark it *C*.

1. Sam if you are planning to make cookies I hope you will not burn them again.

2. Keeping one's head in a crisis shows maturity.

3. Swimming rapidly toward the raft Jack called out repeatedly to his friends.

4. Tim Gloria and Don tried without success to repair the flat tire.

5. She kicked she screamed she had a tantrum and she finally got her way.

6. After working for three hours on his history report Frank took a long refreshing walk in the woods.

7. My professor who is a native Englishman has a marked British accent.

8. Her deadline having been ignored the mayor fired the striking workers.

9. Anyone who thinks that the world owes him a living is headed for disappointment.

10. To write a good essay one must organize well and use proper diction.

11. Billie Jean King a professional tennis player has demonstrated her skill time and again.

12. The dusty rough road to the campsite became difficult to travel after the sun went down.

13. I was amazed at the size of the crowd at the rock concert but my younger sister had expected an even larger one.

14. When I had eaten all the boiled shrimp I wanted I then had a large bowl of crab gumbo.

15. The word *athlete* is frequently misspelled.

16. We plan to leave on August 2 1979 for a trip to Florence Italy.

17. Their beautiful expensive swimming pool will be completed before warm weather comes.

18. The man wearing a hearing aid is my husband's father.

19. Foster not Steve is Mimi's date for the spring dance.

20. Richard the Lionhearted spent much of his early life in France.

21. Oh Pat please bring me my reading glasses.

22. "You are wrong" she answered "in thinking that I will lend you my new mink coat."

23. I was certain as a matter of fact that she had already missed her plane.

24. My brother's new address is 402 Fiftieth Street Savannah Georgia.

25. You do agree that peanut brittle is a delicious candy don't you?

26. Dr. Goodloe Erwin M. D. will be the main speaker at the Heart Association meeting this Thursday.

27. Frances Arnold the new assistant to the dean will be introduced to the faculty today.

28. Wearing a new pair of shoes Sam squeaked his way down the long dark corridor.

29. Jesse James the famous outlaw changed his last name to Howard.

30. Milton's oldest brother Fred has been a police officer for thirty years.

31. Joan is going to buy the material for the bridesmaids' dresses and I am going to do the sewing.

32. Frank O'Connor's short story "The Drunkard" is a funny story about a little Irish boy.

33. The student who will deliver the valedictory graduated from high school at sixteen.

Exercise 69   THE COMMA

In the following sentences insert commas wherever they are needed. If a sentence is correctly punctuated, mark it C.

1. When you make the beds Frank be sure to tuck the blankets in firmly.

2. Reading one spy thriller after another Mary Jo wasted time when she should have been working.

3. Holding back the unruly crowd was a small but determined police officer who kept her head remarkably well.

4. I keep telling Marie to keep her eye on the ball but she always looks down the fairway as she swings her club.

5. Now don't tell anyone the big news until after the official announcement.

6. Before I lived in the South I had some peculiar ideas about Southerners.

7. We wanted to go from Salt Lake City to Provo but decided we did not have time.

8. Writing a letter to his prospective employer was more difficult than he had expected.

9. His new shirt beautifully embroidered in a colorful Mexican design was quite appropriate for the party.

10. The one who gets up first tomorrow morning is the one who should start cooking breakfast.

11. The low rambling brick house sits on a lot wooded with tall graceful pine trees.

12. The famous novelist Thomas Wolfe was a native of Asheville North Carolina.

13. To learn to water ski one must have strength muscular coordination and determination.

14. Creating a warm happy mood with his delightful piano music Teddy Wilson kept us listening for hours.

15. My brother Bill who is a musician is also an expert race driver.

16. I called whistled and waved; but Joyce did not notice me there with my broken bicycle.

17. "I'll never forget" said Janie "the old fig tree we used to climb during summer vacations."

18. Planting lettuce tomatoes and onions in my garden I thought of the wonderful salads I would be having later.

19. The tulips of red yellow and white were handsome when he arranged them in a large copper bowl.

20. Victor Hugo's Restaurant located in Laguna Beach California is set in a beautiful and exotic garden spot.

21. The invitations having been addressed Tommy turned his attention to selecting a menu for his dinner party.

22. Margie Harry Dianne and Fred went to a new seafood restaurant for dinner Saturday night and said that it was wonderful.

23. Isolated from her friends by her illness Rachel depended more and more on reading and painting for occupation.

24. Steve sauntered into the room took a seat in a large wing chair and fell asleep almost immediately.

25. The word *charge* has sixteen meanings as a verb and fifteen as a noun.

26. Mack famous for his grilled steaks is having us over for a backyard cook-out next Friday.

27. The man who is sitting with my mother is her only brother Ted.

28. His remark to tell the truth was lacking in both taste and judgment.

29. Beyond the ocean was gray and menacing as the waves seemed to grow steadily larger.

30. Yes thank you I will have more strawberry shortcake.

31. Since the bill of fare was written in French Jerry was at the mercy of the haughty waiter.

32. Afraid that he would be penniless in a few days Tom cabled his father for additional funds.

33. Ernest Hemingway's story "Soldier's Home" was made into a play for television recently.

Exercise 70   THE COLON AND THE DASH

In the following sentences insert colons and dashes wherever they are needed. If a sentence is correctly punctuated, mark it C.

1. Three girls who visited Mimi last summer Dottie, Sue, and Nancy are planning to share an apartment in New York this fall.

2. Heaven knows what will happen after but why am I telling you my troubles?

3. Dick knew that he had another difficult course to pass before qualifying for medical school organic chemistry.

4. My sisters Beth, Rose, Amy, and Marty can wear one another's clothes.

5. The following utensils belong in the kitchen of any good cook a spatula, a ricer, a sieve, and a pair of shears.

6. Almost everyone I know Jack, Suzanne, Frances, Dolores, and Matt is going out of town in July.

7. Housman conveys his central idea in these lines "I'd face it as a wise man would/ And train for ill and not for good."

8. Trying to find the definition of a word in the dictionary, I came upon an exciting new word *serendipity.*

9. Robin was aware that no one else knew the stranger's intention robbery of the town's only bank.

10. Sally says that she loves motorcycle racing more than it's hard to believe any other form of recreation.

11. There is one role that the famous actress prefers to all others Ophelia in *Hamlet.*

12. The states he has lived in include Tennessee, Arkansas, Texas, Oklahoma, and Oregon.

13. Now Jimmy, you must try to my word, this is outrageous clean up this room before your mother sees it.

14. We can sit in those seats in the fourth oh! I'm sorry! I didn't know that those seats were reserved.

15. The photographer said that he had only one request of the baby's mother to keep the child still.

16. Aunt Gertie and her friend oh, what is the woman's name? love to watch the game shows on television.

17. My flower beds this year have a good variety of perennials asters, phlox, black-eyed Susans, and shasta daisies.

18. I can play bridge, poker, and backgammon; but there is one game I cannot master chess.

19. I don't think that the girls will go hungry on their camping trip; their mothers have supplied them with fried chicken, ham sandwiches, and potato salad.

20. And in closing I would like to say that I wish well, you know what I am trying to say.

Exercise 71   QUOTATION MARKS

In the following sentences insert quotation marks wherever they are needed. If a sentence is correctly punctuated, mark it *C*.

1. Robert Frost's poem Mending Wall has been a favorite of Maria's for years.

2. Jim has a sprained wrist, said Joyce; therefore, he cannot compete in the swimming meet.

3. The angry motorist told the police officer, You have interrupted my honeymoon.

4. Matt told Sarah that she was making a mistake in marrying Fred.

5. When he's asleep, whispered Mother, Billy is an angelic child.

6. When is the last time you heard Bing Crosby's recording of White Christmas ?

7. Kathy is not very happy with her new nickname; her friends call her Stringbean.

8. It seems that every letter I write to my father begins, Dear Dad, I'm short of money again.

9. Julia, what is the botanical name for those flowers we call Johnny-Jump-Ups ?

10. I have just finished reading Anderson's I'm a Fool, a short story about a stable boy.

11. Jack's slang expressions are sometimes insulting; he told Miriam that she had rocks in her head.

12. Was it Romeo or Juliet who said, Parting is such sweet sorrow ?

13. Aunt Ethel asked me whether I would be able to attend the church social next week.

14. Most jazz enthusiasts can tell you that Jelly Roll Morton's real name was Ferdinand.

15. Jed, tell me what you mean by the expression out in left field.

16. I hope the band will play my three old favorites tonight: Begin the Beguine, Stomping at the Savoy, and String of Pearls.

17. Of all the various definitions of a bore, I prefer the one by Ambrose Bierce: A person who talks when you wish him to listen.

18. Mary Anne said, Jim, do you know all the words to The Star Spangled Banner ?

19. Did you know that Simon and Garfunkel wrote a song based on Robinson's poem Richard Cory ?

20. Georgia's so-called rednecks have received tremendous publicity since President Carter's election.

Exercise 72   REVIEW OF PUNCTUATION

In the following sentences insert all necessary marks of punctuation. If a sentence is correctly punctuated, mark it C.

1. Last summer in Vigo Spain a city of a quarter million people the drought was so bad that water was cut off for fifteen hours a day.

2. Jane and I made new evening dresses for the dance that is I cut them out and she finished the job.

3. When I first saw the condition of the boys' room I knew we would need at least three days if not more to clean it up.

4. Thomas Frederick M. D. will complete his residency in surgery next month.

5. Ivan the Terrible was the first czar of Russia according to my reference book.

6. Has Phyllis already left for the track meet or will you be able to ride with her asked Barbara.

7. The dishes were washed the baby was put to bed and the table was set up for a game of bridge.

8. Mary Frances the captain of our soccer team is a superb kicker.

9. There is one mystery that may never be solved what happened to the last piece of chocolate cake.

10. Our European tour will include Paris France Oslo Norway Copenhagen Denmark Helsinki Finland and Munich Germany.

11. Thomas Gray's Elegy Written in a Country Churchyard contains the following line The paths of glory lead but to the grave.

12. About Jerry Lyndon made a rather caustic remark.

13. I heard you and Janice talking about the new boy in what did you say his name is?

14. I'm trying to remember the words of an old nursery rhyme that goes Ride a cock horse to Banbury Cross/ To see an old lady

15. Yesterday I received a letter which said Dear Sir You have been declared the winner in the Super Soap slogan contest.

16. Harvey tried desperately to raise the tightly stuck window then he called out Won't somebody help me?

17. My list of disasters for the day includes sunburn a badly cut finger and a headache.

18. You are planning to spend the night with us on your way to Dallas aren't you?

19. I caught the fish and then fried it in our big iron skillet.

20. I enclose a check for one hundred dollars $100 as a contribution to your annual fund drive.

21. My four cousins Penelope Judy Kitty and Dot are going camping with me at Brasstown Bald Mountain.

22. The women determined to demonstrate their skill won the tennis match rather handily.

23. At 6 45 every day Sid gets up and takes a cold shower before breakfast.

24. A pessimist is a person who believes in Murphy's Law If something can go wrong it will.

25. The kind of friend whom everyone needs is the friend who doesn't carry a grudge.

Exercise 73   REVIEW OF PUNCTUATION

In the following sentences insert all necessary marks of punctuation. If a sentence is correctly punctuated, mark it *C.*

1. My grandfather a man of great determination can still chin himself fifty times without stopping.

2. Of these three faith hope and love the greatest is love.

3. Although he is six feet four and twenty-five years old Mother refers to Fred as her little boy.

4. I told Marie as a matter of fact that she was behaving extremely well under the circumstances.

5. After the wedding we all took a drive along the lakeshore.

6. It was Polonius in *Hamlet* who said To thine own self be true.

7. Perhaps the most famous address in America is 1600 Pennslavania Avenue Washington D. C.

8. Tim likes to jog for fifteen minutes every night before going to bed but I contend that all that exercise keeps me awake.

9. Hamburgers french fries and chocolate malts seem to be his steady diet so I am afraid he will continue to gain weight.

10. Aunt Martha glared at me with a you-ought-to-be-ashamed expression in her flashing brown eyes.

11. By leaving Portland before ten o'clock we hope to arrive in Boston well before twelve.

12. Four boys are planning a trip to the Canadian Rockies in the car that they call their tin lizzie.

13. Having first found a comfortable campsite not far from a cool stream the girls pitched their tent and started cooking supper over the open fire.

14. The tall elegant woman seemed aloof she clearly had a touch-me-not look about her.

15. It was Kurt Vonnegut Jr I believe who said There is no reason why good cannot triumph as often as evil.

16. After I had read Katherine Mansfield's short story Marriage à la Mode I decided that I wanted to read more of her work.

17. Carol here is a list of things you will need in Europe your passport some travelers' checks and a raincoat.

18. Steve I cannot drive you to the airport this afternoon if however you can leave by eleven o'clock I will be glad to take you.

19. To swim expertly is something I have always wished I could do.

20. To be perfectly honest with you I haven't a clue to what Helen was talking about.

21. Why did Don say You'll be sorry you didn't talk things over with me first ?

22. The fire having been laid we set a match to the kindling and watched the flames grow larger and larger.

23. My oldest brother Bob said to me Nan I will teach you to play basketball.

24. The frightened embarrassed little boy jumped on his bicycle and rode away without looking back.

25. Theodosia has been very frank with me she says that I have only one problem my self-consciousness.

Mechanics:
Capital Letters, Italics, the Apostrophe, the Hyphen

20

20a Capital Letters

1. Capitalize the first word of a sentence, of a line of traditional poetry, and of a direct quotation:

> All the students attended the meeting.

> Under a spreading chestnut-tree
> The village smithy stands.

> He said, "She does not wish to see you."

2. Capitalize proper nouns, words used as proper nouns, and adjectives derived from proper nouns:

> Great Britain, William, the Bible

> President, Senator, Captain, University (when these are used with or substituted for the name of a particular president, senator, captain, or university), and similarly

> Mother, Grandfather, Uncle (as in *We told Mother to go to bed, We bought Grandfather a bicycle,* and *We buried Uncle in Arlington Cemetery,* but not in *My mother is ill, His grandfather is eighty-two,* and *Our uncle was wounded at Gettysburg*)

> British, Shakespearean, Biblical, Scandinavian

3. Capitalize the names of days, months, and holidays:

> Monday, February, Fourth of July, Ash Wednesday, Veterans Day

4. Capitalize the names of historical periods and events:

> The Middle Ages, the French Revolution, the Battle of the Bulge, the Reformation

5. Capitalize the first word in the titles of books, chapters, essays, short stories, short

poems, songs, and works of art. Capitalize also all other words in these titles except articles. prepositions, and conjunctions:

> *The Last of the Mohicans,* "Without Benefit of Clergy," "Ode to the West Wind," "Only a Bird in a Gilded Cage," El Greco's *View of Toledo*

6. Capitalize names of the Deity, religions, and religious organizations:

> Jehovah, God, the Redeemer, Buddhism, Church of England, Society of Jesus, Order of St. Francis

7. Capitalize the names of governing bodies, political parties, governmental agencies, and civic and social organizations:

> The House of Commons, the Senate, the Democratic Party, the Internal Revenue Department, the Chamber of Commerce, Daughters of the American Revolution

8. Capitalize the points of the compass when they refer to a specific region but not when they indicate direction:

> He lived in the East all his life.
>
> They traveled west for about a hundred miles and then turned south.

9. Capitalize the names of studies only if they are derived from proper nouns or are the names of specific courses of instruction:

> He was studying physics, chemistry, and German.
>
> He failed in Mathematics 101 and in Human Biology 1.

10. Capitalize personfications:

> O wild West Wind, thou breath of Autumn's being.
>
> Daughters of Time, the hypocritic Days.
>
> Be with me, Beauty, for the fire is dying.

20b Italics

1. Italicize words that you wish to emphasize. (In manuscript indicate italics by underlining.)

> Do you mean to say that she ate them *all*?
>
> It could hardly have been *the* Robert Frost.

NOTE: Use this device sparingly. Frequent use of italics for emphasis is a sign of an immature style.

2. Italicize numbers, letters, and words referred to as such:

> He made his *7* and his *9* very much alike.
>
> She has never yet learned to pronounce *statistics.*
>
> In his handwriting he employs the old-fashioned *s.*

3. Italicize the names of books, magazines, and newspapers. (Smaller units of books, such as chapters, stories, essays, and poems, are usually set in quotation marks.)

A Tale of Two Cities, the *Atlantic Monthly,* the Atlanta *Journal*

NOTE: In the names of newspapers or magazines it is not always necessary to italicize the definite article or the name of a city.

4. Italicize the names of ships, trains, and airplanes:

The *Queen Elizabeth,* the *Twentieth-Century Limited,* the *Spirit of St. Louis*

5. Italicize foreign words and phrases in an English context:

The *coup d'état* led to his becoming emperor.

6. Italicize the titles of paintings, statues, and other works of art:

Gainesborough's *Blue Boy,* Rodin's *The Thinker*

20c   The Apostrophe

1. Use the apostrophe and *s* to form the possessive case of singular nouns:

The boar's head, Mary's lamb, the boss's orders

NOTE: Proper names ending in *s* may form the possessive by adding *'s* if the resulting word is not unpleasant or difficult to sound:

Keats's poems, Charles's work, *but* Ulysses' return

2. Use an apostrophe without *s* to form the possessive of plural nouns ending in *s*:

Soldiers' quarters, boys' clothes

3. Use an apostrophe and *s* to form the possessive of plural nouns not ending in *s*:

Men's coats, children's shoes, the alumni's contributions

4. The possessive of words indicating time is formed like the possessive of other nouns:

A week's delay, a day's journey, *but* a two days' visit

5. The apostrophe is frequently omitted in the names of organizations and institutions:

The Farmers Hardware Company, Boys High School, State Teachers College

6. In forming the possessives of compounds, use the apostrophe according to the meaning and the logic of the construction:

Beaumont and Fletcher's plays [Plays written by Beaumont and Fletcher jointly.]
Smith's and Jones's children [The children of Smith and the children of Jones.]
John and Mary's house [The house belonging to John and Mary.]
Somebody else's business [The business of somebody else.]

7. Use an apostrophe to indicate the omission of letters in contractions and of digits in numerals:

Isn't, don't, 'tis
The cat's had kittens.
The Class of '23

NOTE: Be sure that the apostrophe is placed at the exact point where the letter or digit is omitted. Do not write *is'nt, do'nt.*

8. Use an apostrophe and *s* to indicate the plural of letters, numerals, signs, and words used as such:

Dot your *i*'s and cross your *t*'s.

His telephone number contains four *8*'s.

In your next theme omit the *&* 's.

He uses too many *so*'s.

20d   The Hyphen

In English, compounds are made in three ways:

(1) by writing the words solid (*bedroom, watchmaker, starlight*),

(2) by writing them separately (*ice cream, motion picture, mountain lion*), or

(3) by separating the words with a hyphen (*name-caller, ne'er-do-well, finger-paint*).

The resulting confusion, like so much confusion in English, lies in the fact that the language is constantly changing. A compound may begin its career as two words; then it may move on to the form with a hyphen; and finally it may end as a solid formation—its destiny accomplished, as it were. So we have *bedroom* (written solid) but *dining room* (two words). We have the noun *bluepoint* to refer to an oyster, but we use the two words *blue point* to describe a Siamese cat. A decision may be *far-reaching*, but a forecaster is *farseeing*. The only solution to this confusing problem is to consult a dictionary. But this authority is not always satisfactory because many compounds are made for the occasion and are not in the dictionary— and dictionaries may disagree. Furthermore, a compound with a hyphen may be correct in one part of a sentence and incorrect in another, or it may be correct as a noun and incorrect as a verb. The stylebook of one publisher says, "If you take hyphens seriously, you will surely go mad." Nevertheless, there is a sort of logic in the use of the hyphen, as well as a kind of common sense; furthermore, one can learn some of the pitfalls to avoid.

Consider the following sentences:

He is a great admirer of Henry Kissinger, the ex-Republican Secretary of State. [Is Mr. Kissinger no longer a Republican? The phrase should read *the former Republican Secretary of State.*]

The parents enjoyed their children's recreation of the first Thanksgiving. [In this sentence *re-creation* is the appropriate word, and the hyphen distinguishes it from *recreation.*]

I would think that your sixteen year old brother could scramble an egg. [In this sentence *sixteen, year,* and *old* form a compound modifier and should be hyphenated. The phrase should read *your sixteen-year-old brother.*]

He introduced me to his uncle, an old car enthusiast. [Is his uncle old? Or is his uncle interested in old cars? The phrase is clarified with a hyphen: *an old-car enthusiast.*]

Did you hear the reporter's interview with the singing whale authority? [Did the reporter interview a whale authority who sings or an authority on singing whales? Appropriate hyphenation clears up the confusion; the phrase should read *with the singing-whale authority.*]

The following rules indicate common practice and are fairly reliable:

1. Compound numerals (*twenty-one* through *ninety-nine*) are always written with a hyphen:

> Twenty-six, forty-eight, fifty-two

2. Fractions are written with a hyphen if they are adjectival:

> His speech was one-third fact and two-thirds demagoguery.
> *But*   Three fourths of the apples are rotten.

3. Compounds with *self* are written with a hyphen:

> Self-styled, self-taught, self-centered

Note the exceptions *selfsame, selfhood, selfless.*

4. The hyphen is used in certain expressions of family relationship:

> Great-grandfather, great-aunt

5. Most compounds beginning with *ex, pre,* and *pro* are written with a hyphen:

> Ex-president, pre-Christian, pro-British

6. The hyphen is commonly used with compounds with prepositional phrases:

> Mother-in-law, stick-in-the-mud, heart-to-heart

7. One of the commonest uses of hyphens is to form compound modifiers for nouns and pronouns:

> An eight-year-old child, a well-done steak, a blue-green sea

NOTE: Such compounds are hyphenated when they immediately precede the word they modify, but frequently they are not hyphenated when they are used predicatively:

> His well-spoken words pleased the audience [*but* His words were well spoken].
> She made a number of off-the-record comments [*but* Her comments were made off the record].

8. Hyphens are used in coined or occasional compounds:

> She gave him a kind of you-ought-to-know-better look.
> Her bird-on-the-nest hat was sensational.

9. The hyphen is used in compound nouns that name the same person in two different capacities:

> Author-publisher, musician-statesman, tycoon-playboy

10. The hyphen is frequently used to avoid confusion between words:

> Re-claim [to distinguish from *reclaim*]
> Re-cover [to distinguish from *recover*]

11. Hyphens are used to avoid clumsy spellings:

Bull-like, semi-independent, ante-election, pre-empt

NOTE: *Cooperate* and *coordinate* are common enough to be accepted.

12. The hyphen is used at the end of a line of writing to indicate the division of a word continued on the next line. The division must always come at the end of a syllable. Do not divide words of one syllable:

PROPER DIVISIONS: con-tin-ued, in-di-cate, au-di-ence

IMPROPER DIVISIONS: wo-rd, laugh-ed, comp-ound

NOTE: If you are uncertain about the division of a word, consult your dictionary.

Exercise 74   CAPITALS

In the following sentences change small letters to capital letters wherever necessary and vice versa. Circle the number of any sentence that needs no change.

       F   M   B   D P
EXAMPLE: father, mother, and bill tried without success to get in touch with dr. phillips
             S
            last saturday.

1. Olaf, my friend from sweden, has typical scandinavian coloring: blonde hair, fair skin, and blue eyes.

2. Doesn't it confuse you that veterans day and memorial day are now celebrated on the mondays nearest the actual dates?

3. Dickens's famous novel *A tale of two cities* is on Frank's reading list for Summer.

4. Kim said, "why don't you take harry along with you to the beach today, sis?"

5. When I realized that I was failing mathematics, I became discouraged.

6. We sailed East into the wind for a long while, finally realizing that we had strayed too far from st. simon's island.

7. When they visited the capitol in Washington, my Grandfather and Grandmother met senator Kennedy.

8. My home is in the south, but I am very fond of the great American west.

9. Did you know that Ben Jonson wrote the words to the old song "Drink To Me Only With Thine Eyes"?

10. I understand that aunt Frances has recently joined the Daughters of the American Revolution.

11. Bobbie was elated because she made an *A* in history 152.

12. My Mother's favorite shakespearean play has always been *The Tempest.*

13. Someone said recently that it is surprising how many people don't know the difference between the middle ages and the renaissance.

14. Andy poured italian dressing on the green salad, which contained boston lettuce, mushrooms, and croutons.

15. My Cousin, who lives in Louisiana, says that natives of that State have a certain way of pronouncing its name.

Exercise 75   ITALICS

In the following sentences underline all words that should be italicized. Circle the number of
any sentence that needs no change.

EXAMPLE: Ofter fifty years ago Lindbergh flew his <u>Spirit</u> <u>of</u> <u>St. Louis</u> across the Atlantic
Ocean.

1. The word bedlam, meaning "confusion," came originally from the name of a hospital
in London.

2. One of Agatha Christie's last novels is Curtain, which narrates the death of her fictional
detective Hercule Poirot.

3. Our waiter told us that the soup du jour was Scotch broth.

4. Sailing around the world on the Queen Elizabeth II was the thrill of a lifetime for our
English friends.

5. Mr. Bryan left here to become the editor of the Cleveland Plain Dealer in Cleveland, Ohio.

6. Anyone who has not read Roots or seen the television version seems to belong to a small
minority.

7. The number 13 has traditionally been considered unlucky.

8. I tried my best to explain to her the difference between the words disagreement and
quarrel.

9. To form the possessive of most singular nouns, simply add an apostrophe and an s.

10. She has difficulty in pronouncing the word success because of her lisp.

11. My friend recently gave me a subscription to the beautiful magazine In Britain.

12. The Latin term for an adult male who is head of a family is pater familias.

13. The first time Betty traveled west, she was on that old train The Sunset Limited for four
days.

14. Terry's grandmother, in her old-fashioned way, told him to mind his p's and q's.

15. Frost's poem "The Road Not Taken" appears in a great many anthologies of American
poetry.

16. Fran, I hope you will be able to keep this information strictly entre nous.

17. Suzanne reads the Washington Post every day.

18. I really could not tell whether that word in his letter was more or move.

19. Walter Lord is the author of a fascinating book about the tragic sinking of the Titanic.

20. My handwriting is usually clear, but sometimes I write a q that looks like a g.

Exercise 76   THE APOSTROPHE

In the following sentences underline all words that should have apostrophes, and then write the words with the apostrophes correctly placed. If a sentence is correct, mark it C.

EXAMPLE: <u>Fosters</u> friends who live in Denver have invited him to spend the summer with them.   *Foster's*
....

1. Wheres the insect repellent that I left on the porch last night? ....

2. Clyde, I believe that the responsibility for keeping the room straight should be yours, not mine. ....

3. In my bowl of alphabet soup today I found seven *b*s. ....

4. Although he is a member of the Class of 21, Mr. McWhorter is still a loyal and active alumnus of the University. ....

5. Emily Posts well-known book on etiquette has been brought up to date by her daughter-in-law, whos also an authority on the subject. ....

6. The Johnsons, our next-door neighbors, have offered to cut our lawn as well as theirs while we are away this summer. ....

7. The two candidates for the City Council post are hurling accusations at each other; thats politics, Im told. ....

8. The other day I was lucky enough to catch one of Laurel and Hardys great old comedies on television. ....

9. Billys telephone number is easy to remember because it contains mostly *2*s and *3*s. ....

10. I was envious when I heard about the Joneses three weeks cruise up the fjords of Norway. ....

11. How do you feel about the idea that if one talks to his plants, theyll grow better? ....

12. The remarkable thing about my new weed-cutter is its ability to get into narrow places that the lawn-mower cant reach. ....

13. It seems as though all my free Saturdays lately have been spent doing boring things. ....

14. Frances and Kittys sailboat is a real beauty. ....

253

15. Childrens play-clothes should be rugged and easily washable. ....

16. Unfortunately, Mr. Harris speech was punctuated with *ers*. ....

17. Some of the McCutchens tomato plants are already blooming. ....

18. Isnt it time for the babys nap, or are you going to let him skip it today? ....

19. My opinion is that some of Hopkins poems are difficult to analyze; do you agree? ....

20. The *abc*s of cooking are easy if you own a copy of Mrs. Rombauers book *The Joy of Cooking*. ....

Exercise 77   THE HYPHEN

In the sentences below underline the incorrect compounds and write the correct forms at the right. If a sentence is correct, mark it *C*. Some sentences contain more than one error.

EXAMPLE: Forty three members of our club are going to
participate in the auction to raise funds for the
art museum.   ....*Forty-three*...............

1. Those sweet smelling magnolias remind me of my childhood
in Mobile, Alabama.   ....

2. While I was enjoying a big plate of barbecue hash, I was
interrupted in mid bite by the telephone.   ....

3. The man in the yachting outfit is an ex-English professor.   ....

4. Trying to reach the mountain top, we had to scale a walllike
cliff about thirty feet high.   ....

5. Mother gave Ralph a "don't you dare" look as he started to
take another piece of fruitcake.   ....

6. We decided to recover the old sofa in a striking red velvet
fabric.   ....

7. The forty year old student found that the academic world
had changed since her earlier college days.   ....

8. Reentry into the world of books, classes, and term papers
was a traumatic experience.   ....

9. The hours long wait in a doctor's reception room is often
trying for those who are not feeling well to begin with.   ....

10. Her husband grew up in the Minneapolis Saint Paul area, but
he now seems content to live in California.   ....

11. Peter reports that he works a twelve hour day in his
veterinary clinic.   ....

12. When Maisie and Ed arrived, they found that the party was
wall to wall people.   ....

13. Elsie's mother in law says that her salt free diet has lowered
her blood pressure.   ....

14. A one word description of that terrible bore is "tiresome." ....

15. The soprano's voice has a belllike quality that is most appealing. ....

16. Bobby has been looking everywhere for a part-time job, but he hasn't found one yet. ....

17. We found Jack on the floor in a spread eagle position, reading a science fiction novel. ....

18. My flower bed is full of zinnias, nasturtiums, black eyed Susans, and baby's breath. ....

19. My great grandfather plays golf every day, and he usually beats his partner, who is twenty two years younger than he. ....

20. The reestablishment of a choral society in our town has led to a strong community feeling. ....

| Exercise 78 | **REVIEW OF MECHANICS** |

Underline the errors in mechanics in the following sentences, and then write the correct forms in the spaces at the right. If a sentence is correct, mark it *C*.

EXAMPLE:　Lynn's <u>do or die</u> attitude toward learning to play
tennis will probably help her succeed.

........................*do-or-die*........................

1. How was I to know that the word escargots on the menu is
the French word for snails?

....

....

2. The Edwards library shelves are full of their sons old Hardy
Boys books.

....

....

3. Remember to cross your ts, Meg; otherwise they look like ls.

....

....

4. Mrs. Taylor was upset because the president's news
conference preempted her favorite soap opera.

....

....

5. At the world famous Wimbledon Tennis Matches
spectators enjoy traditional strawberries and cream
refreshment.

....

....

6. Don't forget to look for my favorite novel, Huckleberry
Finn, when you go to the carnegie library, Jim.

....

....

7. After two months stay in Hong Kong I became homesick
for America.

....

....

8. Sara Teasdales poem "Barter" conveys an idealistic message.

....

....

9. We went over to the Simses house after dinner last night
   and watched television with them until after eleven oclock.

   ....

   ....

10. Laura never would say what caused the trouble between
    her and her ex roommate.

    ....

    ....

11. Ellis and Maries children are rather devil may care, arent
    they?

    ....

    ....

12. The firm's president stated that a re-examination of
    existing policy is imperative.

    ....

    ....

13. The Wilson's and the Bentley's are next door neighbors
    and long time friends.

    ....

    ....

14. If theres anyone who annoys me its a know it all trying to
    tell me how to cook in my own kitchen.

    ....

    ....

15. I received my undergraduate degree from the university of
    alabama, and I got my m.a. at Harvard.

    ....

    ....

16. The intersection of Broadway and forty second street in
    New York is known as times square.

    ....

    ....

17. Last summer we took a cruise down the rhine river from
    Strasbourg to Amsterdam on a boat called the Holland Pearl.

    ....

    ....

18. Tommy told his story in such a straight faced manner that
    no one was sure whether or not he was joking.

    ....

    ....

Use of the Dictionary 21

A convenient source of valuable linguistic information which is often overlooked is a standard dictionary. It is easy to use and, if used intelligently, very informative. Many people do not realize that a dictionary contains important facts far beyond simple definitions and guides to pronunciation or spelling. One of the best investments that a college student can make is the purchase and frequent use of a standard collegiate dictionary. It is a necessary step toward the development of an effective vocabulary, but more importantly it is essential to any reader's understanding of the material he encounters daily. In any college course, in the newspapers, and in regular communication with others, the alert student will read and hear unfamiliar words. A desire to learn the meaning, spelling, and pronunciation of a new word should lead him to a dictionary which can provide this information plus other facts such as the derivation of the word, its level of usage, discussions of its synonyms, and usually at least one antonym as a means to illuminate still further its precise shade of meaning.

The best dictionaries have taken years of preparation by hundreds of workers directed by the finest scholars of the time. Unabridged dictionaries are absolutely comprehensive in their explanations and descriptions of words, containing thousands more entries than the more commonly used desk dictionary. In the United States perhaps the best-known unabridged dictionary is *Webster's New International Dictionary of the English Language,* frequently called *Webster's Third* because the current issue is the third edition of the book. It was published by the G. & C. Merriam Company of Springfield, Mass., in 1961. This work, of course, though it is too bulky to be used as a casual desk dictionary (and for most purposes is not really necessary), may be found when you need it in your college library.

Any one of several extremely reliable collegiate dictionaries is the best choice for the college student. Severely abridged paperback editions of these dictionaries are a poor investment, as they do not contain the sometimes vital information which students will find necessary for any detailed or specialized assignment in their courses. Recommended by most language authorities are the following standard college dictionaries: *Webster's Seventh New*

Collegiate Dictionary, published by G. & C. Merriam Co., Springfield, Mass.; *Webster's New World Dictionary of the American Language,* Collins + World Publishing Co., Cleveland; *The American Heritage Dictionary of the English Language,* The American Heritage Publishing Co., Inc., and Houghton Mifflin Co., Boston; *The Random House Dictionary of the English Language,* Random House, New York; *Funk and Wagnall's Standard Collegiate Dictionary,* Harcourt, Brace and World, Inc., New York.

Select one of these dictionaries and buy it as soon as you get to college, and then follow the list of suggestions given below in order to familiarize yourself with the dictionary and the ways in which you can get the maximum use from this very handy and easy-to-use reference work.

1. Read all the introductory material in the front of the dictionary, because this explains what information the book has to offer. If some of it seems too scholarly for you to understand, read on, and at least find out what it is mainly concerned with and what you can expect to find in its entries.

2. Study carefully the key to pronunciation, and check it with words that you know so that you will be sure of understanding it. A need for guidance in pronunciation is one of the most common reasons for consulting a dictionary.

3. To save space, dictionaries necessarily use many abbreviations. These abbreviations are explained at the front of the book, frequently inside the front cover. You should refer often to this table of abbreviations until you know it well, so that no small bit of relevant information can escape you simply through ignorance of its meaning.

4. Examine the appendixes to learn what information is given in them. Some dictionaries list biographical and geographic information in their appendixes; others list them in the main entries in the book. Other information often found in the appendixes of a dictionary includes tables of interpretations of various specialized symbols, like those connected with mathematics, chemistry, music, chess, medicine, and pharmacy; a directory of colleges and universities; a table of weights and measures; a dictionary of English given names, etc.

One of the most important things a dictionary can tell you is the *level of usage* of a certain word. The English language, ever-changing and full of colorful informality, functions on many levels. Many young people use the expression *split* for *go* or *leave.* Politicians and reporters use the term *bottom line* to mean the end result of something. An educated adult may in ordinary conversation refer to *lots of trouble.* And an editor of a magazine may write of the *dichotomy between work and leisure classes* or, in a book review, of an *involuted search for self.* All these expressions are in a sense proper in their context. Good English is usually determined by the level on which it is used. The magazine editor would not normally write about *splitting*; the youth of today would hardly think or write using terms like *dichotomy.* Your dictionary will tell you whether the use of a word in a particular sense is slang, informal (colloquial), dialectal, archaic, obsolete, or none of these, i.e., Standard English.

Slang is the term used to describe the spontaneous, vivid, and sometimes racy inventions used frequently in the speech and writings of groups like teen-agers, gangsters, popular musicians, soldiers, and sports writers—not that these groups necessarily have anything else in common. The life of a slang expression is usually short, but sometimes, if it is striking enough and colorful enough, it may gain universal usage and become at least an informal part of the national vocabulary.

The term *informal* or *colloquial* is applied to words or expressions which are acceptable in the speech of the educated but not in formal writing. It is all right to say, "He's going to have *lots of trouble* explaining his whereabouts on the night of June third," but it is not Standard English to write this statement formally.

Dialect, another usage label, means that a word or expression is common to the speech of a particular group or geographical region. *Archaic* means that the word or term is rarely used today except in certain contexts like church ritual, but that it may be found fairly frequently in early writings. *Obsolete* means that the term is no longer used, but may be found in early writings. In addition, as a part of its usage discussion, a dictionary will inform you if a word or term is commonly considered obscene, vulgar, or profane.

To see how a dictionary presents its information, consider now the following entry from *The Random House Dictionary of the English Language*:*

bur·den[1] (bûr′dᵊn), *n.* **1.** that which is carried; load: *a horse's burden of rider and pack.* **2.** that which is borne with difficulty; obligation or trouble: *the burden of leadership.* **3.** *Naut.* **a.** the weight of a ship's cargo. **b.** the carrying capacity of a ship: *a ship of a hundred-tons burden.* **4.** *Mining.* the earth or rock to be moved by a charge of explosives. **5.** *Accounting.* overhead (def. 6). —*v.t.* **6.** to load heavily. **7.** to load oppressively; trouble. [ME, var. of *burthen,* OE *byrthen;* akin to G *Bürde,* Goth *baurthei;* see BEAR[1]] —**bur′den·er,** *n.* —**bur′den·less,** *adj.* —**Syn. 1.** See **load. 2.** weight, encumbrance, impediment.

Here we are given the correct spelling of the word *burden* and its proper division into syllables. The small numeral[1] after the entry word indicates that this is the first of two or more words which have the same spelling but which differ radically in meaning and derivation and are therefore listed separately. Next the proper pronunciation is given. It becomes clear immediately that you need to learn the significance of the signs, called diacritical marks, that are used to indicate pronunciation. In this entry the first five numbered definitions are preceded by *n* (for *noun*) and the last two by *v.t.* (for *verb, transitive*). After 3, *Naut.* (*Nautical*) means that the definitions given under 3 are special technical senses of the word as used in shipping. The same interpretation is true of definitions 4 and 5. The information in brackets gives the derivation or origin of the word. It tells that *burden* is a variant form of the older word *burthen,* which is derived from the Old English form *byrthen,* and that the word is linguistically akin to the word *bear* as described in the first *bear* entry elsewhere in the dictionary. Finally we learn that the synonyms of *burden*[1] are discussed under the entry *load*. The second entry, *burden*[2], is arranged on the same principles.

---

*Reproduced by permission from *The Random House Dictionary of the English Language,* The Unabridged Edition. Copyright © 1971 by Random House, Inc.

Consider now the following entry from *Webster's New World Dictionary of the American Language*:*

> **drunk** (druŋk) [ME. *dronke* < *drunken:* see DRUNKEN] *pp.* &
> *archaic pt. of* DRINK —*adj.* [*usually used in the predicate*] **1.**
> overcome by alcoholic liquor to the point of losing control
> over one's faculties; intoxicated   **2.** overcome by any
> powerful emotion [*drunk* with joy] **3.** [Colloq.] *same as*
> DRUNKEN (sense 2) —*n.* [Slang] **1.** a drunken person **2.** a
> drinking spree
> *SYN.*—**drunk** is the simple, direct word, usually used in the
> predicate, for one who is overcome by alcoholic liquor [he is
> *drunk*]; **drunken,** usually used attributively, is equivalent to
> **drunk** but sometimes implies habitual, intemperate drinking of
> liquor [a *drunken* bum]; **intoxicated** and **inebriated** are euphe-
> misms, the former often expressing slight drunkenness and the
> latter, a state of drunken exhilaration; there are many euphemistic
> and slang terms in English expressing varying degrees of drunken-
> ness: e.g., **tipsy** (slight), **tight** (moderate, but without great loss
> of muscular coordination), **blind** (great), **blotto** (to the point
> of unconsciousness), etc. —*ANT.* **sober**

Here we learn that the adjective *drunk*, with the specific meanings that follow, is the past participle and was formerly a past tense of the verb *to drink*. Two definitions are given: the first of these is the common one; the second is often used figuratively. The discussion of synonyms gives us the fine shades of distinction among a group of words that mean essentially the same thing. In addition, one antonym, or word of opposite meaning, is given. The final part of the entry, defining *drunk* as a noun, explains that when the word is used as a noun, meaning a person in a drunken condition, or a period of heavy drinking, the word is slang.

The kind of knowledge that a good dictionary can give you far exceeds what has been discussed here. Every good dictionary, for instance, pays special attention to biography and geography. One can learn when Beethoven died and the name of the capital of Peru. One can find the height of Mount Everest and the approximate number of islands in the Philippines. Literature, mythology, and particularly science are well covered in the modern dictionary. Finally, special appendixes sometimes include such miscellaneous information as the meanings of common Christian names, foreign words and phrases, abbreviations, and the symbols used in the preparation of copy for the printer and in proofreading. Some books even contain a dictionary of rhymes. The following exercises illustrate the variety of information one may obtain from a good dictionary.

---

*By permission. From *Webster's New World Dictionary of the American Language,* Second College Edition. Copyright © 1976 by Collins + World Publishing Co., Cleveland, Ohio.

Exercise 79   WORD ORIGINS

After each of the following words indicate in the first space at the right the first systematically recorded language from which the word is derived and in the second space the meaning of the source word.

	LANGUAGE	MEANING
EXAMPLE: contemporary	*Latin*	*together + time*
1. embezzle	....	....
2. bisect	....	....
3. grammar	....	....
4. cellar	....	....
5. envy	....	....
6. geyser	....	....
7. gloom	....	....
8. ignition	....	....
9. denim	....	....
10. kayak	....	....
11. demonstrate	....	....
12. fail	....	....
13. flutter	....	....
14. lubricate	....	....
15. insult	....	....
16. landscape	....	....
17. launch	....	....
18. astronaut	....	....
19. adopt	....	....

20. cider ....

21. cigar ....

22. turquoise ....

23. ski ....

24. mistrust ....

25. neighbor ....

Exercise 80 BRITISH AND AMERICAN USAGE

The following words illustrate differences between British and American usage. Write the American equivalents of these British terms:

EXAMPLE: coach (*n.*) ....*bus*.................................

1. biscuit ....

2. bonnet ....

3. bowler ....

4. chemist ....

5. corn ....

6. croft ....

7. draper ....

8. dustman ....

9. gaol ....

10. geyser ....

11. lift (*n.*) ....

12. lorry ....

13. pasty ....

14. petrol ....

15. pillarbox ....

16. post (*v.*) ....

17. pub ....

18. queue (*v.*) ....

19. rates ....

20. removal ....

21. roundabout (*n.*)   ....

22. sultanas   ....

23. sieve (*v.*)   ....

24. sweet (*n.*)   ....

25. tin   ....

26. tipping (*n.*)   ....

27. torch   ....

28. underground or tube   ....

Exercise 81   PLURALS

Write the plural form of each of the following nouns.

EXAMPLE: calf   ....*calves*........................

1. alumna   ....

2. analysis   ....

3. banjo   ....

4. basis   ....

5. belief   ....

6. bison   ....

7. brother-in-law ....

8. chimney   ....

9. crisis   ....

10. dynamo   ....

11. foot   ....

12. grief   ....

13. half   ....

14. handkerchief ....

15. hero   ....

16. Japanese   ....

17. journey   ....

18. larva   ....

19. lens   ....

20. medium   ....

21. memorandum   ....

22. moth   ....

23. ox   ....

24. parenthesis   ....

25. phenomenon   ....

26. radio   ....

27. radius   ....

28. roof   ....

29. shelf   ....

30. species   ....

31. studio   ....

32. stratum   ....

33. trout   ....

34. turkey   ....

35. worry   ....

Exercise 82   LEVELS OF USAGE

After each of the following sentences indicate the level of usage of the *italicized* words or expressions, using these abbreviations:

A for archaic,   *I* for informal or colloquial,
D for dialectal,   *S* for slang.

(Most standard collegiate dictionaries agree in the classification of these words and expressions. Other dictionaries may differ in their classifications.)

EXAMPLE: He felt torn *betwixt* conflicting loyalties to his two friends.   *A*

1. I really don't think you should take the car, Fred, without your father's *say-so*.   ....

2. Why don't you walk *a piece* down the road with us, Susie?   ....

3. On television dramas the police often use *choppers* to get their man.   ....

4. I have told you *thrice* that it is time for you to begin work on the new quilt you want to make.   ....

5. When they finally got to the *dorm*, the girls were so tired that they kicked off their shoes and went to sleep.   ....

6. My father remembers his childhood in New Orleans, when grocers would give him *lagniappe* with his regular purchase.   ....

7. We all thought Jan looked *right* pretty in her yellow organdie bridesmaid dress.   ....

8. Jeff was going to dive from the high board yesterday, but he *chickened out* at the last second.   ....

9. "I *disremember* the name of the man she is planning to marry," said Uncle Theodore.   ....

10. If *perchance* you meet Mary in Sausalito, tell her we all miss her.   ....

11. I understand that Sam was *sort of* lonely while his family went on a trip to Fripp Island.   ....

12. The sporting goods salesman really did a *snow job* on Vic, selling him equipment he couldn't possibly need.   ....

13. Peggy says she *like to have* lost her mind, with the phone and the doorbell ringing while she was trying to get the baby to sleep.   ....

14. Margaret is fond of saying that her fiancé is from the *upper crust* of Charleston, South Carolina.   ....

15. The *guy* that dented the fender on my new car is going to pay me for the damage.   ....

16. The new *pro* at the golf course has really helped me improve my putting.   ....

17. Mother told Billy that he would be in *a heap of* trouble if he didn't find the lost fishing rod.   ....

18. "Be careful," Dan cried, "*lest* you skid on the slippery pavement."   ....

19. There is a great controversy currently about whether or not possession of *pot* is a criminal offense.   ....

20. The members of the Boy Scout troop were *pretty* worn out after their hike up Sharptop Mountain.   ....

21. Ken spent hours yesterday giving Jack *pointers* on how to develop a strong backhand.   ....

22. "If there is *aught* that can go wrong," said Rosemary, "I am afraid that it will."   ....

23. Jim couldn't understand why a man as rich as his neighbor would be such a *tightwad* about small expenses.   ....

24. Mrs. Johnson specifically warned the boys that they were not to *thumb* a ride to Kansas City.   ....

25. Aunt Polly whispered to us, "*You all* must help me give your father a surprise party for his birthday."   ....

Exercise 83   GENERAL INFORMATION

Refer to your dictionary for the information you will need to fill in the blanks below.

EXAMPLE: Alternate spelling for Maxim Gorky's last name .... *Gorki* ....

1. Coronation year of Queen Elizabeth II ....

2. Location of the Fiji Islands ....

3. Explanation of the term *fielder's choice* ....

4. Invention for which Charles Goodyear is famous ....

5. Diseases transmitted to man by mosquito bites ....

6. Usual number of strings on a guitar ....

7. Physical characteristics of a gull ....

8. Man from whose name the electrical term *farad* is derived ....

9. Modern name of Constantinople ....

10. The name of the developer of psychoanalysis ....

11. Author of a poem about the Pied Piper of Hamelin ....

12. Population of Kyoto, Japan ....

13. Another name for bobcat ....

14. Founder of the Boy Scouts ....

15. Origin of the term *skinflint* ....

16. Profession of Thomas Sheraton ....

17. Name of the person whose estate the game of badminton is named for ....

....

18. Nationality (birthplace) of Pablo Picasso ....

19. Location of Stonehenge ....

20. Author of *The Canterbury Tales* ....

Exercise 84   FOREIGN EXPRESSIONS

The following foreign words and expressions occur frequently in an English context. Write the meaning of each.

EXAMPLE: entre nous .... *between ourselves, confidentially* ....

1. *peccadillo* ....

2. *picaresque* ....

3. *leger de main* ....

4. *legato* ....

5. *lese majesté* ....

6. *potage* ....

7. *post meridiem* ....

8. *sans souci* ....

9. *cul-de-sac* ....

10. *alma mater* ....

11. *rathskeller* ....

12. *stratum* ....

13. *raconteur* ....

14. *poltergeist* ....

15. *dénouement* ....

16. *genre* ....

17. *schnitzel* ....

18. *scherzo* ....

19. *pizza* ....

20. *mesa* ....

Diction 22

Diction is one's choice of words in the expression of ideas. Because one speaks and writes on various levels of usage, the same expression may be appropriate to one level but not to another. The diction, for instance, of formal writing seems overprecise in informal conversation, and the acceptable diction of everyday speech seems out of place in serious, formal composition. But on all levels of speech and writing, faulty diction appears—in wordiness, in trite expressions, and in faulty idiom.

22a Wordiness

Wordiness is the use of too many words—more words, that is, than are necessary to express an idea correctly and clearly. Many sentences written by college students may be greatly improved by reducing the number of words. The following kind of sentence is common in student themes:

WORDY: There is a man in our neighborhood, and he has written three novels.

BETTER: A man in our neighborhood has written three novels.

A neighbor of ours has written three novels.

What is called **excessive predication** is responsible for a common type of wordiness. Usually this fault results from the too frequent use of *and* and *but*. It may usually be remedied by proper subordination:

WORDY: The test was hard, and the students were resentful, and their instructor was irritated.

BETTER: Because the students resented the hard test, their instructor was irritated.

Another kind of wordiness originates in the desire to impress but ends in pretentious nonsense. It is the language of those persons who refer to bad weather as the "inclemency of the elements," who speak of "blessed events" and "passing away" instead of birth and death. Following are further examples of this kind of wordiness:

> Due to the fact that he was enamored of Angela, Thomas comported himself in such a way as to appear ridiculous.
>
> *Because he was in love with Angela, Thomas behaved foolishly.*
>
> I regret extremely the necessity of your departure.
>
> *I am sorry you must go.*
>
> Our horse Hap has gone to the big round-up in the sky.
>
> *Our horse Hap has died.*

Sometimes, of course, expressions like these are used humorously. But do not make a habit of such usage.

Recently a new kind of wordiness has become popular, probably because it is believed to make its users appear knowledgeable. It is the jargon of government officials, social workers, educators on all levels, and others. Its basic principles seem to be these: Never use one word where two or more will do the work. Never use a concrete expression if it is possible to use an abstract one. Never be plain if you can be fancy. The clear sign of this kind of writing and speaking is seen in the repeated use of such phrases as *frame of reference, in terms of, point in time,* and compounds formed with the suffix *-wise.* The writers of this new jargon never simply look at the budget; they "consider the status budget-wise." They don't study crime among the young; they "examine social conditions in terms of juvenile delinquency." They "evaluate," they "utilize," they "expedite," and they "finalize." They speak of the "culturally deprived," the "classroom learning situation," "meaningful experiences," "togetherness," and "lifestyle." All these expressions reflect a desire to be a part of the "in group" (another example of this jargon) by picking up catchwords that seem to show a certain sophistication; what they really show is a loss of precise language and a lack of judgment.

Redundancy, or unnecessary repetition, is another common type of wordiness, due to carelessness or ignorance of the meanings of certain words. Note the following examples of redundancy:

> Repeat that again, please, [Why *again*?]
>
> His solution was equally as good as hers. [Why *equally*?]
>
> The consensus of opinion of the group was that Mrs. Jacobs will make a good mayor. [Use either *consensus of the group* or *the opinion of the group*.]
>
> This location is more preferable to that one. [The word *preferable* means "more desirable"; therefore the word *more* is unnecessary. The sentence should read *This location is preferable to that one.*]
>
> The union continues to remain at odds with factory management. [*Continues* and *remain* mean essentially the same thing. Say, *The union continues at odds with factory management* or *The union remains at odds with factory management.*]
>
> It was a dog large in size and brown in color. [*It was a large brown dog.*]
>
> Mrs. Frost rarely ever wears her fur coat. [*Mrs. Frost rarely wears her fur coat.*]

22b Vagueness

A general impression of vague thinking is given by the too frequent use of abstract words instead of concrete words. Note especially the vagueness of such common words as *asset, factor, phase, case, nature, character, line,* and *field.* All these have basic meanings and should be used cautiously in any other sense. The following examples show that the best way to treat these words is to get rid of them:

> In cases where a person receives a ticket for speeding, he must pay a fine of fifty dollars. [*In cases where* can be replaced with the single word *if.*]

> Industry and intelligence are important assets in business success. [Omit *assets* and the sense remains the same.]

> The course is of a very difficult nature. [*The course is very difficult.*]

> Jerry was aware of the fact that he was risking his savings. [*Jerry was aware that he was risking his savings.*]

Whenever you are tempted to use such words, stop and ask yourself just what you are trying to say. Then find the exact words to say it, cutting out all the "deadwood."

22c Triteness

Trite means worn. Certain phrases have been used so often that they have lost their original freshness. Oratory, sermons, newspaper headlines and captions, and pretentious writing in general are frequently marred by such diction. Expressions of this kind are often called **clichés**. The following list is merely illustrative; you can probably think of numerous ones to add to these:

upset the applecart	proud possessor
an ace up his sleeve	nipped in the bud
dull thud	few and far between
one fell swoop	on pins and needles
up on Cloud Nine	make one's blood boil
grim reaper	eat one's heart out
last but not least	having a ball
face the music	as luck would have it
as straight as a dye	quick as a wink
bitter end	gung ho

Avoid also quotation of trite phrases from literature and proverbs. Expressions like the following have already served their purpose:

a lean and hungry look

a sadder but wiser man

a rolling stone

those who live in glass houses

the best laid plans of mice and men

where angels fear to tread

love never faileth

to be or not to be

22d Euphemisms

Euphemisms are expressions used to avoid the outright statement of disagreeable ideas or to give dignity to something essentially lowly or undignified. The Victorians were notoriously euphemistic: they called their legs "limbs," and instead of the accurate and descriptive terms *sweat* and *spit*, they substituted the vague but more delicate words "perspire" and "expectorate." Unfortunately, the Victorians were not the last to use euphemisms. While we cannot admire or condone some of today's obscenely explicit language, there is little justification for the fuzzy-minded delicacy of euphemisms. There is a decided difference between the choice of an expression which offers a tactful connotation rather than a hurtful one and that of an expression which is deliberately misleading. The condition of pregnancy is euphemistically referred to as "expecting"; a garbage collector is a "sanitation engineer"; a janitor is a "superintendent," etc. *Death*, of course, has numerous euphemistic substitutes such as "passing on," "going to his reward," and many others.

Again, it should be emphasized that the laudable wish to spare the feelings of others is not to be confused with the sort of prudery or false sense of gentility that most often produces euphemisms. Unless the desire to use a euphemism is inspired by the necessity to soften a blow or avoid offensiveness, the more factual term is to be preferred. Ordinarily, avoid euphemisms—or change the subject.

22e Idiom

Construction characteristic of a language is called **idiom**. The established usage of a language, the special way in which a thing is said or a phrase is formed, must be observed if writing is to be properly idiomatic. In English the normal sentence pattern has the subject first, then the verb, and then the direct object. In French, if the direct object is a pronoun, it usually (except in the imperative) precedes the verb. In English an adjective that directly modifies a noun usually precedes it. In French the adjective usually follows the noun. In English we say, "It is hot." The French say, "It makes hot." Such differences make it hard to learn a foreign language.

Another meaning of the word *idiom* is somewhat contrary to this one. The word is also used for all those expressions that seem to defy logical grammatical practice, expressions that cannot be translated literally into another language. "Many is the day" and "You had better" are good examples. Fortunately idioms of this sort cause little trouble to native speakers.

In English, as in most modern European languages, one of the greatest difficulties lies in the idiomatic use of prepositions after certain nouns, adjectives, and verbs. Oddly enough, one agrees *with* a person but *to* a proposal, and several persons may agree *upon* a plan. One may have a desire *for* something but be desirous *of* it. One is angry *at* or *about* an act but *at* or *with* a person. These uses of prepositions may seem strange and perverse. But they are part of the idiomatic structure of English and must be learned. Good dictionaries frequently indicate correct usage in questions of this kind. Do not look up the preposition but rather the word with which it is used. The definition of this word will usually indicate the correct preposition to use with it.

22f Connotation

In selecting words that will express their thoughts accurately, careful writers pay attention to the **connotations** of certain expressions. *Connotation* is the associative meaning, or what the word suggests beyond its literal definition.

Through popular usage certain terms convey favorable or unfavorable impressions beyond their literal meanings; they frequently have emotional or evaluative qualities that are not part of their straightforward definitions. Careless use of a word with strong connotations may cause faulty communication of your ideas. On the other hand, skillful use of connotation can greatly enrich your ability to communicate accurately. For example, you would not refer to a public figure whom you admire and respect as a "politician," a term which suggests such qualities as insincerity and conniving for personal gain. The word *childish* is inappropriate when you mean "childlike"; and the adjective *thin* suggests something scanty or somehow not full enough (especially when describing a person's figure), but *slim* and *slender*, two words close to *thin* in literal meaning, imply grace and good proportion.

Again, your dictionary can provide these shades of meaning that will keep you from writing something far different from your intention and will help you develop a vocabulary you can use accurately.

GLOSSARY OF FAULTY DICTION

The following glossary should help you rid your speech and writing of many errors. The term **colloquial** means that an expression is characteristic of everyday speech. **Dialectal** means that an expression is peculiar to a particular place or class.

NOTE: Remember that colloquialisms, that is the language we use in our everyday conversations with friends and associates, are perfectly acceptable in informal writing and speech. The purpose of this Glossary of Faulty Diction is to point out expressions which should be avoided in formal writing of any kind.

Above. Avoid the use of *above* as a modifier in such phrases as *the **above** reference, the **above** names.* An exception to this rule is that the word is proper in legal documents.

Accept, Except. *To accept is to receive; to except is to make an exception of, to omit. Except* (as a preposition) means *with the exception of.*

Accidently. There is no such word. The correct form is *accidentally,* based on the adjective *accidental.*

A.D. This is an abbreviation of *Anno Domini* (in the year of our Lord). Strictly considered, it should be used only with a date: *A.D. 1492.* But it has recently come to mean *of the Christian era,* and expressions like *the fifth century A.D.* have become common. Here logic has bowed to usage.

Administrate. There is no such word. The verb is *administer;* the noun formed from it is *administration.*

Adverse, Averse. *Adverse* means *unfavorable: The weatherman forecast **adverse** conditions for the yacht race. Averse* means *opposed to: Mother was **averse** to our plans for ice skating at midnight.*

Affect, Effect. In common usage *affect* is a verb meaning *to influence, to have an effect upon* or *to like to have or use* (*He **affects** a gold-headed cane*) or *to pretend* (*She **affects** helplessness*). *Effect* is both verb and noun. *To effect* is *to produce, to bring about.* The noun *effect* is a *result,* a *consequence.*

Aggravate. Colloquial when used to mean *provoke* or *irritate. Aggravate* means to make worse (*The rainy weather **aggravated** his rheumatism*).

Agree to, Agree with. One agrees *to* a proposal but *with* a person. (*We **agree to** his suggestion that we go,* but *The boy did not **agree with** his father*).

Ain't. This form is occasionally defended as a contraction of *am not*, but even those who defend it do not use it in writing.

Alibi. Colloquial for *excuse*. In formal usage *alibi* has legal significance only and means a confirmation of one's absence from the scene of a crime at the time the crime was committed.

All ready, Already. *All ready* means simply that all are ready (*The players were **all ready***). *Already* means *previously* or *before now* (*He has **already** gone*).

All together, Altogether. *All together* means all of a number taken or considered together (*She invited them **all together***). *Altogether* means *entirely, completely* (*He was **altogether** wrong*).

Allusion, Illusion. An *allusion* is a reference to something that does not mention it specifically (*The quotation was an **allusion** to Shakespeare's* Macbeth). An *illusion* is a false or unreal impression of reality (*After his unkind treatment of the puppy Mildred lost her **illusions** about Arthur*).

Alright. This is not a possible alternate spelling for the words *all right*.

Alumnus, Alumna. *Alumnus* is masculine and has the plural *alumni*. *Alumna* is feminine and has the plural *alumnae*.

Among, Between. The common practice is to use *between* with two or more persons or objects (***between** a rock and a hard place*) and *among* with more than two (*The crew quarreled **among** themselves*). Exception: *The plane traveled **between** New York, Chicago, and Miami.* Here *among* would be absurd.

Anymore, Any more. The expression should be written as two words.

Anyone, Any One. *Anyone*, the indefinite pronoun, is one word. *Any one*, meaning any single person or any single thing, should be written as two words (***Any one** of your friends will be glad to help you.*)

Any place, No place. Dialectal corruptions of *anywhere* and *nowhere*.

Apt, Liable, Likely. *Apt* means *suitable, qualified, expert* (*an **apt** phrase, a man **apt** to succeed*). *Liable* means *exposed to something undesirable* (***liable** to be injured, **liable** for damages*). *Likely* means *credible, probable, probably* (*He had a **likely** excuse. Very **likely** it will rain*).

As far as. This expression is frequently misused when it is not followed by a clause (***As far as** her ability she is perfectly able to do the work*). It should always function as a subordinating conjunction, introducing both a subject and a verb (***As far as** her ability is concerned, she is perfectly able to do the work.*)

Asset. In its essential meaning this word is used in law and accounting (*His **assets** exceeded his liabilities*). But it seems to have established itself in the meaning of *something useful or desirable*. When used in this sense, it is frequently redundant.

Attend, Tend. *Attend* means *to be present at.* When meaning *to take care of*, it is followed by *to* (*He **attends to** his own business*). *Tend* without a preposition also means *to take care of* (*He **tends** his own garden*). *Tend to* means *to have a tendency to* (*She **tends to** become nervous when her children are noisy*).

Author, Host, Chair, Position. These nouns are frequently misused as verbs (*She has **authored** three best sellers, The Joneses plan to **host** a party for their friends, The woman who **chairs** the committee is a lawyer, Please **position** the chairs around the table.*). In these four sentences there are perfectly adequate verbs that should be used: *written, give, is* chairwoman of, and *place*.

Awful, Awfully. Either of these is colloquial when used to mean *very*.

Awhile, A While. *Awhile* is used as an adverb (*They stayed **awhile** at their friend's house*). When used after the preposition *for*, *while* is a noun, the object of the preposition (*I thought for **a while** that you were going to miss the plane*). The adverb is written as one word; the object of the preposition and its article are written as two.

Bad, Badly. *Bad* is an adjective, *badly* an adverb.

Balance. Except in accounting, the use of *balance* for *difference, remainder, the rest* is colloquial.

Being As. Dialectal for *since* or *because*.

Beside, Besides. *Beside* is a preposition meaning *by the side of* (*Along came a spider and sat down **beside** her*). *Besides* is a preposition meaning *except* (*He had nothing **besides** his good name*) and an adverb meaning *in addition, moreover* (*He received a medal and fifty dollars **besides***).

Blame On. Correct idiom calls for the use of *to blame* with *for*, not *on*. (*They **blamed** the driver for the accident*, not *They **blamed** the accident on the driver*.) *Blame on* is colloquial.

Boyfriend, Girlfriend. These two terms are colloquial, meaning *a favored male or female friend, a sweetheart.* If no other term seems appropriate, write them as two words: *boy friend, girl friend.*

Burst, Bursted, Bust. The principal parts of the verb *burst* are *burst, burst,* and *burst.* The use of *bursted* or *busted* for the past tense is incorrect. *Bust* is either sculpture or a part of the human body. Used for *failure* or as a verb for *burst* or *break*, it is slang.

But What. Use *that* or *but that* instead of *but what* (*They had no doubt **that** help would come*).

Cannot. This word is the negative form of *can*. It is written as one word.

Cannot Help But. This is a mixed construction. *Cannot help* and *cannot but* are separate expressions, either of which is correct (*He **cannot but** attempt it,* or *He **cannot help** attempting it*).

Capital, Capitol. *Capital* is a city; *capitol* is a building. *Capital* is also an adjective, usually meaning *chief, excellent.*

Case. This is a vague and unnecessary word in many of its common uses today. Avoid *case* and seek the exact word.

Calvary, Cavalry. Mistakes here are chiefly a matter of spelling, but it is important to be aware of the difference: *Calvary* is the name of the hill where Jesus was crucified; *cavalry* refers to troops trained to fight on horseback, or more recently in armored vehicles.

Chairperson. Use the terms *chairman* and *chairwoman* in preference to *chairperson*, which should be used only if it is an official title in an organization or if you are quoting directly someone who has used the term.

Claim. Do not use simply to mean *say*. In the correct use of claim some disputed right is involved (*He **claims** to be the heir of a very wealthy man*).

Complement, Compliment. In its usual sense *complement* means *something that completes* (*Her navy blue shoes and bag were a **complement** for her gray suit*). A *compliment* is an expression of courtesy or praise (*My **compliments** to the chef*).

Connotate. There is no such verb as *connotate*; the verb is *connote,* and its noun form is *connotation.*

Considerable. This word is an adjective meaning *worthy of consideration, important* (*The idea is at least **considerable***). When used to denote a great deal or a great many, *considerable* is colloquial or informal.

Contact. Colloquial and sometimes vague when used for *see, meet, communicate with*, as in *I must **contact** my agent.*

Continual, Continuous. *Continual* means *repeated often* (*The interruptions were **continual***). *Continuous* means *going on without interruption* (*For two days the pain was **continuous***).

Convince, Persuade. Do not use *convince* for *persuade* as in *I **convinced** him to wash the dishes. Convince* means *to overcome doubt* (*I **convinced** him of the soundness of my plan*). *Persuade* means *to win over by argument or entreaty* (*I **persuaded** him to wash the dishes*).

Couple. This word, followed by *of* is informal for *two* or *a few*.

Credible, Creditable. *Credible* mean *believable* (*His evidence was not **credible***). *Creditable* means *deserving esteem or admiration* (*The acting of the male lead was a **creditable** performance*).

Critique. This word is a noun, not a verb; it means a critical review or comment dealing with an artistic work. The verb form is *criticize*.

Cupfuls, Cupsful. The plural of cupful is *cupfuls,* not *cupsful.*

Data. *Data* is the plural of *datum, something given or known.* It usually refers to a body of facts or figures. It normally takes a plural verb (*These **data** are important*). At times, however, *data* may be considered a collective noun and used with a singular verb.

Definitely. This is frequently used to mean *very* or *quite.* It is a trite expression and should be avoided for this reason as well as for its lack of accuracy.

Different Than. Most good writers use *different from*, not *different than.*

Disinterested. Often confused with *uninterested. Disinterested* means *unbiased, impartial; uninterested* means *lacking interest in.*

Don't. A contraction of *do not.* Do not write *he, she,* or *it don't.*

Drapes. Incorrect when used as a noun to mean *curtains. Drape* is the verb; *draperies* is the correct noun form.

Due To. Do not use *due to* for *because of* as in ***Due to** a lengthy illness, he left college. Due to* is correctly used after a noun or linking verb (*His failure, **due to** laziness, was not surprising. The accident was **due to** carelessness*).

Dyeing, Dying. *Dyeing* refers to the coloring of materials with dye. Do not omit the *e,* which would confuse the word with *dying,* meaning *expiring.*

Emigrant, Immigrant. A person who moves from one place to another is both an *emigrant* and an *immigrant*, but he emigrates *from* one place and immigrates *to* the other.

Equally As. Do not use these two words together; omit either *equally* or *as.* Do not write *Water is **equally as** necessary as air*; write *Water is **as** necessary as air* or *Water and air are **equally** necessary.*

Enthuse, Enthused. These words are colloquial and always unacceptable in writing.

Etc. An abbreviation of Latin *et* (*and*) and *cetera* (*other things*). It should not be preceded by *and*, nor should it be used as a catch-all expression to avoid a clear and exact ending of an idea or a sentence.

Everyday, Every day. When written as one word (*everyday*), this expression is an adjective (*Mother's **everyday** china is ironstone*). When used adverbially to indicate how often something happens, it is written as two words (***Every day** at noon I eat an apple and drink a glass of milk*).

Exam. A colloquial abbreviation for *examination.* Compare *gym, dorm, lab,* and *prof.*

Expect. This word means *to look forward to* or *foresee.* Do not use it to mean *suspect* or *suppose.*

Fact That. This is an example of wordiness, usually amounting to redundancy. Most sentences can omit the phrase *the fact that* without changing the sense of what is said (*The fact that he wanted a new bicycle was the reason why he stole the money* may be effectively reduced to *He stole the money because he wanted a new bicycle*). Whenever you are tempted to use this expression, try rewording the sentence without it, and you will have a more concise and a clearer statement.

Farther, Further. The two words are often confused. *Farther* means *at or to a more distant point in space or time; further* means *to a greater extent, in addition.* One says *It is farther to Minneapolis from Chicago than from here*, but *We will talk further about this tomorrow.*

Faze. Colloquial for *to disturb* to *to agitate.* Most commonly used in the negative (*Mother's angry looks didn't faze Jimmy*).

Feel. *Feel* means to perceive through the physical senses or through the emotions. This word should not be used as a careless equivalent of *think* or *believe,* both of which refer to mental activity.

Fellow. Colloquial when used to mean a *person.*

Fewer, Less. Use *fewer* to refer to a number, *less* to refer to amount (*Where there are fewer persons, there is less noise*).

Fine. Colloquial when used as a term of general approval.

Fix. *Fix* is a verb, meaning *to make firm or stable.* Used as a noun meaning *a bad condition* or a verb meaning *to repair,* it is colloquial.

Flaunt, flout. *Flaunt* means *to exhibit ostentatiously, to show off* (*She flaunted her new mink coat before her friends*). *Flout* means to show *contempt for, to scorn* (*Margaret often flouts the rules of good sportsmanship*).

Forego, Forgo. *Forego* means to *precede* or *go before* (*The foregoing data were gathered two years ago. Forgo* means *to give up, reliquish* (*I am afraid I must forgo the pleasure of meeting your friends today*).

Formally, Formerly. *Formally* means *in a formal manner* (*He was formally initiated into his fraternity last night*). *Formerly* means *at a former time* (*They formerly lived in Ohio*).

Gentlemen, Lady. Do not use these words as synonyms for *man* and *woman.*

Got. This is a correct past participle of the verb *to get* (*He had got three traffic tickets in two days*). *Gotten* is an alternative past participle of *to get.*

Guess. Colloquial when used for *suppose* or *believe.*

Guy. Slang when used for *boy* or *man.*

Hanged, Hung. *Hanged* is the correct past tense or past participle of *hang* when capital punishment is meant (*The cattle rustlers were hanged at daybreak*). *Hung* is the past tense and past participle in every other sense of the term (*We hung popcorn and cranberries on the Christmas tree*).

Hardly, Scarcely. Do not use with a negative. *I can't hardly see it* borders on the illiterate. Write *I can hardly see it* or (if you cannot see it at all) *I can't see it.*

Healthful, Healthy. Places are *healthful* if persons may be *healthy* living in them.

Hopefully. This word means *in a hopeful manner* (*She hopefully began getting ready for her blind date*). Do not use this modifier to mean *it is hoped* or *let us hope* (*Hopefully, the new rail system for Atlanta will be completed within five years*).

If, Whether. In careful writing do not use *if* for *whether. Let me know if you are coming* does not mean exactly the same thing as *Let me know whether you are coming.* The latter leaves no doubt that a reply is expected.

Imply, Infer. *Imply* means *to suggest, to express indirectly. Infer* means *to conclude*, as on the basis of suggestion or implication. A writer *implies* to a reader; a reader *infers* from a writer.

Incidently. There is no such word. The correct form is *incidentally*, based on the adjective *incidental.*

Into, In To. *Into* is a preposition meaning *toward the inside* and is followed by an object of the preposition. Do not use the one-word form of this expression when the object of the preposition is the object of *to* only, and *in* is an adverbial modifier. Say *He went into the building* but *The men handed their application forms in to the personnel manager.*

Irregardless. No such word exists. *Regardless* is the correct word.

Its, It's. The form *its* is possessive (*Every dog has its day*). *It's* is a contraction of *it is* (*It's a pity she's a bore*).

It's Me. Formal English requires *It is I. It's me* is informal or colloquial, perfectly acceptable in conversation but not proper for written English. Compare the French idiom *C'est moi.*

Kid. Used to mean a child or young person, *kid* is slang.

Kind, Sort. These are singular forms and should be modified accordingly (*this kind, that sort*). *Kinds* and *sorts* are plural, and they, of course, have plural modifiers.

Kind Of, Sort Of. Do not use these to mean *rather* as in *He was kind of* (or *sort of*) *lazy.*

Last, Latest. *Last* implies that there will be no more. *Latest* does not prevent the possibility of another appearance later. The proper sense of both is seen in the sentence *After seeing his latest play, we hope that it is his last.*

Lend, Loan. The use of *loan* as a verb is incorrect. *Loan* is a noun. The distinction between the two words may be seen in the sentence *If you will lend me ten dollars until Friday, I will appreciate the loan.*

Like, As. Confusion in the use of these two words results from using *like* as a conjunction. The preposition *like* should be followed by an object (*He ran like an antelope*). The conjunction *as* is followed by a clause (*He did as he wished, He talked as though he were crazy*). The incorrect use of *as* as a preposition is a kind of reaction against the use of *like* as a conjunction. Consider the sentence: *Many species of oaks, as the red oak, the white oak, the water oak, are found in the Southeast.* Here the correct word is *like*, not *as.*

Literally. The word means *faithfully, to the letter, letter for letter, exactly.* Do not use in the sense of *completely,* or *in effect.* A sentence may be copied *literally* ; but one never, except under extraordinary circumstances, *literally devours a book.* Frequently, the word *virtually,* meaning *in effect or essence, though not in fact,* is the correct word.

Lot, Lots. Colloquial or informal when used to mean *many* or *much.*

Mad. The essential meaning of *mad* is *insane.* When used to mean *angry,* it is informal.

May Be, Maybe. *May be* is a verb phrase (*It may be that you are right*). *Maybe* used as an an adverb means *perhaps* (*Maybe you are right*).

Mean. Used for disagreeable (*He has a mean disposition, He is mean to me*), the word is informal or colloquial.

Media. *Media* is the plural of *medium, a means, agency,* or *instrumentality.* It is often incorrectly used in the plural as though it were singular, as in *The media is playing an important role in political races this year.*

Midnight, Noon. Neither of these words needs the word *twelve* before it. They themselves refer to specific times, so *twelve* is redundant.

Most. Do not use for *almost. Almost all of them are here* or *Most of them are here* is correct. *Most all of them are here* is incorrect.

Muchly. There is no such word as *muchly*. *Much* is both adjective and adverb (***Much** water has flowed over the dam, Thank you very **much***). Compare *thusly*.

Mutual. The use of *mutual* for *common* is usually avoided by careful writers. ***Common** knowledge, **common** property, **common** dislikes* are things shared by two or more persons. *Mutual admiration means admiration of each for the other.*

Myself. Colloquial when used as a substitute for *I* or *me*, as in *He and **myself** were there*. It is correctly used intensively (*I **myself** shall do it*) and reflexively (*I blame only **myself***).

Nice. *Nice* is a catch-all word that has lost its force because it has no clearcut, specific meaning as a modifier. When writing in praise of something, select an adjective that conveys more specific information than *nice* does.

Of. Unnecessary after such prepositions as *off, inside, outside* (not *He fell **off of** the cliff* but *He fell **off** the cliff*).

On Account Of. Do not use as a conjunction; the phrase should be followed by an object of the preposition *of* (***on account of** his illness*). *He was absent **on account of** he was sick* is bad grammar.

Oral, Verbal, Written. Use *oral* to refer to spoken words (*An **oral** examination is sometimes nerve-wracking for a student*); use *verbal* to contrast a communication in words to some other kind of communication (*His scowl told me more than any **verbal** message could*); use *written* when referring to anything put on paper.

Orientate. There is no such word. The verb is *orient*, meaning *to cause to become familiar with or adjusted to facts or a situation* (*He **oriented** himself by finding the North Star*). The noun is *orientation*.

Over With. The *with* in unnecessary in such expression as *The game was **over with** by five o'clock*.

Party. Colloquial when used to mean *a person*. Properly used in legal documents (***party** of the first part*).

Peeve. Either as a verb or noun, *peeve* is informal diction.

Personally. This word is often redundant and is a hackneyed, sometimes irritating expression, as in ***Personally**, I think you are making a big mistake*.

Plan On. Omit *on*. In standard practice idiom calls for an infinitive or a direct object after *plan*. *They **planned** to go* or *They **planned** a reception* are both correct usage.

Plenty. This word is a noun, not an adverb. Do not write *He was **plenty** worried*.

Pore, Pour. *Pore*, meaning *to meditate* or *to study intently and with steady application*, is a verb used with the preposition *over*. (*She **pored** over her chemistry assignment for several hours*.) It should not be confused with *pour*, meaning *to set a liquid flowing or falling*. (*They **poured** the tea into fragile china cups*.)

Principal, Principle. *Principal* is both adjective and noun (***principal** parts, **principal** of the school, **principal** and interest*). *Principle* is a noun only (***principles** of philosophy, a man of **principle***).

Pupil, Student. School children in the elementary grades are called *pupils*; in grades nine through twelve *student* or *pupil* is correct; for college the term must always be *student*.

Quite. The word means *altogether, entirely* (*He was **quite** exhausted from his exertion*). It is colloquial when used for *moderately* or *very* and in expressions like ***quite** a few, **quite** a number*.

Quote, Quotation. *Quote* is a verb and should not be used as a noun, as in *The **quote** you gave is from Shakespeare, not the Bible*.

Real. Do not use for *really. Real* is an adjective; *really* is an adverb (*The **real** gems are **really** beautiful*).

Reason Is Because. This is not idiomatic English. The subject-linking verb construction calls for a predicate nominative, but *because* is a subordinating conjunction that introduces an adverbial clause. Write *The **reason** I was late **is that** I had an accident,* not *The **reason** I was late **is because** I had an accident.*

Respectfully, Respectively. *Respectfully* means *with respect,* as in *The young used to act **respectfully** toward their elders. Respectively* is a word seldom needed; it means *in the order designated,* as in *The men and women took their seats on the right and left **respectively.***

Reverend. This word, like *Honorable,* is not a noun, but an honorific adjective. It is not a title like *doctor* or *president.* It is properly used preceding *Mr.* or the given name or initials, as in *the **Reverend** Mr. Gilbreath, the **Reverend** Earl Gilbreath, the **Reverend** J. E. Gilbreath.* To use the word as a title as in ***Reverend,** will you lead us in prayer?* or *Is there a **Reverend** in the house?* is plainly absurd. ***Reverend** Gilbreath* instead of *the **Reverend** Mr. Gilbreath* is almost as bad.

Right. In the sense of *very* or *extremely, right* is colloquial. Do not write (or say) *I'm **right** glad to know you.*

Same. The word is an adjective, not a pronoun. Do not use it as in *We received your order and will give **same** immediate attention.* Substitute *it* for *same.*

Savings. This word is frequently misused in the plural when the singular is the correct form. It is particularly puzzling that many people use this plural with a singular article, as in *The ten per cent discount gives you a **savings** of nine dollars. A saving* is the proper usage here. Another common error occurs in reference to *Daylight **Saving** Time;* the right form again is *Saving,* not *Savings.*

Shape. In formal writing do not use *shape* for *condition* as in *He played badly because he was in poor **shape.*** In this sense *shape* is informal.

Situation. This is another catch-all term, frequently used redundantly, as in *It was a fourth down **situation.*** Fourth down *is* a situation, so the word itself is repetitious. This vague term can usually be omitted or replaced with a more specific word.

Should Of, Would Of. Do not use these terms for *should have, would have.*

So, Such. Avoid the use of *so* and *such* for *very,* as in *Thank you **so** much; you are **such** a darling.* These words are subordinating conjunctions, calling for a dependent clause expressing result, as in *He was **so** late **that** the others left without him,* or *Her hair was **such** a mess **that** she could not go to the party.*

Some. Do not use for *somewhat,* as in *She is **some** better after her illness.*

Species. This word is both singular and plural. One may speak of *one species* or *three species.* The word usually refers to a kind of plant or animal.

Sprightly, Spritely. *Sprightly* means *animated, vivacious, lively.* There is no such word as *spritely,* but many people use this term, probably because it suggests the word *sprite,* an *elf* or *fairy.* Do not write *her **spritely** conversation was fascinating.*

Stationary, Stationery. *Stationary* means *fixed, not moving.* Remember that *stationery,* which is paper for writing letters, is sold by a *stationer.*

Statue, Stature, Statute. A *statue* is a piece of sculpture. *Stature* is bodily height, often used figuratively to mean *level of achievement, status,* or *importance.* A *statute* is a law or regulation.

Strata. This is the plural of the Latin *stratum.* One speaks of *a stratum* of rock but of *several strata.*

Super, Fantastic, Incredible, etc. When used to describe something exciting or marvelous, these overworked words actually add little to our everyday conversation because they have lost their original force. At any rate, they must never be a part of written formal English, as they are simply slang, and trite slang at that.

Suppose, Supposed. Many people incorrectly use the first form *suppose* before an infinitive when the second form *supposed* is needed, as in *Am I suppose to meet you at five o'clock?* The past participle *supposed* must go along with the auxiliary verb *am* to form the passive voice. This error almost certainly arises from an inability to hear the final *d* when it precedes the *t* in the *to* of the infinitive. The correct form is *Am I supposed to meet you at five o'clock?*

Sure, Surely. Do not use the adjective *sure* for the adverb *surely. I am sure that you are right* and *I am surely glad to be here* are correct.

Trustee, Trusty. The word *trustee* means *a person elected or appointed to direct funds or policy* for a person or an institution, as in *Mr. Higginbotham is a trustee on the bank's board of directors.* A *trusty*, on the other hand, is a prisoner granted special privileges because he is believed trustworthy, as in *Although he was a trusty, Harris escaped from prison early today.*

Too. *Too* means *in addition,* or *excessively.* It is incorrect to use the word to mean *very* or *very much,* as in *I was not too impressed with her latest book* or *I'm afraid I don't know him too well.*

Toward, Towards. The first form is greatly preferred over the second.

Try And. Use *try to*, not *try and*, in such expressions as *Try to get here on time* (not *Try and get here on time*).

Type. Colloquial in expressions like *this type book;* write *this type of book.*

Undoubtably, Undoubtedly. There is no such word as *undoubtably.* The correct word is *undoubtedly.*

Unique. If referring to something as the only one of its kind, you may correctly use *unique.* (*The Grand Canyon is a unique geological formation.*) The word does not mean *rare, strange,* or *remarkable,* and there are no degrees of *uniqueness*; to say that something is *the most unique thing one has ever seen* is faulty diction.

Use (Used) To Could. Do not use for *once could* or *used to be able to.*

Very. Do not use as a modifier of a past participle, as in *very broken.* English idiom calls for *badly broken* or *very badly broken.*

Wait For, Wait On. To *wait for* means *to look forward to, to expect* (*For two hours I have waited for you*). To *wait on* means *to serve* (*The butler and two maids waited on the guests at dinner*).

Want In, Want Off, Want Out. These forms are dialectal. Do not use them for *want to come in, want to get off, want to get out.*

Way. Colloquial when used for *away* as in *Way down upon the Swanee River.*

Ways. Colloquial when used for *way* as in *a long ways to go.*

Whose, Who's. The possesive form is *whose* (*Whose book is this?*). *Who's* is a contraction of *who is* (*Who's at the door?*). The use of *whose* as a neuter possessive is confirmed by the history of the word and the practice of good writers. *The house whose roof is leaking* is more natural and less clumsy than *the house the roof of which is leaking.*

Your, You're. The possessive form is *your* (*Tell me your name*). *You're* is a contraction of *you are.*

Exercise 85   DICTION

Rewrite the following sentences, reducing wordiness as much as possible.

EXAMPLE: According to what the paper says, tomorrow's heat, in terms of unusually high temperature, will in all probability be a record-setting situation.

The paper says that tomorrow's high temperature will probably set a record.

1. I was going to take a hike, and my mother and father had decided to take a swim in the lake, but just about that time company arrived.

2. Carey exclaimed that he thought the itinerary for our trip through the English Lake District was equally as interesting as the itinerary of the Johnsons, and that, as a matter of fact, he preferred it more than he did theirs.

3. There is a mountain in North Carolina, and it is called King's Mountain, and one of the important battles of the Revolutionary War was fought there.

4. Harry's Rolls-Royce is silver in color and tremendous in size, and in terms of Harry's feelings about it, he is full of happiness and joy.

5. Skyline-wise, the city of Atlanta, Georgia, has changed and altered significantly during the last decade of ten years, as Mr. Franklin pointed out and mentioned to me at our conference several days ago last week.

6. I was very tired and shaky, but I continued to remain standing at the rear of the conference hall, and I thought my back would break if I did not sit down soon.

7. Margaret, I think that you should take into consideration your status salary-wise and try to come to some reasonable conclusion in terms of your future before you finalize your plans to change your job at this point in time.

8. Used for health purposes, regular exercise is beneficial to people in most cases.

9. In spite of the fact that he has been smoking for a period of twenty-five years, Arthur has announced that he is going to discontinue his use of tobacco and stop smoking immediately.

10. In a sneering manner Ruth laughed at our attempts to activate the motor and start it going, and she is one person whom I cannot help but dislike.

Exercise 86   DICTION

Rewrite the sentences below, reducing the wordiness as much as possible.

EXAMPLE: I would like to call your attention to the fact that it is time for the annual check-up that you should have every year with your doctor.

I should remind you that it is time for your annual physical check-up.

1. She was hostess for an annual party every spring, to which she invited everyone who was a friend of hers.

2. With a great deal of thoughtfulness Marguerite conveyed the information to her guests that the concert would commence to begin immediately with no further delay.

3. In discussing the relative merits of smooth versus chunky style peanut butter, I would say that I consider the chunky style to be infinitely superior to the smooth.

4. The Senator remarked that in cases where his constituents' welfare is concerned, he will firmly support a measure and stand squarely behind it.

5. His sport coat, which is of seersucker material, is somewhat short in length in terms of today's fashion.

6. Jim still persists in his statement that the consensus of opinion is in confirmation of his own views.

7. Please leave your luggage, coats, cameras, and etc., in the bus until we determine the necessary number of hotel rooms required for our group.

8. Our house, which is of the split-level variety, is made of red brick and is located on the corner of two streets, Elm Street and Tenth Street.

9. We really felt that it was an emergency situation, and we felt that it was absolutely necessary and essential that something be done in the case of Suzanne's terrible sunburn.

10. In my opinion, I think that John is reverting back to his childhood and wants to relive again those memorable teen-age days of his youth.

Exercise 87   DICTION

The following sentences contain one or more trite expressions or euphemisms. Underline the trite and euphemistic phrases and for each one write *T* or *E* in the space at the right.

EXAMPLE: It was <u>raining cats and dogs,</u> but Mother went ahead with her plans
to spend the day at the lake.   *T*
....

1. As luck would have it, Millie ran into Tom when she went on a date with
   Fred.   ....

2. Victorian ladies considered it improper for their limbs to be seen in public.   ....

3. My sister told me that she had a bone to pick with me about my wearing
   her new sweater without asking.   ....

4. First and foremost, in my humble opinion, is one's duty to his own beliefs.   ....

5. Billy got the tummy ache last night from eating green apples.   ....

6. It was a foregone conclusion that Albert was in for a rude awakening from
   his delusions of grandeur.   ....

7. Statistics show that many senior citizens must live in sub-standard housing.   ....

8. Walter got red as a beet when I suggested that there is more than meets the
   eye in his friendship with Eloise.   ....

9. He is a trusting soul who believes that every youthful offender is as innocent
   as a lamb.   ....

10. The tiny tots ran like streaks of lightning for the pool, having the time of
    their lives on that never-to-be-forgotten day.   ....

11. I am sorry to say that Charles was inebriated last night, although he will
    never admit that he is under the influence of alcohol.   ....

12. Mr. and Mrs. Williams are anticipating a blessed event in November; it goes
    without saying that they are hoping for a boy.   ....

13. The ominous silence that followed her statement indicated beyond the
    shadow of a doubt that Lady Luck had deserted her in her hour of need.   ....

14. We concluded, when we saw the wreath on the door, that the ninety-year-old
    man had gone to his reward.   ....

15. Mark rose to the occasion and did his usual masterly job of striking while the iron was hot.   ....

16. Everyone agreed that Coach Merriwell was a tower of strength when he urged the girls to get out there and give their all for the dear old Alma Mater.   ....

17. Jack had to admit that he was financially embarrassed when he asked to have dinner and spend the night in our humble abode.   ....

18. It struck Hank like a bolt from the blue when the manager terminated his employment.   ....

19. Jenny's parents are concerned that she is falling behind in her studies and also having trouble adjusting to her peer group.   ....

20. Most educationally disadvantaged children seem to come from families in the lower income bracket.   ....

B. Select any ten of the above sentences and replace the trite expressions and euphemisms with more suitable diction.

1. ....

....

2. ....

....

3. ....

....

4. ....

....

5. ....

....

6. ....

....

7. ....

....

8. ....

....

9. ....

....

10. ....

....

Exercise 88   DICTION

The following sentences contain unidiomatic uses of prepositions. Underline each preposition that is incorrectly used and write the correct form at the right.

EXAMPLE: Marcella was angry <u>with</u> the outcome of yesterday's election.   *about*

1. I hear that the reason of Tom's happiness is that he has just become engaged.   ....

2. Although the girls are sisters, Toni's interests differ with Marie's.   ....

3. The two men talked to great length about the need for a systematic approach to pollution control.   ....

4. John said to Ralph, "Just listen at that great clarinet of Benny Goodman's."   ....

5. After the mayor had agreed with the request for higher wages, the firefighters went back to work.   ....

6. The rivals were temporarily aligned to each other in their efforts for the common good.   ....

7. The leader of the scout troop made it clear that he expected cooperation in all members.   ....

8. I must say that I do not hold to the modern idea that doing one's own thing is all that matters.   ....

9. It is not easy for everyone to abide with the rules of good sportsmanship in the heat of a spirited game.   ....

10. As the screen star walked in the restaurant, all eyes followed him.   ....

11. William is pleased with his new skateboard, which he says is superior than his old one.   ....

12. The distinguished scientist spent her entire professional life in search for a cure for leukemia.   ....

13. Theo said that she waited thirty minutes on Frances before starting out alone.   ....

14. If you can think of a solution of the problem, please let me know.   ....

15. I think we should make every effort to comply to the request of the clean-up crew concerning trash.   ....

Exercise 89   DICTION

The following exercises (89–92) are based on the Glossary of Faulty Diction. Underline all errors and colloquialisms (informal expressions) and write the correct or preferred form at the right.

EXAMPLE: Irregardless of what Jan told you, I am sure that the beer
party starts at five o'clock.   *Regardless*

1. Dottie and myself went shopping in San Antonio and had lunch by the river.

2. Melissa handed her essay into her English teacher three days late.

3. Our friends the Sawyers immigrated to Australia last year, and they are quite happy there.

4. When washing a silk blouse, dip it thusly into warm soap suds, being careful not to wring it too vigorously.

5. I never dreamed that Connie was the type of person who would boldly flaunt the rules of social conduct.

6. Mother said that my gym instructor paid me a fine complement about my performance on the trampoline.

7. The amount of people gathered to listen to the politician's speech was pitifully small.

8. I have never seen a more disinterested group than the captive audience hearing about her pet poodle's newest trick.

9. The dreams of striking oil on the run-down old farm turned out to be just another bursted bubble.

10. We couldn't find a good campsite anyplace, so we decided to spend the night in our station wagon.

11. "No," Father said, "it is not alright for you to eat another hamburger."

12. I wish I knew which brand of toothpaste would really insure that I will have less cavities.

13. Can you think of any way that I can convince Maggie to have a blind date with Sam?

14. We have lots of time left before we need to leave for the airport. ....

15. The reason I like Donna is because she is unselfish. ....

Exercise 90   DICTION

Underline all errors and colloquialisms and write the correct or preferred form at the right.

EXAMPLE: Jerry was <u>pretty well</u> exhausted after wrestling with the boa
                    constrictor.   ....*quite*.........

1. The reason I don't feel well is because I ate three slices of watermelon.   ....

2. The pianist's final selection was a spritely Chopin waltz.   ....

3. I used to could twirl a baton, but lately I have lost the knack.   ....

4. "You are so right," Erica said, "in saying that Gus is catty."   ....

5. I am positive from the look in your eyes that your hiding something
   from me.   ....

6. Sue sent me some beautiful monogrammed stationary for Christmas.   ....

7. A television commercial says that Zesty Mustard compliments the
   flavor of a hamburger.   ....

8. "Reverend Fitzhugh, I thought you preached a lovely sermon," said
   Mrs. Calabash.   ....

9. My principle reason for writing is to inform you of a large inheritance.   ....

10. Her name, incidently, is spelled with two *b*'s.   ....

11. The two little girls couldn't hardly keep from giggling when they
    saw the dog wearing a straw hat.   ....

12. Won't it be wonderful when there is harmony between the countries
    of the world?   ....

13. If you are inferring that you disapprove of my actions, why not go
    ahead and say so?   ....

14. The dome of the capital is painted with gold leaf.   ....

15. Everyone knows that there are less calories in milk than in cream.   ....

16. I expect you think that I am behaving foolishly in entering the polka
    contest.   ....

17. Dad says that I'm apt to have trouble with my bicycle if I don't have the brakes adjusted. ....

18. It is aggravating to have to change a flat tire in the rain. ....

19. My brother is an alumni of the same college my father and grandfather attended. ....

20. I suppose it is alright for you to go swimming in the lake, but the water is very cold this time of year. ....

Exercise 91   DICTION

Underline all errors, colloquialisms, and trite expressions. Then write the correct or preferred form at the right.

EXAMPLE: The sheriff told the speeding driver that she was in
a <u>heap of</u> trouble.   *a great deal of*

1. It troubles me that I cannot agree with your suggestion that we
divide the money equally.   ....

2. His parents' support has had a wonderful affect on Frank's
attitude.   ....

3. Sports fans in Detroit are enthused about their hockey team,
the Red Wings.   ....

4. Some people like football, and some like baseball, but basket-
ball is my bag.   ....

5. And now, last but not least, I present our great coach, Fred
Abernathy, who will talk about sportsmanship.   ....

6. A tried and true method of making friends is being interested
in others.   ....

7. The two boys worked like Trojans to help their friend get his
motorboat running again.   ....

8. Eugenia is the only person I know who says that turnip greens
and cornbread really turn her on.   ....

9. I suspicioned that we were going to lose the game when I heard
that our starting quarterback had mumps.   ....

10. Mrs. Judkins wants to know if you are going to cut her grass this
week.   ....

11. Though we had not planned on staying overnight, the thunder
and lightning made us decide to stay.   ....

12. Rumors about who would be the new bishop spread like
wildfire through the town.   ....

13. Jim said he was sort of uneasy about his chances of getting the
job he had applied for.   ....

14. The group of educators returned from their conference with reports of a really meaningful dialogue.   ....

15. I was literally knocked off my feet when the judge fined me fifty dollars for littering.   ....

16. Johnny asked Joan to loan him her car for a week, but she refused him.   ....

17. Quick as a wink, I accepted Matt's proposal of marriage.   ....

18. Margie's last impractical scheme involves selling frozen yogurt at the sidwalk art exhibit.   ....

19. Judy fell hook, line, and sinker for Jack's charm; no one else ever interested her.   ....

20. To make a long story short, they fell in love and were married last June.   ....

Exercise 92   DICTION

Underline all errors and colloquialisms. Then write the correct or preferred form at the right.

EXAMPLE: I am surprised that Peter is <u>disinterested</u> in going to camp
this year.   *uninterested*
....

1. Terry kept warning Lucy that those kind of tactics never succeeds.   ....

2. That woman spends money like she had a million dollars.   ....

3. I may can get Doris to lend us her pocket calculator just for
tonight.   ....

4. Lots of people actually enjoy backpacking, although I am not
among them.   ....

5. The grouchy old man ordered the young people off of his
property.   ....

6. Lars is one of a family of Danes who emigrated here to the United
States in 1950.   ....

7. We all think that Marianna should cook the steaks being as she
has had experience.   ....

8. Annette's slice of cake was equally as big as Dan's, but Annette
has a bigger appetite.   ....

9. Mother was horrified when she accidently threw her diamond
ring into the garbage disposal.   ....

10. The police detective maintained that the suspect's alibi was not
creditable.   ....

11. The Talmadges will contact us when the time comes for our trip
to the mountains.   ....

12. Miriam's parents were awfully proud of her excellent performance
in the swimming meet.   ....

13. I will try to persuade Mr. Levenson that our approach to the sales
promotion is a sound one.   ....

14. Newspaper journalism is a media that requires broad knowledge
and great precision of its practitioners.   ....

15. Jed's pants were very torn after his encounter with the English bulldog.

    ....

16. We could see the two boys way across the lake, swimming toward the opposite shore.

    ....

17. No one seems to know yet whose going to be appointed to the Board of Regents.

    ....

18. Henry said that he would of been glad to baby sit for us if he had known we needed him.

    ....

19. That modern sculpture in front of the libary is supposed to be the stature of a woman.

    ....

20. Quite a few people have signed up for the community arts program that our club is sponsoring.

    ....

Building 23
a Vocabulary

As you know from your own experience, one of your greatest needs for successful composition is to improve your vocabulary. One of the best ways to build a vocabulary, of course, is always to look up in a dictionary the meanings of unfamiliar words which you hear spoken or come across in your reading. This chapter on vocabulary will provide you with a minimal body of information concerning word formation and the derivations of the various words which comprise the English language. For a more intensified study of all aspects of this fascinating subject, including ways to strengthen your own vocabulary, consult and use frequently a book devoted exclusively to this purpose.

Learning the derivation of a word will fix in your mind the meaning and spelling of that word. Since the largest part of our English vocabulary comes from three main sources—the Anglo-Saxon, the Greek, and the Latin languages—a knowledge of commonly used prefixes, roots, and suffixes from these languages will prove very useful.

A **prefix** is a short element, a syllable or syllables, that comes before the main part of the word, which is the **root**. A **suffix** is added to the end of the word. Thus the word *hypodermic* has *hypo-*, meaning "under," as its *prefix*; *derm*, meaning "skin," as its *root*; and *-ic*, meaning "having to do with," as its *suffix*. You see that the *prefix* and *suffix* of a word modify the meaning of the *root*. The word, then, *hypodermic,* when used as an adjective, means "having to do with something under the skin."

So basic is Anglo-Saxon that, though the words of classical origin outnumber those from Anglo-Saxon, we use most commonly in our speech words of Anglo-Saxon origin. For instance, the Anglo-Saxon prefixes *un-* (not) and *for-* (from) are found in many of our words, such as *unfair* and *forbid.* The Anglo-Saxon root word *hlaf* (loaf) gives us the word *lord*, a lord being a loafkeeper or warden (*hlaf-weard*). The root word *god* (God) gives us *goodbye*, a contraction of *God be with ye.* Anglo-Saxon suffixes such as *-ish* (having the qualities of) and *-ly* (like) are seen in many words such as *foolish* and *courtly.*

If you combine the Greeek root *tele*, meaning "at a distance," with *graph* (writing), *phone* (sound), *scope* (seeing), *pathy* (feeling), you have *telegraph* (writing at a distance), *telephone* (sound at a distance), *telescope* (seeing at a distance), *telepathy* (feeling at a distance).

The Latin root *duc* is seen in such words as *adduce, aqueduct, conduce, conduct, induce, produce, reduce, seduce, conductor, ducal,* and *ductile.* If you know that *duc* means "to lead," and if you know the meanings of the prefixes and suffixes combined with it, you can make out the meanings of most of these words.

Each prefix, root, and suffix that you learn may lead to a knowledge of many new words or give a clearer understanding of many you already know. Therefore, a list of some of the most common prefixes, roots, and suffixes is given below. Look up others in your dictionary, or as suggested earlier, get a good vocabulary text book and use it often.

23a Prefixes

Prefixes Showing Number or Amount

BI– (*bis–*) two	*(bi)*annual, *(bis)*sextile
CENT– (*centi–*) hundred	*(cent)*enarian, *(centi)*pede
DEC– (*deca–*) ten	*(dec)*ade, *(Deca)*logue
HEMI– half	*(hemi)*sphere, *(hemi)*stich
MILLI– (*mille–*) thousand	*(milli)*on, *(mille)*nnium
MULTI– many, much	*(multi)*form, *(multi)*graph
MON– (*mono–*) one	*(mono)*gyny, *(mono)*tone
OCTA– (*octo–*) eight	*(octa)*ve, *(octo)*pus
PAN– all	*(pan)*acea, *(pan)*demonium, *(pan)*orama
PENTA– five	*(penta)*gon, *(Penta)*teuch
POLY– much, many	*(poly)*glot, *(poly)*chrome
PROT– (*proto–*) first	*(prot)*agonist, *(proto)*type
SEMI– half	*(semi)*circle, *(semi)*final
TRI– three	*(tri)*angle, *(tri)*ad
UNI– one	*(uni)*fy, *(uni)*cameral

Prefixes Showing Relationship in Place and Time

AB– (*a–, abs–*) from, away from	*(a)*vert, *(ab)*sent, *(abs)*tract
AD– (*ac–, af–, al–, ag–, an–, ap–, ar–, as–, at–*) to, at	*(ad)*mit, *(ac)*cede, *(af)*fect, *(al)*lude, *(ag)*gregate, *(an)*nounce, *(ap)*pear, *(ar)*rive, *(as)*sume, *(at)*tain
AMB– (*ambi–*) around, both	*(ambi)*dextrous, *(ambi)*guous
ANTE– before	*(ante)*cedent, *(ante)*date
ANTI– (*ant–*) against	*(anti)*thesis, *(ant)*agonist
CATA– away, against, down	*(cata)*clysm, *(cata)*strophe
CIRCUM– around, about	*(circum)*scribe, *(circum)*stance
CON– (*com–, col–, cor–*) with, together, at the same time	*(con)*tract, *(com)*pete, *(col)*league, *(cor)*relate
CONTRA– (*counter–*) opposite, against	*(contra)*dict, *(counter)*mand
DE– from, away from, down	*(de)*pend, *(de)*form, *(de)*tract
DIA– through, across	*(dia)*gram, *(dia)*meter
DIS– (*di, dif–*) off, away from	*(dis)*tract, *(di)*verge, *(dif)*fuse
EN– (*em–, in-*) in, into	*(en)*counter, *(em)*brace, *(in)*duct
EPI– on, over, among, outside	*(epi)*dermis, *(epi)*demic
EX– (*e–, ec–, ef–*) out of, from	*(ex)*pel, *(e)*lect, *(ec)*centric, *(ef)*face

EXTRA–*(extro–)* outside, beyond *(extra)*mural, *(extro)*vert
HYPO– under *(hypo)*dermic, *(hypo)*crite
INTER– among, between, within *(inter)*fere, *(inter)*rupt
INTRO– *(intra–)* within *(intro)*spection, *(intra)*mural
OB– *(oc–, of–, op–)* against, to, before *(ob)*ject, *(oc)*casion, *(of)*fer, *(op)*press
   toward
PER– through, by *(per)*ceiver, *(per)*ennial
PERI– around, about *(peri)*meter, *(peri)*odical
POST– after *(post)*script, *(post)*erity
PRE– before *(pre)*cedent, *(pre)*decessor
PRO– before in time or position *(pro)*logue, *(pro)*bate
RETRO– back, backward *(retro)*gress, *(retro)*spect
SE– aside, apart *(se)*clude, *(se)*duce
SUB– *(suc–, suf–, sug–, sum–, sup–,* *(sub)*scribe, *(suc)*cumb, *(suf)*fer, *(sug)*-
   sus–) under, below   gest, *(sum)*mon, *(sup)*pose, *(sus)*pect
SUPER– *(sur–)* above, over *(super)*sede, *(super)*b, *(sur)*pass
TRANS– *(tra–, traf–, tres–)* across *(trans)*port, *(tra)*vesty, *(traf)*fic, *(tres)*-
   pass
ULTRA– beyond *(ultra)*marine, *(ultra)*modern

Prefixes Showing Negation

A– *(an–)* without *(an)*onymous, *(a)*theist
IN– *(ig–, im–, il–, ir–)* not *(in)*accurate, *(ig)*nore, *(im)*pair, *(il)*-
   legal, *(ir)*responsible
NON– not *(non)*essential, *(non)*entity
UN– not *(un)*tidy, *(un)*happy

23b   Greek Roots

ARCH	chief, rule	*(arch)*bishop, an*(archy)*, mon*(archy)*
AUTO	self	*(auto)*graph, *(auto)*mobile, *(auto)*matic
BIO	life	*(bio)*logy, *(bio)*graphy, *(bio)*chemistry
CAU(S)T	burn	*(caust)*ic, holo*(caust)*, *(caut)*erize
CHRON(O)	time	*(chron)*icle, *(chron)*ic, *(chrono)*logy
COSM(O)	order, arrangement	*(cosm)*os, *(cosm)*ic, *(cosmo)*graphy
CRIT	judge, discern	*(crit)*ic, *(crit)*erion
DEM(O)	people	*(demo)*crat, *(demo)*cracy, *(dem)*agogue
DERM	skin	epi*(dermis)*, *(derm)*a, pachy*(derm)*, *(derm)*-ophobe
DYN(A) (M)	power	*(dynam)*ic, *(dynam)*o, *(dyn)*asty
GRAPH	write	auto*(graph)*, *(graph)*ic, geo*(graphy)*
HIPPO	horse	*(hippo)*potamus, *(hippo)*drome
HYDR(O)	water	*(hydr)*ant, *(hydr)*a, *(hydro)*gen
LOG(Y), LOGUE	saying, science	*(log)*ic, bio*(logy)*, eu*(logy)*, dia*(logue)*
MET(E)R	measure	thermo*(meter)*, speedo*(meter)*, *(metr)*ic
MICRO	small	*(micro)*be, *(micro)*scope, *(micro)*cosm
MOR(O)	fool	*(moro)*n, sopho*(more)*
NYM	name	ano*(nym)*ous, pseudo*(nym)*
PATH	experience, suffer	a*(path)*y, sym*(path)*y, *(path)*os

PED	child	*(ped)*agogue, *(ped)*ant, *(ped)*iatrician
PHIL	love	*(phil)*antrophy, *(phil)*osophy, *(phil)*ander
PHON(O)	sound	*(phono)*graph, *(phon)*etic, *(phono)*gram
PSYCH(O)	mind, soul	*(psycho)*logy, *(psych)*ic, *(Psych)*e
SOPH	wisdom	philo*(sopher)*, *(soph)*ist, *(soph)*istication
THEO	God	*(theo)*logy, *(theo)*sophy, *(theo)*cratic
THERM	heat	*(therm)*ostat, *(therm)*ometer, *(therm)*os

23c Latin Roots

AM	love	*(am)*ity, *(am)*orist, *(am)*orous
ANIM	breath, soul, spirit	*(anim)*al, *(anim)*ate, un*(anim)*ous
AQU(A)	water	*(aqu)*educt, *(aqua)*tic, *(aqua)*rium
AUD	hear	*(aud)*itor, *(aud)*ience, *(aud)*itorium
CAPIT	head	*(capit)*al, *(capit)*ate, *(capit)*alize
CAP(T), CEP(T), CIP(T)	take	*(cap)*tive, pre*(cept)*, pre*(cip)*itate
CED, CESS	go, yield	ante*(ced)*ent, con*(cede)*, ex*(cess)*ive
CENT	hundred	*(cent)*ury, *(cent)*urion, per*(cent)*(age)
CER(N), CRI(M,T), CRE(M,T)	separate, judge, choose	dis*(cern)*, *(crim)*inal, dis*(crete)*
CRED	believe, trust	*(cred)*it, in*(cred)*ible, *(cred)*ulity
CLAR	clear, bright	*(clar)*ity, *(clar)*ify, de*(clar)*ation
CORD	heart	dis*(cord)*, con*(cord)*, *(cord)*ial
CORP(OR)	body, substance	*(corpor)*al, *(corp)*se, *(corp)*ulent
DON	give	*(don)*or, *(don)*ate
DOM(IN)	tame, subdue	*(domin)*ant, *(domin)*ate, *(domin)*ion
DORM	sleep	*(dorm)*ant, *(dorm)*itory, *(dorm)*ient
DUC	lead	con*(duc)*t, *(duc)*tile, aque*(duc)*t
FER	bear	in*(fer)*ence, *(fer)*tile, re*(fer)*
FORT	strong	*(fort)*ress, *(fort)*e, *(fort)*itude
FRAG, FRING FRACT	break	*(frag)*ile, in*(fring)*e, *(fract)*ure
GEN	beget, origin	en*(gen)*der, con*(gen)*ital, *(gen)*-eration
JAC(T), JEC(T)	cast	e*(jac)*ulate, pro*(ject)*, e*(ject)*
LATE	carry	col*(late)*, vacil*(late)*, re*(late)*
MI(SS,T)	send	dis*(miss)*, *(miss)*ionary, re*(mit)*
NOMIN, NOMEN	name	*(nomin)*ate, *(nomen)*clature
NOV	new	*(nov)*el, *(nov)*ice, in*(nov)*ation
PED	foot	*(ped)*al, centi*(pede)*, *(ped)*estrian
PLEN, PLET	full	*(plen)*ty, *(plen)*itude, re*(plete)*
PORT	bear	*(port)*er, de*(port)*, im*(port)*ance
POTENT	able, powerful	*(potent)*, *(potent)*ial, *(potent)*ate
SECT	cut	dis*(sect)*, in*(sect)*, *(sect)*ion

23d Suffixes

NOUN SUFFIXES

1. *Suffixes Denoting an Agent*

   —ANT (*—ent*) one who, that which ten*(ant)*, ag*(ent)*
   —AR (*—er*) one who schol*(ar)*, farm*(er)*
   —ARD (*—art*) one who (often deprecative) cow*(ard)*, bragg*(art)*
   —EER one who privat*(eer)*, auction*(eer)*
   —ESS a woman who waitr*(ess)*, seamstr*(ess)*
   —IER (*—yer*) one who cash*(ier)*, law*(yer)*
   —IST one who novel*(ist)*, Commun*(ist)*
   —OR one who, that which act*(or)*, tract*(or)*
   —STER one who, that which young*(ster)*, road*(ster)*

2. *Suffix Denoting the Receiver of an Action*

   —EE one who is the object of some action appoint*(ee)*, divorc*(ee)*

3. *Suffixes Denoting Smallness or Diminutiveness*

   —CULE (*—cle*) mole*(cule)*, ventri*(cle)*
   —ETTE din*(ette)*, cigar*(ette)*
   —LET ring*(let)*, brace*(let)*
   —LING duck*(ling)*, prince*(ling)*

4. *Suffixes Denoting Place*

   —ARY indicating location or repository diction*(ary)*, api*(ary)*
   —ERY place or establishment bak*(ery)*, nunn*(ery)*
   —ORY (*—arium, —orium*) place for, concerned
   with dormit*(ory)*), audit*(orium)*

5. *Suffixes Denoting Act, State, Quality,*
   or Condition

   —ACY denoting quality, state accur*(acy)*, delic*(acy)*
   —AL pertaining to action refus*(al)*, deni*(al)*
   —ANCE (*—ancy*) denoting action or state brilli*(ance)*, buoy*(ancy)*
   —ATION denoting result migr*(ation)*, el*(ation)*
   —DOM denoting a general condition wis*(dom)*, bore*(dom)*
   —ENCE (*—ency*) state, quality of abstin*(ence)*, consist*(ency)*
   —ERY denoting quality, action fool*(ery)*, prud*(ery)*
   —HOOD state, quality knight*(hood)*, false*(hood)*
   —ICE condition or quality serv*(ice)*, just*(ice)*
   —ION (*—sion*) state or condition un*(ion)*, ten*(sion)*
   —ISM denoting action, state, or condition bapt*(ism)*, plagiar*(ism)*
   —ITY (*—ety*) action, state, or condition joll*(ity)*, gai*(ety)*
   —MENT action or state resulting from punish*(ment)*, frag*(ment)*

—NESS quality, state of	good*(ness)*, prepared*(ness)*
—OR denoting action, state, or quality	hon*(or)*, lab*(or)*
—TH pertaining to condition, state, or action	warm*(th)*, steal*(th)*
—URE denoting action, result, or instrument	legislat*(ure)*, pleas*(ure)*

ADJECTIVES SUFFIXES

—ABLE (*–ible, –ile*) capable of being	lov*(able)*, ed*(ible)*, contract*(ile)*
—AC relating to, like	elegi*(ac)*, cardi*(ac)*
—ACIOUS inclined to	pugn*(acious)*, aud*(acious)*
—AL pertaining to	radic*(al)*, cordi*(al)*
—AN pertaining to	sylv*(an)*, urb*(an)*
—ANT (*–ent*) inclined to	pleas*(ant)*, converg*(ent)*
—AR pertaining to	sol*(ar)*, regul*(ar)*
—ARY pertaining to	contr*(ary)*, revolution*(ary)*
—ATIVE inclined to	demonstr*(ative)*, talk*(ative)*
—FUL full of	joy*(ful)*, pain*(ful)*
—IC (*–ical*) pertaining to	volcan*(ic)*, angel*(ical)*
—ISH like, relating to, being	devil*(ish)*, boy*(ish)*
—IVE inclined to, having the nature of	elus*(ive)*, nat*(ive)*
—LESS without, unable to be	piti*(less)*, resist*(less)*
—OSE full of	bellic*(ose)*, mor*(ose)*
—OUS full of	pi*(ous)*, fam*(ous)*
—ULENT (*–olent*) full of	fraud*(ulent)*, vi*(olent)*

VERB SUFFIXES

The following verb suffixes usually mean "to make" (to become, to increase, etc.).

—ATE	toler*(ate)*, vener*(ate)*
—EN	madd*(en)*, wid*(en)*
—FY	magni*(fy)*, beauti*(fy)*
—IZE (*–ise*)	colon*(ize)*, exerc*(ise)*

Exercise 93   WORD ANALYSIS: PREFIXES

Break the following English words into their parts, and give the literal meaning of each part as derived from its source. Consult the lists of prefixes and roots given on previous pages. Use your dictionary if you find a part not given in these lists. Be able to use each word in a sentence.

WORD	PREFIX (and literal meaning)	ROOT (and literal meaning)	MEANING OF WHOLE WORD
bicycle	*bi*, two	*cycle*, wheel	two-wheeled vehicle
abhor			
absent			
adapt			
addict			
admire			
advertise			
anarchy			
antacid			
antecedent			

WORD	PREFIX (and literal meaning)	ROOT (and literal meaning)	MEANING OF WHOLE WORD
anticlimax	....	....	....
			....
autobiography	....	....	....
			....
bicentennial	....	....	....
			....
biology	....	....	....
			....
chronological	....	....	....
			....
circumference	....	....	....
			....
circulate	....	....	....
			....
collide	....	....	....
			....
combine	....	....	....
			....
contradict	....	....	....
			....
contrast	....	....	....
			....

WORD	PREFIX (and literal meaning)	ROOT (and literal meaning)	MEANING OF WHOLE WORD
controversial	....	....	....
counteract	....	....	....
derive	....	....	....
hypothesis	....	....	....
intercept	....	....	....
malignant	....	....	....
postgraduate	....	....	....
precaution	....	....	....
surpass	....	....	....
transparent	....	....	....

Exercise 94   WORD ANALYSIS: SUFFIXES

Break the following English words into their parts, and give the literal meaning of each part as derived from its source. Consult the lists of suffixes and roots given on previous pages. Use your dictionary if you find a part not given in these lists. Be able to use each word in a sentence.

WORD	ROOT (and literal meaning)	SUFFIX (and literal meaning)	MEANING OF WHOLE WORD
amplify	*ampli*, large	*fy*, to make	to increase, make large
amazement			
braggart			
changeable			
clannish			
complicate			
corrective			
darkness			
dependent			
dissonance			

WORD	ROOT (and literal meaning)	SUFFIX (and literal meaning)	MEANING OF WHOLE WORD
engineer	....	....	....
			....
foundling	....	....	....
			....
hardship	....	....	....
			....
heroism	....	....	....
			....
historic	....	....	....
			....
joyous	....	....	....
			....
legal	....	....	....
			....
legible	....	....	....
			....
library	....	....	....
			....
lubricant	....	....	....
			....
missionary	....	....	....
			....

WORD	ROOT (and literal meaning)	SUFFIX (and literal meaning)	MEANING OF WHOLE WORD
nominee	....	....	....
			....
nutrition	....	....	....
			....
observation	....	....	....
			....
occurrence	....	....	....
			....
penalize	....	....	....
			....
pianist	....	....	....
			....
roadster	....	....	....
			....
satisfy	....	....	....
			....
sensitivity	....	....	....
			....
tactless	....	....	....
			....
wisdom	....	....	....
			....

Exercise 95   WORD ANALYSIS

For each root listed below write the meaning and at least three words containing the root. Do not use the same word with two roots. Be able to explain the meaning of the root as related to the word.

ROOT	MEANING	WORDS CONTAINING ROOT
graph	*write*	*autograph, graphic, telegraph*
ann, enn		
cept		
cur(r), curs		
dic, dict		
duc		
fac(t)		
fer		
fin		
fort		
logue, log(y)		
miss, mit(t)		
pend, pens		
phon		
potent		
script, scrib		
tele		
theo		
tors		

ROOT	MEANING	WORDS CONTAINING ROOT
vert, vers	....	....
vid, vis	....	....
viv	....	....

Exercise 96   VOCABULARY: PREFIXES AND SUFFIXES

A. Underline the prefix in each of the following words, give its meaning, and use the word in a sentence so as to show the meaning of the prefix.

	MEANING OF PREFIX	SENTENCE
<u>sub</u>way	*under*	*A complex network of subway tracks lies under New York City.*
1. aquarium	....	....
2. audition	....	....
3. automatic	....	....
4. biography	....	....
5. chronic	....	....
6. dermatitis	....	....
7. octagonal	....	....
8. pediatrician	....	....

	MEANING OF PREFIX	SENTENCE
9. prewar	....	....
10. semicircle	....	....

B. In the following list of words underline each suffix, give its meaning, and use the word in a sentence.

	MEANING OF SUFFIX	SENTENCE
lyricist	*one who*	*Johnny Mercer, the lyricist whose songs are well known, was from Savannah, Georgia.*
1. glamorous	....	....
2. edible	....	....
3. boredom	....	....
4. motherhood	....	....
5. stupidity	....	....
6. waitress	....	....

	MEANING OF SUFFIX	SENTENCE
7. painful	....	....
8. lengthen	....	....
9. honor	....	....
10. democracy	....	....

Exercise 97   VOCABULARY: LATIN AND GREEK ROOTS

A. Use derivatives of *arch* meaning "chief, leader, rule," to complete the following sentences:

1. The .... of a country is its sole and single ruler.

2. The form of government in which the ruling power belongs to a few persons is called an ....

3. A chief duke, especially a prince of a former Austrian royal family, has the title of ....

4. An .... is an angel of the highest rank.

5. A specialist who designs buildings and supervises construction is an ....

B. Use derivatives of *cred*, meaning "believe, trust," to complete the following sentences:

1. When a person shows doubt or disbelief, seeming incapable of belief, he is said to be ....

2. Letters given a person for the purpose of proving that he has a right to be trusted are called ....

3. A .... , sometimes known as a confession of faith, is a brief statement of religious or moral belief.

4. Something which is worthy of being believed may be described as ....

5. A person to whom one is indebted in his ....

C. Use derivatives of *gen*, meaning "beget, origin," to complete the following sentences:

1. In grammar nouns and pronouns are grouped by .... , according to their sex or lack of it.

2. The recorded history of one's ancestors is a ....

3. A race, species, kind, or class of anything may be called a................................. .

4. A study of .... involves reference to the origin of something.

5. In Great Britain people of good birth and social standing, those ranking just below the nobility, are known as the ....

D. Use derivatives of *hydro*, meaning "water," to complete the following sentences:

1. A fireplug, which is a large pipe with a valve for drawing water, is also called a
....

2. .... , an abnormal fear of water, is another name for rabies.

3. Removal of water from fruits or vegetables in order to preserve them is the process of
....

4. The production of electricity by water power is called .... power.

5. A .... is a winglike structure attached to the hull of a boat, lifting it
off the water and causing it to skim along at great speed.

Spelling 24

Spelling is an important aspect of written communication. Instructors seldom have the opportunity, however, to spend adequate classroom time on the subject. The responsibility for the mastery of spelling, therefore, rests almost solely on the individual student.

Here are a few practical suggestions on how to approach the problem of spelling:

1. Always use the dictionary when you are in doubt about the spelling of a word.
2. If there is a rule applicable to the type of words which you misspell, learn that rule.
3. Employ any "tricks" which might assist you in remembering the spelling of particular words that give you trouble. If, for example, you confuse the meaning and hence the spelling of *statue* and *stature,* remember that the longer word refers to bodily "longness." Certain troublesome words can be spelled correctly if you will remember their prefixes (as in *dis/appoint*) or their suffixes (as in *cool/ly*). Also it might help you to remember that there are only three *-ceed* words: *exceed, proceed,* and *succeed.*
4. Keep a list of the words which you misspell. In writing down these words, observe their syllabication and any peculiarities of construction. Try to "see" — that is, to have a mental picture of — these words.
5. Practice the correct pronunciation of troublesome words. Misspelling is often the result of mispronunciation.

Of the many rules governing spelling four are particularly useful since they are widely applicable. Study these four rules carefully.

24a   Final *e*

Drop the final *e* before a suffix beginning with a vowel (*-ing, -ous,* etc.) but retain the final *e* before a suffix beginning with a consonant (*-ment, -ly,* etc.):

Final *e* dropped: come + ing = coming
fame + ous = famous

love + able = lovable
guide + ance = guidance

Final *e* retained: move + ment = movement
fate + ful = fateful
sole + ly = solely

EXCEPTIONS: Acknowledge, acknowledgment; abridge, abridgment; judge, judgment; dye, dyeing; singe, singeing; hoe, hoeing; mile, mileage; due, duly; awe, awful; whole, wholly. The final **e** is retained after **c** or **g** when the suffix begins with **a** or **o**: peace, peaceable; courage, courageous.

24b   Final Consonant

Double a final consonant before a suffix beginning with a vowel if (1) the word is of one syllable or is accented on the last syllable and (2) the final consonant is preceded by a single vowel:

Word of one syllable: stop + ed = stopped

Word in which the accent falls on the last syllable: occur + ence = occurrence

Word in which the accent does not fall on the last syllable: differ + ence = difference

24c   *ei* and *ie*

When **ei** and **ie** have the long **ee** sound (as in *keep*), use **i** before **e** except after **c**. (The word *lice* will aid you in remembering this rule; **i** follows **l** and all other consonants except **c**, while **e** follows **c**.)

ie	*ei* (after *c*)
chief	ceiling
field	receive
niece	deceive
siege	conceit

EXCEPTIONS (grouped to form a sentence): Neither financier seized either species of weird leisure.

24d   Final *y*

In words ending in *y* preceded by a consonant, change the *y* to *i* before any suffix except one beginning with *i*.

Suffix beginning with a letter other than *i*:

fly + es = flies
ally + es = allies
easy + ly = easily
mercy + ful = merciful
study + ous = studious

Suffix beginning with *i*:

fly + ing = flying
study + ing = studying

24e   Spelling List

The following list is made up of approximately 450 frequently misspelled words. Since these are commonly used words, you should learn to spell all of them after you have mastered the words on your individual list.

absence	audience	competent	dining
academic	autumn	competition	diphtheria
accept	auxiliary	complement	disappear
accidentally	awkward	completely	disappoint
accommodate	bankruptcy	compliment	disastrous
accumulate	barbarous	compulsory	discipline
accustomed	becoming	confident	discussion
acknowledge	beginning	congratulate	disease
acquaintance	believe	connoisseur	dissatisfied
across	beneficial	conqueror	dissipate
address	benefited	conscience	distribute
advantage	brilliant	conscientious	divine
aggravate	Britain	conscious	division
allege	buoyant	contemptible	dormitories
all right	bureau	continuous	drudgery
altogether	business	convenient	dual
always	cafeteria	coolly	duchess
amateur	calendar	council	duel
among	camouflage	counsel	dyeing
amount	candidate	courteous	dying
analysis	captain	criticism	ecstasy
angel	carburetor	curiosity	efficiency
anonymous	carriage	curriculum	eighth
anxiety	cavalry	dealt	eligible
any more	ceiling	deceit	eliminate
apology	cemetery	decide	embarrassed
apparatus	certain	defendant	eminent
apparent	changeable	definite	emphasize
appearance	characteristic	dependent	enthusiastic
appreciate	chauffeur	descend	environment
appropriate	choose	descent	equipped
arctic	chosen	describe	equivalent
argument	clothes	description	erroneous
arithmetic	colloquial	desert	especially
around	colonel	desirable	exaggerate
arrangement	column	despair	excellent
ascend	coming	desperate	except
assassin	commission	dessert	exercise
association	committee	dictionary	exhaust
athletics	comparative	dietitian	exhilaration
attendance	compel	difference	existence
attractive	compelled	dilapidated	expel

expelled	immediately	momentous	permanent
experience	incidentally	morale	permissible
explanation	independence	mortgage	perseverance
extraordinary	indispensable	murmur	persistent
familiar	inevitable	muscle	personal
fascinate	infinite	mysterious	personnel
February	influential	naturally	perspiration
finally	innocence	necessary	persuade
financial	instance	nevertheless	physically
financier	instant	nickel	physician
forehead	intellectual	niece	picnicking
foreign	intelligence	ninety	piece
foreword	intentionally	ninth	pleasant
forfeit	interested	noticeable	politician
formally	irrevelant	notoriety	politics
formerly	irresistible	nowadays	politicking
forth	its	nucleus	possession
forty	it's	obedience	possible
fourth	judgment	obstacle	practically
fraternity	kindergarten	occasion	precede
friend	knowledge	occasionally	preference
fulfill	laboratory	occurrence	preferred
fundamental	led	o'clock	prejudice
futile	legitimate	off	preparation
furniture	leisure	omission	prevalent
gauge	library	omitted	principal
generally	likable	operate	principle
genius	literature	opinion	privilege
government	livelihood	opportunity	probably
grammar	loose	optimism	procedure
granddaughter	lose	organization	professor
grandeur	lovable	original	prominent
grievance	magazine	outrageous	pronunciation
guarantee	maintain	overrun	propaganda
handkerchief	maintenance	paid	psychology
harass	maneuver	pamphlet	publicly
having	manual	parallel	purchase
height	manufacture	paralysis	pursue
hindrance	mathematics	paralyzed	quantity
hitchhike	meant	parliament	quarter
hoping	medicine	particularly	questionnaire
hygiene	mediocre	partner	quiet
hypocrisy	miniature	passed	quite
illusion	mirror	past	quiz
imaginary	mischievous	pastime	quizzes
imitation	misspell	perform	realize

really
recognize
recommend
region
reign
relevant
religious
remembrance
repetition
representative
resistance
respectfully
respectively
restaurant
rhetoric
rheumatism
ridiculous
sacrifice
sacrilegious
salable
salary
sandwich
schedule
science
secretary

seize
sense
sentence
separate
sergeant
severely
sheriff
shining
shriek
siege
significant
similar
sincerely
sophomore
source
speak
specimen
speech
stationary
stationery
statue
stature
statute
strength
strenuous

stretch
studying
superintendent
supersede
surprise
susceptible
syllable
symmetry
temperature
tendency
their
thorough
too
tournament
tragedy
transferred
tremendous
truly
Tuesday
twelfth
tying
tyranny
unanimous
undoubtedly
universally

unnecessary
until
unusual
using
usually
vaccine
vacuum
valuable
vegetable
vengeance
vigilance
vigorous
village
villain
weather
Wednesday
weird
whether
who's
whose
women
writing
written

Exercise 98   SPELLING

A. Combine the specified suffix with each of the following words and write the correct form in the blank space.

EXAMPLE: move + ing   ....*moving*...............

1. fry + ed   ....

2. begin + ing   ....

3. apply + ance   ....

4. come + ing   ....

5. valley + s   ....

6. lovely + ness   ....

7. excite + able   ....

8. apology + ize   ....

9. assure + ance   ....

10. defy + ance   ....

11. announce + er   ....

12. create + or   ....

13. shine + ing   ....

14. dye + ing   ....

15. grieve + ous   ....

16. value + able   ....

17. journey + s   ....

18. activity + s   ....

19. win + er   ....

20. differ + ent   ....

21. transmit + ed   ....

22. forgot + en   ....

23. lie + ing   ....

24. victory + ous   ....

25. persecute + ion   ....

26. endure + ance   ....

27. justify + ed   ....

28. travel + er   ....

29. desire + able   ....

30. arrive + al   ....

B. Supply *ie* **or** *ei* **in each of the following words. Then write the correct form in the blank space.**

EXAMPLE: rec*ei*ve   ....*receive*.........

1. dec__t   ....

2. __ther   ....

3. l__sure   ....

4. fr__ght   ....

5. gr__f   ....

6. v__n   ....

7. n__ce   ....

8. y__ld   ....

9. shr__k   ....

10. pr__st   ....

11. th__r   ....

12. sh__ld ....

13. p__˙rce ....

14. c__ling ....

15. sl__gh ....

16. f__nd ....

17. ach__vement ....

18. front__r ....

19. l__utenant ....

20. w__rd ....

Exercise 99   SPELLING

If there is a misspelled word in any line of five words given below, underline it and write it correctly at the right. If all five words are correctly spelled, write *C* in the blank.

EXAMPLE: quarter, speech, fraternity, <u>permanant</u>, purchase   ....*permanent*............

1. accidentally, enthusiastic, advantadge, confident, ceiling   ....

2. atheletics, around, desirable, eliminate, council   ....

3. laboratory, relevant, mirrow, region, symmetry   ....

4. persuade, ridiculous, carriage, carburator, exercise   ....

5. descent, concience, dealt, shining, villain   ....

6. unusual, subordination, untill, source, remembrance   ....

7. restaraunt, unnecessary, tournament, personnel, similar   ....

8. sophomore, grievous, arouse, questionnaire, recede   ....

9. picnicking, license, mischievious, heroes, category   ....

10. hypocrite, frantically, lightening, earnest, condemn   ....

11. monotonous, maintenance, interrupt, proceed, fullfil   ....

12. loneliness, fiery, incessant, occurence, muscle   ....

13. rheumatism, rememberance, forfeit, quantity, lose   ....

14. guarantee, handkerchief, original, incidently, eighth   ....

15. dessert, dilapidated, Britian, colonel, arithmetic   ....

16. cemetery, ecstacy, discipline, compel, barbarous   ....

17. column, enviroment, conqueror, assassin, erroneous   ....

18. buoyant, undoubtedly, writting, studying, ninth   ....

19. paralyzed, operate, procedure, overrun, misspell   ....

20. tradgedy, repetition, quizzes, psychology, infinite   ....

21. supersede, mortgage, morale, mathematics, nuculus   ....

22. grammar, hypocrisy, grandeur, harrass, leisure   ....

23. sacrilegious, prejudice, forword, livelihood, parallel   ....

24. campaign, control, acquitted, payed, rhythm, receive   ....

25. fourth, extraordinary, exhilaration, congradulate, sandwich   ....

Exercise 100   SPELLING

Underline any word which is misspelled. Then write it correctly at the right. If a sentence contains no misspelled word, write *C* in the blank.

EXAMPLE: The camp counselor thought it best to <u>seperate</u> the
quarreling boys.   *separate*

1. A famous poet wrote the forword for my cousin's latest anthology
of American poetry.   ....

2. It is definitely not alright with me, Susan, for you to borrow my
dictionary without permission.   ....

3. Mother has had a seige of sinus trouble that gives her terrible
headaches.   ....

4. The deputies on the police force do not support the sherriff in
his views on law enforcement.   ....

5. The mortgage on our house will be paid off on the nineth of
September.   ....

6. Sometimes one can fullfil his obligations only by sacrificing his
own wishes.   ....

7. The hypocricy of the politician's friendly maneuvers was apparent
to everyone present.   ....

8. I'm not acustomed to breakfast in bed, but it is a delightful idea.   ....

9. The oil dealer said that it is almost impossible to guage the amount
of oil we will burn this winter.   ....

10. Those rushing frantically to congradulate the winner were disappointed when she disappeared into her dressing room.   ....

11. Following a disasterous first half, the Falcons rallied surprisingly
and came out with an extraordinary win.   ....

12. It is significant that almost everyone in our city has publically
denounced the mayor's questionable procedure.   ....

13. Solitude can be a pleasant condition and need not give rise to
lonliness.   ....

14. Since I sprained my ankle last summer, I can't play tennis
anymore. ....

15. John's ability to reconize the good qualities of others makes him
a lovable person. ....

16. We were throughly disgusted with her insistence that she must
precede us all in the registration line. ....

17. Dan refused to except my apology for having torn his new coat. ....

18. The defendant coolly answered all questions put to her by the
district attorney. ....

19. It is difficult to conceive of the effects that constant harrassment
can have on an individual. ....

20. The seafood dishes at Tassey's Pier in Savannah are delicious, and
the crabmeat cocktail is especially exellent. ....

21. Actually, I would say that my salary puts me into the lowest
income catagory. ....

22. Jonathan has now decided to be an antique dealer instead of a
proffessor. ....

23. Ken sent his complements to the chef for the wonderful dinner
of barbecued ribs and cornbread. ....

24. If I couldn't live in the United States, I believe that I would choose
to make my home in Great Britian. ....

25. It is your priviledge, Frances, to have your own opinion of John,
but it is futile for you to try to change mine. ....

TEST ON LESSONS 1-7

A. In each of the following sentences underline the subject once and the verb twice, and circle the complement (or complements). On the first line at the right tell whether the verb is transitive active (*TA*), transitive passive (*TP*), or intransitive (*I*). On the second line tell whether the complement is a direct object (*DO*), indirect object (*IO*), predicate nominative (*PN*), predicate adjective (*PA*), objective complement (*OC*), or retained object (*RO*).

1. Jeff's classmates considered him the most intelligent boy in the class. ....

2. Golf is Ed's chief form of exercise. ....

3. The council meeting was held yesterday. ....

4. The ownership of a dog requires patience, understanding, and love. ....

5. The fraternity elected Virginia its sponsor. ....

6. Well, perhaps I can go. ....

7. The atmosphere seems violent and explosive. ....

8. The courageous life is often a lonely life. ....

9. John Ciardi writes poetry not only for adults but also for children. ....

10. Everyone is expected to furnish her own books. ....

B. What part of speech is each of the following underscored words?

1. most in the first sentence above ....

2. Golf in the second sentence above ....

3. council in the third sentence above ....

4. of in the fourth sentence above ....

5. sponsor in the fifth sentence above ....

6. Well in the sixth sentence above ....

7. and in the seventh sentence above ....

8. lonely in the eighth sentence above ....

9. poetry in the ninth sentence above ....

10. her in the tenth sentence above ....

C. In each of the sentences below identify the *italicized* expression by writing one of the following numbers in the space at the right:

1 if it is a prepositional phrase,	*6* if it is an absolute phrase,
2 if it is a participial phrase,	*7* if it is a noun clause,
3 if it is a gerund phrase,	*8* if it is an adjective clause,
4 if it is an infinitive phrase,	*9* if it is an adverbial clause.
5 if it is an appositive phrase,	

1. Four students were involved *in the accident.* ....

2. The formations *pointing upward* are called stalagmites. ....

3. *Although I have not seen Jessica,* she should be here by noon. ....

4. I know *that I left my keys at Lenox Square.* ....

5. Neal and I wanted *to visit the Heath Gallery.* ....

6. The truck *sitting in the driveway* blocked my view. ....

7. "The Wide Net," *a favorite story of mine,* was written by Eudora Welty. ....

8. *Reading poetry* can be very satisfying. ....

9. *The meeting having ended,* we went immediately to the dining room. ....

10. The little boy *who always behaved badly* was sorely missed when he was absent. ....

D. Underline the dependent clause (or clauses) in each of the following sentences. In the first space at the right tell whether the clause is a noun clause (*N*), adjective clause (*ADJ*), or adverbial clause (*ADV*). In the second space tell how the noun clause is used (that is, whether it is a *subject, direct object*, etc.) or what the adjective or adverbial clause modifies.

1. My mother always said that no news is good news. ....

2. After I finish law school, I want to get a doctorate in history. ....

3. Thackeray said that the world is a looking glass which gives ....
   back to everyone a reflection of his own face. ....

4. They did not tell us why you were leaving. ....

5. If you cannot play, will you send a substitute? ....

6. The folk festival was cancelled because the weather was
   terrible. ....

7. I did not know that Beth was your sister. ....

8. The old millionaire who lived on the hill was seldom seen
   by his neighbors. ....

9. The cartoons that he drew were caricatures of his family. ....

10. While I was in Scotland last summer, I visited Burns's
    birthplace. ....

E. In the following sentences insert all necessary commas and semicolons. Rewrite sentence fragments in such a way as to make complete sentences. If a sentence is correct, mark it *C*.

1. Eight wagon trains left Comer, Georgia, last week, the trip to Washington will take several months.

2. Many of Eugene O'Neill's plays are autobiographical, such as *Long Day's Journey Into Night*. Which is a moving account of O'Neill's search for identity.

3. Sarah an excellent cook but I am not sure how clean her kitchen is.

4. Even though they both liked the idea of owning a home neither was eager to assume the large mortgage.

5. Serena writing to Caroline Shaw thanking her for her invitation but saying that she would be unable to accept.

6. Mimi will work for a stockbroker she will begin her new job on Monday.

7. A fat, middle-aged man with squinty eyes entered the room everyone turned toward him and looked at him suspiciously.

8. Erick looked affectionately at the little child then he turned and walked away.

9. Agatha Christie who is one of my favorite detective story writers died in 1977.

10. A compost pile which improves the soil's structure making a compost pile is not difficult.

TEST ON LESSONS 8-18

Correct all errors in the following sentences. Errors may be crossed out and corrections written above the sentence. A misplaced element may be underscored and its proper place in the sentence indicated by placing a caret (∧) there. In some cases the entire sentence will have to be rewritten. If a sentence is correct, write *C* in the space below the sentence.

1. Having hung the curtains and put down the rug, the room became warm and inviting.

2. The young banker is bright, confident, and has ability.

3. Saturday morning he shoveled the snow off the walk, and he swept the steps clear, and then he watched the Army-Navy game.

4. My professor considers Emily Dickinson to be more gifted than any American poet.

5. I can easily understand why a stranger could not find their way to the waterfall.

6. Who do you suppose writes this column for the newspaper?

7. Neither Howard nor Ed were able to lift the sack of cabbages onto the truck.

8. You will find my address book laying on the desk in my study.

9. To succeed as a student or an athlete, self-discipline is essential.

10. Mae not only wanted to study her lessons but also to write a letter home.

11. Once deep in the woods, the children found the wildflowers they were looking for.

12. A man of experience in the kitchen, my brother cooks some better than I do.

13. After arranging the flowers in the earthenware pitcher, the coffee table seemed to be the logical place to set them.

14. The waitress brought silver for the table, poured the water, and then she went to look for the menus.

15. Because I did not have a program made the concert difficult to follow.

16. He sure does hope that we will have boiled shrimp for lunch.

17. The bedroom was painted a pale pink at the north end of the house.

18. Although he has gardened for years, he still enjoys it as much as ever.

19. Julia is one of those women who happily manages a family and a career.

20. I am certain that it was him who composed the music.

21. The geraniums bloomed in red profusion on her porch which attracted passers-by.

22. My mother was pleased that while I was at home how I picked up my clothes.

23. The mountain cabin was small, rustic, and was located across the cove from us.

24. Last week Hortense hoped to have finished her Christmas shopping.

25. We only reached the ferry for Ocracoke a few minutes before it sailed.

26. I still cannot tell the brothers apart: I took Robert to be he.

27. Gertrude can paint a barn as well as any man, if not better.

28. To entertain her child, the woman brought along a tablet, pair of scissors, and a box of crayons.

29. Max told Warren that he had missed another excellent movie.

30. If I was an artist, I would use this room as my studio.

31. Albert turned off the light in the living room, which caused him to stumble over the footstool.

32. I think that Ben and her plan to refinish the table they bought at the garage sale.

33. Stanley wishes that he were as tall as me.

34. It was a fine spring morning, and the boy was acting as friskily as a colt.

35. No member of the city commission has expressed their opinion about moving the historical marker.

36. Sam along with the rest of his family have been sitting in the same church pew every Sunday for a decade.

37. This morning we were surprised to see a blanket of snow laying over the entire town.

38. Whom do you suppose is playing in the late show tonight?

39. Neither of Guy's cronies are going to the Brass Rail tonight.

40. While hurrying through the heavy rain, Susan's umbrella turned inside out.

41. I am always surprised to discover that June's days are longer than May.

42. Have you noticed how good she can serve a ball?

43. One has no way of knowing if the witness will appear in court.

44. Catherine is such a gracious person that everyone feels warmly toward her.

45. The spaniel climbed out of the fishpond and shaken himself off.

46. The swan floated on the lake, preening it's feathers.

47. Because Jones is in a hurry, he will neither eat breakfast nor stop by the Post Office.

48. It was the most perfect diamond the jeweler had ever seen.

49. Having been repeatedly bitten by mosquitoes, the screen porch was a welcome retreat.

50. Finding time to read is more of a problem for me.

TEST ON LESSONS 19–24

A. In the following sentences insert all the necessary marks of punctuation, and correct all errors of mechanics.

1. My Mother my Aunt and my Grandmother spent four days last week making pickled peaches and ginger pears.

2. Josephine Tey's book the Singing Sands raises the mystery novel to a very high level.

3. I wanted to finish my jigsaw puzzle before lunch however I had trouble with five odd-shaped pieces of blue sky.

4. Millicient asked How can I finish this chapter if you keep talking to me

5. Tom said that there is one food that he cannot enjoy raw oysters.

6. Many people use the word awfully when the word very is more accurate.

7. Those three courses history 279 english 101 and french 203 will certainly keep you busy this fall Eugenia.

8. When Frank Sinatra sang with the Tommy Dorsey band he popularized the song I'll never smile again.

9. At about 1 30 a m by the way there will be a spectacular meteor shower.

10. Why did Billy say Its too late now

11. Joanna remarked What mother calls her drawing room is really just the living room.

12. When we had played tennis hiked on the beach and gone for a swim we were more than ready for a long nap.

13. Helen MacInnes a popular mystery writer is the wife of the noted literary critic Gilbert Highet.

14. Janet went to the shelf and selected the book Sanctuary which I immediately told her she would not like.

15. We believe furthermore that there is a sensible solution to the pollution problem recycling.

B. After each of the following groups of words indicate the level of usage of the *italicized* words, using the following abbreviations: *A* for archaic, *I* for informal (colloquial), and *S* for slang.

1. a *piker*   ....
2. *quoth* the raven   ....
3. *flabbergasted*   ....
4. We had a *neat* time.   ....
5. Hurry, *lest* you be late.   ....

6. a *fouled-up* situation   ....
7. *He's* a *jerk.*   ....
8. a *mean* old *codger*   ....
9. *You're* a sweet *kid.*   ....
10. I think *oft* of you.   ....

C. The following section of the test is based on the Glossary of Faulty Diction. Cross out all the errors or colloquialisms, and write the preferred forms above each sentence.

1. A couple of days ago I felt badly, but I am OK now.

2. If you will hold your racket thusly, your forehand will be fantastic.

3. Laying in that hot sun all day sort of gave me a headache.

4. He couldn't hardly keep his mind on his work on account of he was bugged about being stood up by his girlfriend.

5. Irregardless of what you say, I think the latest Peter Benchley book is a real bomb.

6. That little twerp deserves no sympathy after the way he chickened out.

7. The commercial for a new light beer insists that it has less calories, but I am not much enthused over its flavor.

8. The game was over with by five o'clock, just like I had said it would be.

9. The police officer inferred by his tone that he thought the boys were tight, saying, "Kids, you're in lots of trouble."

10. I asked Myra to loan Jim and myself her water skis, but she is still mad at me for keeping them too long the last time.

11. When those four women play bridge, they quarrel between themselves, keeping up a continuous spat.

12. Whose going to wait on the mail today, and whose going to be real nice and make up all the beds?

13. It's always me that she wants to put on her boring committees; I wish I knew if she is going to ask me this year.

14. Don is always full of half-cocked schemes; his last is a plan to build an ice-skating rink in Jamaica.

15. The principal of current programming is all wrong; the media is underestimating the intelligence of its audience.

D. Give the meaning of each of the following prefixes or roots. Then write two words containing each prefix or root.

1. *post-* ....

   (1) .... (2) ....

2. *graph* ....

   (1) .... (2) ....

3. *retro-* ....

   (1) .... (2) ....

4. *ced, cess* ....

   (1) .... (2) ....

5. *anim* ....

   (1) .... (2) ....

6. *mono-* ....

   (1) .... (2) ....

7. *capit* ....

   (1) .... (2) ....

8. *duc* ....

   (1) .... (2) ....

9. *micro-* ....

   (1) .... (2) ....

10. *cord* ....

   (1) .... (2) ....

E. If there is a misspelled word in any line of five words given below, write it correctly in the space at the right. If all five words are correctly spelled, write *C* in the space.

1. sophomore, restaurant, medcine, recommend, personnel ....

2. rhetoric, source, temperature, nickle, realize ....

3. tendency, until, tournament, original, neice ....

4. sincerely, ascend, connoisseur, hankerchief, angel ....

5. recieve, cemetery, changeable, eighth, barbarous ....

6. amateur, colloquial, dependant, definite, magazine ....

7. permanent, bouyant, nevertheless, sacrilegious, syllable ....

8. sheriff, diptheria, sandwich, writing, twelfth ....

9. equivalant, significant, villain, Wednesday, obstacle ....

10. propaganda, procedure, exagerrate, usually, valuable ....

11. symmetry, pamphlet, miniature, accomodate, parallel ....

12. rheumatism, resistence, surprise, ninth, probably ....

13. nucleus, anymore, mathematics, forehead, privilege ....

14. pastime, overrun, innocence, financier, publicly ....

15. omitted, salary, column, quanity, committee ....

ACHIEVEMENT TEST

In the following sentences identify the part of speech of each *italicized* word by writing one of the following numbers in the space at the right:

1 if it is a noun,	*5* if it is an adverb,
2 if it is a pronoun,	*6* if it is a preposition,
3 if it is a verb,	*7* if it is a conjunction,
4 if it is an adjective,	*8* if it is an interjection.

1. A crowd of spectators *had gathered* to watch the fire. ....
2. Jake wore a *blue* suit. ....
3. I bought season tickets, *but* I missed every game. ....
4. What you suggest is *reasonable.* ....
5. Everyone came to the dance *but* Hal. ....
6. Yes, I do remember seeing *him*. ....
7. *When* I am angry, I cry. ....
8. The old *hound* sleeps all day on the porch. ....
9. Traveling across the country, we met many *interesting* people. ....
10. I think that Ellie is very mature *for* her age. ....
11. I have never read any of his *poetry.* ....
12. *We* decided to visit our relatives in Africa. ....
13. Clyde, you have *but* a few minutes to catch your bus. ....
14. Janet, a classical *guitarist*, is preparing herself to be a professional. ....
15. If I were you, I would *not* go to the game alone. ....
16. She is *looking* forward to attending college. ....
17. Every Saturday *we* visited my grandmother. ....
18. Bob has a friend who *traveled* through Mexico on a bicycle. ....
19. How many books have *you* read? ....
20. *If* she agrees, then we will go. ....
21. The honor guard was *carefully* selected. ....
22. President Carter is *from* Plains, Georgia. ....
23. Ruth *and* Alexa are my cousins. ....
24. I have no *desire* to participate in this witch-hunt. ....
25. Mrs. Gibson had high standards *for* her students. ....

Each of the following sentences either contains an error in grammar or is correct. Indicate the error or the correctness by writing one of the following numbers in the space at the right:

> *1* if the case of the pronoun is incorrect,
> *2* if the subject and the verb do not agree,
> *3* if a pronoun and its antecedent do not agree,
> *4* if an adjective or an adverb is used incorrectly,
> *5* if the sentence is correct.

26. They work together very good. ....
27. If I was you, I would not eat too much ice cream. ....
28. Either the players or the coach are going to order our tickets. ....
29. Each of the actors wanted their own studio. ....
30. Between you and I, I do not believe that Ralph can do the work. ....
31. Everyone left the class but me. ....
32. Do you think that Harland will mind me going? ....
33. Rain sure would help my tomatoes. ....
34. Every one of the artists plans to exhibit their paintings. ....
35. Appearing sadly, the chairman announced the retirement of his old friend. ....
36. Mother's apple turnovers taste more tartly than these. ....
37. The judge considered Joy and she to be the best swimmers in the meet. ....
38. Marjorie along with her roommates are interested in the mythology course. ....
39. Who have you addressed the invitations to? ....
40. Her favorite dessert is peaches and cream. ....
41. At noon the alumni is meeting to hear the annual report. ....
42. Each one of the boys has brought their own bat to practice. ....
43. The music on the radio sure is loud this morning. ....
44. In the drawer is a tarnished bracelet, some ribbon, and an old playbill. ....
45. Why should I, who turns in every paper on time, be penalized? ....
46. Do either of the twins object to dressing alike? ....
47. The legislative committee published their report concerning the state parks. ....
48. Mr. Winkle has asked you and I to his house for tea. ....
49. The hat she wore to the wedding is the most unique one I have ever seen. ....
50. Do you think that Gerald is as tall as he? ....

Each of the following sentences either contains an error in sentence structure or is correct. Indicate the error or the correctness by writing one of the following numbers in the space at the right:

> *1* if the sentence contains a dangling modifier,
> *2* if the sentence contains a misplaced modifier,
> *3* if the sentence contains a faulty reference of a pronoun,
> *4* if the sentence contains faulty parallelism,
> *5* if the sentence is correct.

51. While climbing the stairs, her heel caught in the worn carpet. ....
52. He ordered a hamburger, a cup of coffee, and added French fries as an afterthought. ....
53. From here it is as far to New Orleans as it is to Washington. ....
54. Pat is a pianist with talent and who practices faithfully. ....
55. One must read his assignment every night if you are to keep up with the lectures. ....
56. She wrote a letter to the newspaper which expressed disagreement with the editor. ....
57. Failing to find a table for two, the counter seemed to be their only alternative. ....
58. He is a good insurance salesman and plans to make a career of it. ....
59. Lou told her sister that she had forgotten to put on any suntan lotion. ....
60. I believe that the pine seedlings only grew a few inches this summer. ....
61. To sum up, one must write her essays clearly and concisely. ....
62. The architect hopes to soon complete the plans for the new courthouse. ....
63. To be a good correspondent, letters must be answered promptly. ....
64. The old woman who had climbed the steps slowly sat down to rest at the top. ....
65. He practiced on his trombone until after midnight, which annoyed our neighbors. ....
66. My room is as warm if not warmer than my sister's. ....
67. As a young girl Father thought his daughter should be interested in music and needlework. ....
68. When Jack was explaining to Uncle Jim about the accident, he was trembling with fear. ....
69. It was disgusting that I was not only late for work already but also that I was caught in a terrible traffic jam. ....
70. After hearing Hank's guitar concert, I certainly wish I had one. ....
71. The car collided with a telephone post that whizzed around the curve. ....
72. Before one finishes college, you should have gained considerable maturity. ....
73. Susan discovered that she only had one aspirin in her purse. ....
74. What he had confessed suddenly disturbed me. ....
75. He had nearly driven ten miles before he realized that he was on the wrong road. ....

Each of the following sentences contains an error in punctuation or mechanics, or is correct. Indicate the error or correctness by writing one of the following numbers in the space at the right:

> *1* if a comma has been omitted,
> *2* if a semicolon has been omitted,
> *3* if an apostrophe has been omitted,
> *4* if quotation marks have been omitted,
> *5* if the sentence is correct.

76. I told Mrs. Wiggs "I cannot leave my work unfinished." ....
77. It is high time Steve that you start to make your own decisions. ....
78. James is ill, said Joyce; therefore, he cannot be in the play. ....
79. Robert Frosts poem "Mending Wall" has been on our reading list for years. ....
80. Hoping to drive the runner in Matt bunted. ....
81. When he was ready to perform the star, an English actor, walked confidently to the platform. ....
82. Fathers going to drive us all down to Franklin this afternoon. ....
83. The boy walked slowly out of the bakery then he plodded down the path toward home. ....
84. I am really sorry that this has happened but I promise that it will not happen again. ....
85. Alice made a delicious apple pie I would offer you a piece, but I ate it all myself. ....
86. Entering the building I came face to face with my mother-in-law. ....
87. The cruise to St. Thomas having been quite enjoyable the Browns decided to try a Scandinavian one. ....
88. My cousin Arthur has qualified for the Olympics in gymnastics. ....
89. My brother grills steaks beautifully he is the best cook in our family. ....
90. The new car was standing in the driveway and Father was staring at the dent in the fender. ....
91. Wait! cried Stan; I will be ready in two minutes. ....
92. The boy riding the unicycle has a good sense of balance. ....
93. Does anyone know all the words to the old hymn Bringing in the Sheaves? ....
94. I was the first person to arrive at the scene of the accident I later had to testify in court. ....
95. Joanna and John both like the mountains but they argue about everything else. ....
96. To Peggy Reed was a puzzling individual. ....
97. On January 20, 1977 Jimmy Carter was inaugurated. ....
98. The thoughtful considerate man offered his seat on the bus to the tired woman. ....
99. Its going to be a long time before the energy crisis is over. ....
100. To be on time for the concert many people began arriving several hours early. ....

Index